PRAISE FOR JULIA NGUYEN AND *AWAKEN THE HERO WITHIN*

∽✺∾

"*Awaken the Hero Within* is an inspiring and effective step-by-step guide that shows you how to move from self-sabotage into the light of your true power. This book is an impactful read for anyone who is ready to embark on a journey of personal healing and self-discovery."

—*Kelly Graver, Stress Management Coach*

"Your program is amazing. It's a combination of hypnotherapy, coaching and business mentoring. That's a killer combo! I learned that I'm capable of getting things done and it was an absolute pleasure to be able to talk to someone who's been where I was. In itself that's priceless. I also loved the recording that was made for the 21 days we worked together. I'm sure I'm going to continue listening to it even after the coaching program." —*Angel*

"Before working with Julia, I had zero motivation to work, extreme procrastination, and that was going on for almost four years. I needed to start working again, focusing on my business, focusing on growing it, and getting rid of the debts I'd accumulated. I was still skeptical even immediately after the (initial) session, but in a couple weeks I started seeing very measurable, positive results. I started working 10-12 hour days, 6 days a week. I restructured my company, hired a really good team to work with, and paid $150,000 debt. I now feel super positive and have high hopes." —*Baris*

"Before working with Julia I waited for life to change for me. I felt stuck, but unsure how to get myself un-stuck on my own. Julia is completely accepting, gently guiding without pushing, and she held a greater vision for my life than even I've dreamt possible (until now). Julia gave me a connection to my sense of purpose again. Don't wait any longer to feel connected to your true calling and the life of your dreams. Reach out to Julia today and start hearing, seeing, feeling, tasting, breathing and living the possibilities for greatness in your life!" —*Rayme*

Awaken

— *the* —

Hero Within

ALSO BY JULIA NGUYEN

Dream Life Workbook

Hero's Journey Workbook

From Passion to Profit: How to Build a Business Ebook

Blog: *www.TheDreamLifeFoundation.com/Blog*

My Podcast is available on the following platforms under
The Dream Life Foundation:

Apple iTunes

Spotify

AWAKEN

the

HERO WITHIN

A Practical Guide for Tapping into Your Limitless Potential

JULIA NGUYEN

"The wound is the place where the
Light enters you."

—Rumi

To my mom who gave me life and everything that I possess.

To my sister who has always been there for me, no matter what.

To my two brothers who are with me on this journey.

To anyone with a dream:

It was my dream to write a book that will positively impact and change lives throughout the world. If I can make my dreams happen, you can, too! I believe in you and hope that this book will help you believe in yourself.

Remember there is a "hero" within you.

Contents

PREFACE

Life is a "DIY" Project

So, get to work and transform your life today!

T HERE IS A GOOD CHANCE that you, like most people, are not yet living your dream life. This tragic phenomenon transcends the boundaries of age, sex, race, and income. Many people find themselves feeling stuck where they are in life. They work at jobs they don't enjoy or have a routine that leaves them feeling unfulfilled. Like you, they face setback after setback as they watch other people reach their dreams and wonder, "Why can't that be me?"

Well, I have great news for you! This book will equip you with the building blocks and practical tools you need to eliminate the unsupportive beliefs and habits that hold you back. You'll learn to ask the right questions, identify and eliminate the bad habits, and easily adopt the best practices that build a life of success and happiness. Best of all, you'll have fun as you take the wheel and create your own version of a life of purpose and happiness!

For any of us to live a life that's truly amazing, we must first learn how to master ourselves. This means recognizing our own strengths and weaknesses, and then creating habits that develop our strengths and compensate for those weaknesses. Once we learn how to master ourselves, we will be able to show up in the world 1,000 times more powerfully and have a real impact on the lives of others. FYI: Mastering yourself is a process, so it will not happen overnight. But if you are serious about becoming your very best self, IT WILL HAPPEN.

This book is a Rx prescription for a happy life!
YOUR life!

What would make you happy? The chance to make a difference in the lives of others? A successful or fulfilling career? Loving and satisfying relationships? Financial gain?

Before we get started, I want you to be clear about your expectations. Think about what you hope this book will do for you. Imagine what your life would look like if you could have everything you ever wanted. If you take what you learn in this book seriously, you can be on your way to a brand-new future.

Hesitating? If you're waiting for a sign before taking the plunge, this is it! The very fact that you are here now means that you are ready! You are reading this book for a reason! This can be the beginning of a whole new chapter for you. So, think about how you want this new chapter to unfold. What do you want the next phase of your life to look like?

Get ready to embark on an adventure of a lifetime—your own "Hero's Journey"!

This book is packed full of practical tools that will equip you for your "Hero's Journey." Your Hero's Journey is a trek that takes you deep into your inner self where your past has deposited roadblocks that are keeping you from your future.

I am going to show you how to clear away those roadblocks. I have combined the techniques of cognitive behavioral therapy (CBT), positive psychology, meditation, hypnosis, and self-reflection into a well-rounded approach for adjusting behavior that will help you create permanent and lasting changes. *These techniques are laid out for you all along your Hero's Journey. All you have to do is follow the steps.* You will be amazed at how simply changing your thinking and perspective will change your life.

I will give you tools to heal unhealed wounds. You will learn how to release your pain, let go of the past, and create a life of purpose. Stepping into your new chapter of life will mean stepping out of the old and familiar, one step at a time. Change is a natural and normal part of life, and the steps you're about to take are easy, doable, and bite-sized. You don't have to make massive and uncomfortable changes. Just take it one guided step at a time!

Always remember that the biggest investment you will ever make is the investment in yourself. This investment can be of time, effort, or money, and will return to you tenfold. Whether you are reading a book, attending conferences or a seminar, joining a community, or taking a class to better your skills, the more you put into it, the greater the results you will obtain. So, as you read this book, dedicate the time and energy to really go through the exercises and complete them. Give yourself the gift of self-improvement, and remember, small, consistent actions will yield extraordinary results!

This book combines my story about overcoming depression and an explanation of practical tools that helped me. If you are serious about your Hero's Journey, you need to understand how these tools work. This book also contains powerful exercises for you to complete. These exercises are VITAL to progressing in your journey.

In order for you to master the skills provided, it is essential that you not only complete the exercises once but that you repeat these exercises over time. Some exercises may not make sense initially but will begin to resonate as you progress through your journey, so it's important to work through them continuously.

If there were a way for you to transform your life easily and powerfully, would you do it?

Check out this Self-Mastery Pyramid[1]. It will be your guide toward self-mastery during this journey to connect with your internal "Hero." All of us who embark on our own personal "Hero's Journey" need this pyramid to maintain honesty and self-awareness as we progress. Honesty helps reveal the truth about what is holding us back in life. Knowing the truth frees us to step forward into our amazing future.

THE SELF MASTERY PYRAMID

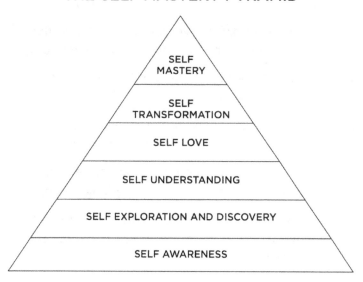

Each of us begins the journey of self-mastery at the bottom of this pyramid. As we develop self-awareness, particularly in regard to our personal values, we move up the pyramid to the top. Remember, each stage of progression is an opportunity to gain additional self-awareness, so this journey is not a race, but an experience to be traveled deliberately at one's own pace. Each stage of the self-mastery pyramid builds upon the preceding stage, but it is *not* necessary to master one stage before beginning to explore the next. The self-mastery pyramid should be viewed as a guide to the process of becoming whole. Some stages may take longer than others to master, and individual progress speed will vary.

At each level, consider the following aspects of development and ask yourself about each of them:

1. **Self-awareness**: Know yourself. Who are you, what drives you, what habits are holding you back?

2. **Self-exploration/Discovery**: Digging deeper, describe your *why*, your purpose, your desires, and your goals.

3. **Self-understanding**: Understanding your worldview and what shaped it.

4. **Self-love**: Building confidence. Healing from past traumas, letting go of things that no longer serve you.

5. **Self-transformation**: Changing habits. Developing healthy routines, rewiring your thinking process.

6. **Self-mastery***: Feeling whole and complete. Pure happiness, bliss, able to accept any situation. Living the life of your dreams.

*Note that *self-mastery* does not equal perfection. Perfection is not real, but you can master yourself and be happy and content with who you are and what you want out of life.

So, how can this book make a difference in YOUR life?

If you take it seriously, you will be able to:

◇ Overcome your mental blocks and change the way you think about things.

◇ Closely examine the "life story" that has brought you to where you are today.

◇ Learn how to focus on life as a journey to be experienced fully, rather than a means to an end.

◇ Align your "life" and "work" views—because making money and having meaning in your life do not always align.

◇ Fix dysfunctional attitudes by discovering the roots in your thinking.

◇ Understand what gives you energy and what sucks you dry, so that you can design a fulfilling life instead of one that drains you.

◇ Identify barriers and obstacles that prevent you from realizing happiness, contentment and satisfaction in your life.

If you feel like something is holding you back from being everything you want to be, then this book holds answers for you, but it requires you to be completely and ruthlessly honest with yourself.

Be prepared to embark upon the amazing journey of discovering who you are deep down, and how you can truly become happy with your life!

*** DISCLOSURE ***

I WANT YOU TO KNOW where I am coming from: I do not believe in pure positive thinking. Although I am an optimist, I believe in the benefits of practicing positive thought processes and in taking consistent action. We are all driven by our beliefs and conditioning, which means it's time to take the wheel and work on yourself so you can get off autopilot, overcome the obstacles that hold you back, and live the life you've only dreamed about.

I do not claim to solve all of your problems. I can only provide the tools to help you get to where you want to be. The rest is up to you. I aim to inspire you to create change for yourself through my own personal story and transformation.

Always honor your past and the stories that make you, you. However, do not let them define who you are forever and stop you from embracing your true potential.

Mental health is a serious issue and although I was able to help myself overcome depression, some people need additional resources. Besides doing mindset training, I highly recommend seeing a therapist or a professional, whichever is more appealing to you. We all need someone we can talk to who is objective and can give us a different perspective, and someone who will pull us outside of our drama.

This book is meant to inspire fresh hope within you and is not a cure-all solution. It provides the tools and resources to guide you towards self-awareness and contentment, but merely reading this book is not the answer. You must act. You are the creator of your own life. You are the only one who can make powerful changes in your life—remember that!

What you do today will affect the rest of your life!

As you read this book, you can begin to make genuine changes to your thinking and to your life—starting right now. If you methodically follow the principles and exercises of The Hero's Journey, it will not take long for you to feel a transformation happening within your mind and body. Allow yourself to be motivated by each small victory and continue to take the next steps toward your amazing future!

THE HERO'S JOURNEY

"Don't forget, you are the hero of your own story."
—Greg Boyle[J]

JULIA NGUYEN

INTRODUCTION: THE HERO'S JOURNEY

Your Roadmap to Self-Actualization

"A hero ventures forth from the world of common day into a region of supernatural wonder: fabulous forces are there encountered and a decisive victory is won: the hero comes back from this mysterious adventure with the power to bestow boons on his fellow man."[1]

—Joseph Campbell
The Hero with a Thousand Faces

FOR GENERATIONS, humans have been awestruck by superhero stories. From myths and legends to the worlds of Marvel and DC, to real life stories of rising above adversity, we crave the adventure of a hero who overcomes, triumphs, and saves the world. The hero is the most sought-out archetype. Maybe this is because heroes are relatable on a deep level. The truth is that the "hero" archetype is one that resides deep in the psyche of every individual. We sense that this "hero" is patiently waiting to be unleashed. *The Hero's Journey* is a map for self-discovery and actualization. It provides the blueprint we need in order to master ourselves and unleash our inner "hero." It's a compass, showing us the way to find ourselves along life's journey.

The Hero's Journey was a concept discovered by Joseph Campbell, a famous American mythologist and philosopher. As he studied mythology, he noticed that the myths and religions of many cultures had a similar storyline, as specific elements of each story seemed to appear in stories from different legends and myths. This storyline became known as a "monomyth," or "universal story structure," a pattern that transcends all cultures.

The Hero's Journey monomyth generalizes a three-phased template progression of a hero's experiences from beginning to end: *separation, initiation*, and *return*. This book is laid out to guide you through the monomyth of *The Hero's Journey* wherein you discover the role you play as the hero in your own life.

◇ During the *separation* phase, as the hero, you will learn to separate yourself from your past. Here you will relive an old story that is keeping you stuck in old patterns of thinking and behaving. At one point, you will separate from the ego, the part of you that is glued to the seductive material world and keeps you in misery.

◇ During the *initiation* phase you will explore the deeper parts of who you are and how you came to be. You will learn how to overcome the struggles of your mind, gaining an inner wisdom that will help you transform your life.

◇ Your journey will culminate in the *return* phase. Once you've mastered your art and completed your transformation, it's time to return home and share your gift with the world.

The Hero's Journey is not only the basis of mythology, but it is the basis of psychological development and the actualization of one's own potential in the best possible way. *The Hero's Journey* combines death, birth and transformation, requiring both destruction of the old self and creation of the new. Along the way, *The Hero's Journey* encompasses love, honor, approval, freedom, and survival, all part of the human process of self-actualization. You will need to overcome setbacks and limitations as you battle both inner and outer demons, confront the darkest parts of who you are, and find a treasure that is the secret to self-discovery and individuation. At the end of the journey, you are equipped to take on the world.

The Hero's Journey is divided into 12 stages. Each stage gives you more clues as to what it takes to achieve ultimate happiness in life. Think of this as a scavenger hunt where you collect clues and rewards. These stages are your golden compass and map as you embark on your lifelong journey of transformation. Each chapter of this book focuses on one of the 12 stages and its role in *The Hero's Journey* monomyth:

1. THE ORDINARY WORLD

This stage is considered the beginning of *The Hero's Journey* and can be nicknamed the "still sleeping" stage. Traversing the *Ordinary World* marks the beginning for every hero. Expect to feel major dissatisfaction with your life during this initial stage. In this stage, you don't know what you don't know, and in ignorance, you are probably just drifting along with the currents of life. It is marked by life in the conventional world, a world influenced by family, friends, and society. It's a stagnant phase where you're stuck in inertia and you likely don't see a clear path forward.

2. THE CALL TO ADVENTURE

The *Call to Adventure* is a triggering point in your life. After staying silent and suffering alone in the *Ordinary World* you realize that you are destined for greatness but settling for mediocrity. This stage is where you experience a spark of curiosity. You become curious about the world, your reason for being here, and how to overcome obstacles you realize are holding you back or causing you to struggle. You're getting the call to transformation, to begin a new journey, whatever that may be for yourself. It may be to change your environment, your career, or merely to try something new. However, this new adventure means you have to leave your familiar territory. It's time to travel to the "Land of the Unknown." Leaving your current world means that you are leaving the comfort of familiar surroundings and people. At the same time, the prospect of traveling to this new land offers up endless possibilities. You may begin to have a sense of wanderlust, restlessness, and a fascination for what's to come. Welcome those feelings as progress in your journey!

3. REFUSAL OF THE CALL

This stage is known as the *resistance* stage. You're ready to embark on this new adventure of self-discovery and mastering yourself, however, your ego and familiarity have a strong hold over you. Picture this stage as a battle between your current and future selves. Though you may desire to move forward and actualize happiness, your old belief patterns are still prevalent and threaten to suck you backward. You are plagued by victimhood and not yet ready to face your inner demons. You are curious but stuck because of fear.

4. MEETING THE MENTOR

The *mentor* may not come into your life at exactly this moment, but at this stage in the journey you become intellectually open to realizing the influence and impact that mentors can have on your future. Mentors are people who will physically or virtually guide you on your journey of self-discovery. They will have wisdom gleaned from their own experiences and will relay their wisdom to you to help you along the way. A mentor is the person who helps push you to take this path to transformation. Your mentor can come in many shapes and forms. It could be someone you admire, or someone you ran into who has a great influence on you. The mentor does not have to have an active presence in your physical world, only an influence over it. My mentors were authors of the self-development books I read.

5. CROSSING THE FIRST THRESHOLD

In the fifth stage of the process you have decided to leave the past behind. You've made the choice and the commitment, so now it's time to take action. The first threshold to cross is challenging the belief systems and hard-wiring that you've developed up until this point in your life. This process is a series of tests and tasks you must complete to detach yourself from false, destructive, and limiting beliefs and to open yourself to new realizations. In this stage, you are gaining momentum and clarity as you forge your path forward.

6. TESTS, ALLIES, ENEMIES

Similar to mentors, *tests, allies*, and *enemies* also come in many forms, from actual physical people in your life, to feelings of resistance and frustration. You will be dealing with risks, challenges, and even some failures in this stage. During this stage, you may be letting go of friends or people who are not aligned with your path. You have reached a level of awareness to realize that these individuals are not supportive, do not understand your journey, and may even have a negative influence on you and your behavior. Somewhere in this turmoil, though, you will begin to develop the skills to distinguish between enemies and true allies.

7. INNERMOST CAVE

In the innermost cave you will conduct your deepest internal work and focus on healing old wounds. This stage is where you are really developing your internal strength. You are consciously and subconsciously letting go of negative belief systems that you've held on to for your entire life, as well as building practices that are helping you align with your inner self. You challenge your inner negotiators and start to discover your true identity, your true self.

8. Ordeal

During this stage, you might face a final test of faith and patience. This could be a period of time when it feels like the whole world is against you. Some refer to this as the "rock bottom phase." You might feel extreme loneliness, sadness, and confusion. However, through this pain comes remarkable growth. This stage marks another test to see if you've learned the Hero's lessons and can implement that knowledge in life's future challenges.

9. Reward

Finally, you reach your reward! In this ninth stage you've been committed to your Hero's Journey and the universe is delivering your reward. This reward can be awesome moments of bliss and happiness, or a sense of freedom from fear and depression. It can be the satisfaction of what you have accomplished. It can be material rewards. It can be love and support from the people around you. This is where the results of all your efforts and struggles begin to manifest! You will finally see the fruits of your labor.

10. The Road Back

The *road back* is a time to reflect on your journey and see how far you've truly come. It's a time to celebrate the new habits you've developed as you continue on this transformational road and your success in separating yourself from the old habits that previously held you back. You now have the skills and tools

7

necessary to move past any trying situation. You've grown a lot, made a ton of progress, and now you can take a deep breath with a sigh of relief... ahhhh! You've made it this far.

11. RESURRECTION

Your journey is coming close to an end. You are being reborn as you rise up to your full potential and embody your highest self. You've taken all that you have learned and incorporated it into your life. The wisdom you've gained along your journey resides in your mind and heart now. It is integrated into your very being. You are enlightened, fully awake, and connected to the hero within you.

12. RETURN WITH THE ELIXIR—THE ELIXIR OF LIFE

When you've learned all that you need to learn, it's time to bring the *elixir* of your knowledge home. This "elixir" is the essence of what you have learned about yourself. "The highest expression of self," to quote a phrase from David Hartman's *The Hero's Journey of Self-Transformation*[2], is when you use this elixir to help other people through their own journey. You can share your story, your wounds and battles. Most importantly, you offer how you managed to overcome it all. You will become the source of light and inspiration for others. Together, with other "heroes" like yourself, you can change the world.

The Hero's Journey becomes a homecoming to your eternal truth.

MY STORY

Loneliness. Self-hate. Low self-esteem. Fear. Failure. Self-harm. Hopelessness. Confusion. These crippling words have ruled my life for as long as I can remember. My story is the story of a girl who lived life in constant fear. A girl who was unhappy with herself and felt broken and wounded in unimaginable ways. For a long time, I lived in a state of perpetual victimhood, blaming the world for my misery. My days were filled with thoughts that kept me in a state of toxicity. I suffered from endless depression, succumbing to the negative voice in my mind. I was my own worst critic and my own enemy, breaking myself down to nothingness. Actually, it was beyond nothingness. It was a numbness where I floated around with a dark cloud hanging over my head.

When people looked at me, they thought that my life was perfect. They saw my warm smile that covered my pain. They saw my nice car and material things. They saw where I lived and the vacations I got to go on. They saw my successful career and thought I seemed to have it all. They only saw the surface layer, the beautifully masked version of who I really was—my persona, a superficial construct for the world to see. Little did they know of my internal struggle. Every single day, I faced a constant battle within myself.

I attributed my misery to my external surroundings. Every person, place, or thing took on the role of my scapegoat, from my family to friends, and ex-boyfriends. I hated the universe for giving me a life with so much adversity. I could not understand why all of this suffering was happening to me. I felt small. I was a victim of a broken family with parents who were divorced, growing up with poor finances, and going through trauma in my early teenage years which led to an avalanche of negative self-beliefs. I let life happen to me because I believed I had no control over it. The turmoil I felt inside me never subsided. The story I have told myself for so long—of not being good enough, of not being worthy, and of being a failure—took control of my life and kept me captive in its dark prison cell. It wasn't until one day, when I was so unhappy with myself and my life, that I was forced to reevaluate who I was and answer the universe's call to step into my power so that I could stop my endless suffering.

This magnitude of misery sparked the beginning of a magical awakening for me. I woke up to the endless possibilities that life had to offer.

So, I began my healing journey, a journey to connect with my higher self and with the "hero" within—the version of myself who is full of hope, love, and happiness.

It has been a constant journey and I still continually work towards healing. Through my own transformation, I realized what my purpose in life was: The reason for all of my suffering was so that I can learn to heal myself, and in turn, heal others.

If my story resonates with you or touches some part of your soul, maybe it's time for you to embark on your own journey of self-discovery. Maybe it's time for you to discover the *Hero Within*...

You have a choice. Instead of fear, anxiety, depression, or self-hate, you can choose happiness, hope, and love.

It is time to release those self-deprecating beliefs about yourself and step into your power.

It is time to take back control of your life and not be a victim of your negative thoughts and emotions.

If your perceived shortcomings have ruled your life and you are ready to take back control, I am here to help guide you through your challenges and help you find the power within yourself to create a magical and meaningful life.

◇ I am here to help you develop a healthy and positive mindset to enable you to pursue your biggest passions and goals.

◇ I am here to help you create a self-care ritual that will fill you with love and confidence so that you can chase your dreams.

◇ I am here to help you learn what it means to be alive—fully alive.

◇ I am here to help you come out of a "victim mentality" and come into a "hero mentality."

◇ I am here to help you uncover the depths of your soul.

◇ I am here to be a catalyst for your change and growth.

◇ I am here to transform you into your light.

"My role and gift in life is not to teach, preach, or convince anyone of anything. I am here to empower others to get their own answers, access their true dreams, and overcome anything that gets in the way of making those dreams a reality."[1]

—Bruce D. Schneider

Beginnings

For many years I struggled with my identity. I struggled with who I was, and who I was supposed to be according to other people's expectations. Struggling with this question led me to go on this search—to understand the meaning of life. More importantly, to understand the meaning of MY life, and my role in it.

When each of us first arrived on this planet as an innocent and loving newborn baby, we looked at the world in awe. Our first breath of air was incredible! As we exited our mother's womb, we were greeted with smiling faces and so much love. This defining moment that marked the beginning of our life was pure bliss. We had no way to imagine that there was so much more to come our way, a perplexing mixture of good and bad experiences.

Between the ages of 0 and 7, our conditioning began. We started to gain input and insight from our external environment, such as our families and schools, showing us what to do, what not to do, and telling us that if we expressed ourselves a certain way, we would be punished. We were punished by rejection, causing us to instinctively obey what we were taught. Our need to belong surpassed our true identity. We were introduced to the rigid dichotomy of the world, the good versus the bad. Through this conditioning, we learned how to act, how to behave and how to present ourselves within society.

But there is a problem with societal pressures like this. They can lead us astray. The conditioning that formed us may seduce us and cause us to lead a life not worth living, a life that is far away from our dreams. Meanwhile, we have developed an identity that is incongruent with our internal nature. We have become a perfectly molded version of ourselves that we feel is acceptable to those around us. In order to please others, we did whatever it took to fit into social norms, not realizing that we were neglecting the innermost part of who we really are. We put on this mask and created a persona that was acceptable to the outside world. A persona is an image we leave behind. It is the identity we show to the external world. Over time we became engulfed by this facade and forgot the essence of our inner selves. We became a puppet in this show called "life," while in the process many of us lost our true identities.

Are you going down this road? At some point, did you disconnect from your true self because you were so busy making other people happy, trying to fit in, never once putting your own happiness first?

This disconnection from our true identities can make us feel lost and being lost can lead us to feelings of unhappiness. You may feel lost because you don't know why you are so unhappy. The natural reaction to unhappiness or feeling lost is to seek ways to numb the pain. It all begins here. We feel lost and alone, but we refuse to look within ourselves for the answers. Instead, we use our external environment to filter out our negative emotions.

We might immerse ourselves in work and distractions like alcohol, drugs, and a super-busy social life. Our goal is to numb the pain that we feel deep inside. We refuse to face the growing emptiness that has taken up residence within us. We do anything and everything we can so that we don't have to face who we are, or at least the perception of who we think we are.

If this resonates on some level with you, keep reading.

Pain and fear from your past have kept you frozen where you are. You want to fill this void, but what you realize is that the more you try to fill it with things around you—whether it's a luxury car, a new designer item or the trendiest clothing—for a short while things seem better, but soon you feel emptier than before. How can that possibly be? Is there any way to fix this? Yes!

The world has been happening to you for a long time. It has jaded you, wounded you, and caused you to feel like a child in an unsafe situation living in constant fear. How are you supposed to thrive when your most basic needs are not being met?

Abraham Maslow, as far back as the 1940s, saw this as a real problem. He developed a psychological model called the "Hierarchy of Needs"[2] that shows how critical the sense of safety and security is for every human being. He considered feeling safe so important to every person's wellbeing that he put it right above necessities and basic needs like food and water. He also believed that for us to reach self-actualization, we must go through each of the following levels in ascending order.[3]

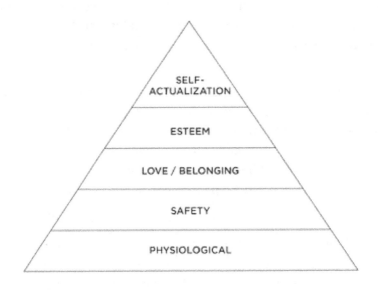

If we struggle with feeling insecure or feeling unsafe, we may be stuck in the "Safety" level of Maslow's Hierarchy. If we constantly depend on other people or other things to make us feel good about ourselves, we are hovering between the "Love/Belonging" and "Esteem" stages. If we are living in constant fear of being judged or always have a fear of failing, can we really thrive? Where are you on Maslow's Hierarchy?

In this book, we are aiming for that top level: "Self-Actualization." You can get there if you try. But first, you have to understand where you are right now.

In order to reach self-actualization, we have to cultivate self-awareness and take responsibility. Let's face it, most of us have had some type of event happen to us in the past, that has left a painful mark on us and changed our lives in a negative way. The world may have been cruel to you, but if you are looking for a way to transform your life, you have to realize that it is now 100% entirely up to you to make that transformation. I'm sorry to say, but no one is going to do this for you. We each have ONE life, ONE chance, and ONE opportunity to live, so it's time for you to stand up and take charge of your own life.

Remember, although people might have hurt you in the past, most often they were only doing the best they could with the knowledge they had at the time. If you are still blaming them for the way your life is now, STOP IT. Holding a life-long grudge against someone who did you wrongly will only destroy you—not them.

***This journey you are embarking on
is an adventure of a lifetime!***

At the heart of the *Hero's Journey* is an introspective adventure with profound spiritual and psychological implications, where you will discover the path that leads you to genuine happiness and fulfillment. It is a journey that changes you as you travel from the past to the present and toward your future self. As you complete the journey, you cycle back home with unexpected knowledge, wisdom, and strength. Your struggles along the journey will infuse you with a resilience that keeps you moving ahead as you transform from the inside out. *The Hero's Journey* is full of insights and fresh meaning that will help you through every challenge you face during the rest of your life. So, embrace these insights as victorious milestones along the way. As you become your own "Inner Hero," dare to live with a bold heart, eager to give and spread love as you face each new challenge.

◇ You will begin your *Hero's Journey* at the first stage, The Ordinary World, living a life of quiet desperation behind your false persona, unaware of who you are.

◇ Then you are Called to Adventure, a journey of exploring your mind and transforming who you are now to the hero within.

◇ You might resist the change in the beginning, your Refusal of the Call.

◇ Along the way, you meet a Mentor, one or more individuals who come in to guide you on your journey. The mentor gives you insights and wisdom, so now you can better understand yourself.

◇ Crossing the First Threshold is an eye-opening experience. You start cultivating a sense of awareness about who you are and how your beliefs have formed.

◇ Nothing makes an adventure like Tests, Allies, and Enemies! There will be many tests along the way, gauging to see if you are resilient on your path.

◇ The most challenging work is what goes on inside you as you tread deep waters and approach the Innermost Cave of your being. Now is the time to buckle down and focus because there's a lot to uncover and change about yourself. Fortunately, you have gathered all the right tools as you traveled through each previous stage—you can do this!

◇ A final Ordeal appears next, really testing your faith, seeing if you are ready to risk it all as you get closer to your destination.

◇ Overcoming your ordeal means you will receive Rewards for your efforts. You begin to notice easier transitions and smoother-sailing waters.

◇ You're almost at the end of your Hero's Journey, so it becomes time to reflect on how far you've come as you take The Road Back.

◇ The journey has been long: you've let go of the past, healed from old wounds, and the old version of you has died while the Hero within you is being reborn, a Resurrection.

◇ With all the wisdom and the lessons you've learned, you have obtained the Elixir of Life, a true treasure that is so amazing, you can't keep it to yourself. You are now ready to share your journey and guide others on theirs.

As I read Joseph Campbell's *The Hero with a Thousand Faces*, I was reminded of my own journey and the stages I went through. As my cloud of depression started to dissipate, I became aware that I was, in fact, my own hero and that I had meaning and something valuable to contribute to our world. As you go through this book, you, too, will find your meaning and purpose for existing.

Once you take 100% responsibility for your life and decide to no longer be a victim, you can really begin to radically change your life and step into your "superhero" suit.

As you embark on your Hero's Journey, what is it that you are really searching for?

You are the one you've been searching for. Not the past you. Not the future you.

But the *you* who is present in the here and now, in this very moment.

Life can be as beautiful as you want to make it. I hope you find the courage to believe in yourself and embark on this journey because, for me, it has been an amazing journey. I hope to share this cosmic journey with you and inspire you to connect with the hero within you that has always been there.

The world needs your brilliance to shine. Let's light up the dark sky with our shining lights, together.

XO,

~ *Julia*

THE HERO'S JOURNEY...

PART ONE:
SEPARATION

"Self-discovery is the process of throwing away
your mask, standing in front of the mirror, and
daring to see the depths of who you truly are—
the hero of your own life."

~ *Julia*

CHAPTER 1:

SELF-DISCOVERY AND THE ORDINARY WORLD

❧

S O, WHAT EXACTLY IS *self-discovery*? The *Collins English Dictionary* defines it as "a becoming aware of one's true potential, character, motives, etc."[1] In other words, *self-discovery* is the act of finding your true purpose in life. It means discovering and realizing your true beliefs and then living a life based on those beliefs. It means understanding the experiences that you have encountered from your childhood up to the present and their importance in shaping who you are. Self-discovery is the process of throwing away your mask, standing in front of the mirror, and daring to see the depths of who you truly are—*the hero of your own life*.

"Know Thyself." This is a common platitude that we often overlook because it seems so simple. However, we cannot deny that most adults struggle to know themselves, and many simply don't care to. We are so busy chasing the dreams that other people have created for us that we eventually lose our "self." One day we wake up and realize that we have no idea who we are and what we want because, for so long, we succumbed to the expectations of the people around us.

Self-discovery is a necessary step in order for us to reach individuation. *Individuation* refers to the process where we realize our *individuality*, separate from others and become conscious of our own unique identity. We start to realize the meaning for our existence on Earth and ponder the blueprint that we will leave behind for future generations. It is part of the process of "self-actualization" at the top of Maslow's Hierarchy of Needs. Furthermore, individuation is essential to our sense of self. It will give us the ability to have emotional well-being and to go after our dreams.

SELF-DISCOVERY IN MENTAL HEALTH

The process of self-discovery plays an important role because it can be put to good use in more than one area of your personal life. For example, discovering yourself as an individual will help you accept yourself through the process of self-awareness and by reprogramming your mind psychologically. You'll begin to feel much more comfortable in your own skin and not have to depend on the approval of others. In the area of relationships, being true to yourself and standing up for yourself will very likely push away people seeking only to criticize and control. As you become stronger, you will discover that these negative people will eventually be replaced by those who accept and love you for the person that you truly are and are becoming. When you are true to who you are, you will have clear, healthy boundaries and not allow others to take advantage of you. Being true to yourself can mean saying "no" when necessary or simply avoiding things like peer pressure.

Self-discovery is a welcome change for most people. Many of us have difficulty accepting ourselves and our weaknesses. So, when others criticize us or make negative comments about our appearance, our socioeconomic status, or our idiosyncrasies, we are crushed. Negativity like this can result in unnecessary stress, a bad mood, depression, anxiety and overall unhappiness. We cannot help it—external judgment creates a roadblock in our lives that holds us back from our truest potential.

This is why you need to learn to block the negativity of others and instead focus on your own positive thoughts. Whenever you feel yourself bristling at someone's insensitive or cruel remark about you, just stop. Create a new habit of refocusing your energy away from reacting in anger or bitterness. Remember that you have talents and abilities that they do not even know about, and that those inner strengths are going to help you turn your life around. Replacing negativity with purposeful positivity will make your stress levels drop like a rock.

SELF-DISCOVERY IN PHYSICAL HEALTH

Aside from the mental aspect, self-discovery can also help us improve our physical health. If you become mindful about your body, listening to what it is telling you and developing healthy habits, you will discover empowering ways of taking care of it. Morning walks and a day at the gym are great ways to connect with your physical self. Eating healthily and supplementing with vitamins you are deficient in will build up your strength and endurance not only for physical activity, but also for dealing with emotional situations because they supply the nutrients you need for stamina and mental clarity.

Taking care of your body also reduces stress so your cortisol levels can drop. Less cortisol coursing through your veins will reduce your risk of stress-induced conditions such as high blood pressure, diabetes and, surprisingly, depression.

"Ongoing stress means that stress hormones are operating throughout the day for most of the day. This is exhausting to the body and may cause the neurotransmitters in your brain like serotonin—the 'feel good' chemical that appears to influence mood, appetite, and sleep, among other things—to stop functioning correctly, potentially leading to depression."[2]

Who knew? So, getting those cortisol levels down should be the first priority if you have been struggling with depression.

SELF-DISCOVERY IN YOUR CAREER

Undoubtedly, many people are unhappy with their jobs. How many times have you heard friends or co-workers complain about their job and why they are so miserable in their work environment? How many times have you complained of this yourself? Oftentimes this dissatisfaction is the result of letting themselves be pushed into a career they really didn't want in the first place. Maybe a family member or other authority figure pressured and encouraged you into a career field with promises of money or prestige, but did YOU ever set a goal for what YOU wanted to do with your own life?

You may need to work in a job that is not fulfilling for a while or even for a long time for logistical reasons. Circumstances such as taking care of your family, providing for your spouse, getting through school, paying rent, and having a dependable means of taking care of yourself, as well as overcoming financial difficulties could force you to do that. If that is the case, you can continue to pursue your self-discovery journey during your free time. Do activities that refocus your attention away from the things that stress you out. Try hiking, gardening, sports or volunteering. Read-up on topics that interest you. *Learn everything you can about your dream life.*

The most important point at this stage in the process is that if there is something you really want to do with your life, find a way to go for it! Take college courses or, if you feel it is necessary, get a degree in your chosen field of work. Just remember that there are many alternative avenues to achieve a career path without taking the traditional route and getting a degree: Become an apprentice and learn a skill under a mentor. Seek out an entry-level job in the kind of work you want to do and work your way up. Attend webinars and seminars. These can all be positive steps in your Self-Discovery Journey.

STARTING YOUR SELF-DISCOVERY JOURNEY

Taking your path to self-discovery allows you to realize your strengths and weaknesses, your talents and abilities, and enables you to figure out how to develop these further. When you discover your passion, your self-discovery journey becomes a lot easier because your passion will drive you forward. You will see how all your talents and abilities align. *So, think about what you are passionate about*. What impact do YOU want to make in this world? If you let your dreams energize your self-discovery journey, you have a much greater chance of being happy, because you will know what you want, and be able to leverage your abilities to achieve it.

Regardless of where you are in life, whether you are already successful or feeling stuck—not sure of which direction you are heading, you are either on a journey or being called to one. A journey does not have to be the means to an end, but rather its purpose may be to enable you to thrive through your experiences. I encourage you to embark on a journey of self-discovery, and to learn the depths of who you are. Ask yourself, "Who am I?" Really think about it. Who are you? What makes you really happy? What would you do if you knew there were no limitations?

Finding yourself is a challenging journey. However, it is the best journey that you can go on to experience the kind of pure bliss and happiness you experienced at the moment of birth—before you were side-tracked from who you were meant to become.

*As you are reading and absorbing all of this, don't be afraid to let go of your inhibitions, or the things that have been holding you back. **If you really reach for your passion and all the possibilities that go with it, you will discover a sense of wonder awakening within you!***

EXERCISE E1-1:
DEFINING WHO YOU ARE

Grab a paper and pen or journal. Spend a few minutes answering these questions:

ASK YOURSELF

WHO AM I?

WHAT MAKES ME REALLY HAPPY?

WHAT WOULD MY LIFE BE LIKE IF NOTHING GOT IN MY WAY?

STILL SLEEPING ~ ORDINARY WORLD

The Conscious and the Subconscious—How to Get from your Ordinary World to a Special World

The Hero's Journey is a personal map of transformation, helping you go from where you are to where you want to be by exploring your conscious and subconscious minds. Furthermore, it is an exploration of the complexities of the self—everything that embodies who you are.

As you begin your own Hero's Journey, you travel along a path of self-discovery, starting with the exploration of your conscious mind, then working through your subconscious to create new beliefs, behaviors and patterns that will support you as a hero and become embedded in your unconscious mind.

You've likely heard about the famous psychoanalyst, Sigmund Freud. Freud believed that the mind operates from three different levels:

1. the *conscious*,

2. the *subconscious*,

3. and the *unconscious*.

As he studied the mind, he realized that all three parts have a significant role in human behavior.[3]

The *conscious mind* is the mind of awareness. It combines all of the mental processes that we have on a daily basis. It is everything that we think, feel, and can see at any given moment. It's the part of the mind that you utilize every single day. It helps you with analysis and logical reasoning and is the rational mind. The conscious mind is incredible in its ability to visualize and filter out anything that it feels is not necessary. However, it has limited processing capabilities compared to the subconscious and unconscious mind.

Most of us discover this when we try to use our conscious mind to break a habit, for instance. We are usually not successful because the *subconscious* and *unconscious* minds are in the background running the show. We have to first address the subconscious and unconscious reasons for our bad habits.

The *subconscious mind* is responsible for regulating your entire body system. It monitors and regulates your reflexes, responses, and movements. It's the mind that helps you do things automatically, things that you do not even think about. For example, it regulates your heart rhythm, pumps blood from your heart to the rest of your body, digests food, and sends white blood cells to a wound site to heal after an injury. It also stores thoughts, feelings, urges, and memories that are out of your conscious awareness but can be recalled when necessary, including short-term memories. Freud originally used the term "preconscious mind," when referring to the subconscious, but over time, the two were used interchangeably.

The *unconscious mind* stores all of your past experiences, beliefs, and behavioral patterns. It stores deep feelings and motives that we cannot access. The unconscious mind is not accessible to the conscious mind, although you can use your subconscious mind to help reprogram beliefs and behaviors that are stored in the unconscious. The unconscious processes much more information than the conscious mind.

It's important to be aware of these three minds as you embark on *The Hero's Journey*. You will be challenged to analyze your conscious mind as well as to dive deeper into your subconscious mind. Once you become aware of your thoughts, feelings, and actions (conscious mind) and what drives them (subconscious), you can begin to create lasting change in yourself (unconscious).

The Hero's Journey begins at the "ordinary world." The ordinary world is a place where you may be living your day-to-day life on autopilot. You're living your life according to the status quo, working very hard, and striving toward the "American Dream." You're chasing external satisfaction, doing what everyone else is doing, while also trying your best to blend in with everyone else. You're unaware that you still have so much potential to tap into. You just cruise through life, spending your days doing the same things over and over again. You're in your safe space, not seeking out change. You might feel unhappy, but you're unsure why, so you do things to avoid facing why you really feel that way. In the "ordinary world" you are oblivious of the adventures to come.

As I was studying the Hero's Journey, I began to realize that my life was filled with stages that mirrored the stages of a hero's journey. The Hero's Journey modeled my own journey as I tried to overcome depression and become aware that I was, in fact, *my own hero*. The stages of the Hero's Journey showed me how to move beyond my crushing past. Through my pain, I learned my purpose in life and realized the contribution I could make to the world.

Everyone's "Hero's Journey" is marked by traveling a cycle through which we overcome life's trials, become the hero within, and end where we began. This time around, though, we are enlightened and transcended from who we once were to who we can be!

MY ORDINARY WORLD

It was a bright and sunny day in 2005 when I made a fateful decision and first attempted to take my life. I was 14 years old, extremely depressed, and just couldn't face the world anymore. What should have been normal teenage years, instead was a period of quiet desperation wherein I experienced hatred for myself and others, taking the zest out of my life. I had never felt so alone, lost, and confused. I was struggling with my parents' divorce, in a toxic relationship with an alcoholic, had few reliable friends, and hated the fact that we had no money.

The feelings of sadness, hopelessness, and desperation overtook me as I contemplated sinking into the oblivion. It was like an earthquake was shaking in me, bringing tumultuous amounts of turmoil. The pain I felt every single day was like the feeling of a thousand heartbreaks, piercing through me and making my heart ache so fiercely. It was so unbearable that I felt as if there was no other way out. The pain was gut-wrenching, so this had to be the answer. I did not have an exact plan, I just knew I wanted to end it and disappear from this world. I walked into the bathroom, opening the mirrored cabinet to an array of bottles of medications. I pulled one off the shelf and stared in the mirror for what I thought would be the last time. "It'll all be over soon," I thought to myself as I observed this distorted version of myself in the reflection.

I took the bottle of pills outside with me, yanked open a door of my family's car, an old brown Toyota, and sat inside. I tilted the bottle of medication and watched as a few yellow pills dropped into my hand. Determined to go big or go home, I emptied the entire bottle and swallowed every last pill. As the medication hit me, I began to feel hazy. Everything slowed down. I felt numb, tingly. Everything started spinning and I felt sick to my stomach. Extreme nausea and discomfort flooded over me. The world around me suddenly seemed bleak and meaningless. Slowly my pain started to dissipate.

I was lucky that the medications I took did nothing but perhaps damage my liver. No one knew about this attempt and I definitely did not want to tell anyone. The next three days of my life were hell. Fortunately, it was the weekend and I didn't have to deal with school. I remember going to my part-time job feeling drowsy and completely out of it. It was all a blur. When I got to work, my coworker noticed that something was off and asked me if I was okay, and I casually answered, "Yes, I'm fine," even though I felt miserable on the inside. The day passed and came to an end.

The next two days I spent in bed, sleeping through it as the medications detoxed from my body. I kept this incident to myself, feeling guilt and shame for a failed attempt. I didn't

31

want to burden anyone with my problems so instead, I internalized them.

I was lucky that the medications I took were not enough to help me succeed in ending my life because that's not the result I wanted. At the end of the day what I truly wanted was help, love, and understanding, but I had no idea how to ask for it. Although I had my family and knew that they cared about me, they were unaware of the depth of my despair. I didn't have the words to describe my feelings and my needs. So, instead of turning to my loved ones for support, I felt I had to shoulder my burden alone. Adolescence was the beginning of a depression that would stay with me for years.

Throughout high school, I lost focus on everything except the depression that took the front seat in my consciousness. I kept switching schools every few months. I felt alone and kept my distance from most people. At 15-years-old I decided to move away from my family to live in Las Vegas on my own. I originally went out to Las Vegas to meet a modeling agent, however, upon my arrival there with my mother, we realized that he was a complete scam. He wanted me to live in his home and "manage" my modeling. Both my mother and I immediately felt like something was off. We decided not to sign with him.

However, this brief break away from Albuquerque, my hometown, gave me the urge to move away. I saw Albuquerque as a miserable place and I had always wanted to escape from there. This was the perfect chance for me to leave the past behind. Although my mother hesitated, she knew she couldn't stop me. I moved to Las Vegas all on my own, found a Vietnamese family to stay with until a few months later when I met my best friend and her family took me in. Throughout this time, my depression persisted and it became worse the longer I was away from home. After one year of living there, I decided it was time for me to move back home. When I went back home, the depression was still present but I managed to cover it up from the people around me. I used drinking and sexual promiscuity to help me feel better about myself, but nothing I tried worked. I was left feeling even more pathetic.

When I turned 18 I moved back to Las Vegas, hoping for better luck this time. But by the time I was 23, my life was the epitome of disaster. I had been there for five long years but I was no happier. My life consisted of drinking myself to sleep, hooking up with strangers, and many nights that I could not recall. I was cruising through life with no sense of direction. Every morning when I woke up, I felt worse than the night before. Still, I repeated the same cycle day after day, sinking further into my own demise. I hated who I was when I looked in the mirror. I was so ashamed of the person staring back at me. I sought external validation, never feeling like I was good enough. Not pretty enough. Not skinny enough. Not smart enough. I continued drifting aimlessly through life, repeating the same mistakes. I was lost and confused. I didn't understand why everything was happening to me the way it did. I was a victim, letting my external environment control who I was because, deep down inside, I really did not know who I was. I always had this deep feeling that I was not good enough. A feeling that everything I did, no matter what it was, was never enough. So, I lived like this, in pain, in fear, in scarcity because I didn't know that I was, in fact, "good enough" and perfect in all that I am.

These terrible emotions eventually led me to do things that I am not extremely proud of. One evening, I went out with two of my friends to a nightclub at the Cosmopolitan Hotel in Las Vegas. We got there around 11:30 p.m., but then time seemed to warp and pass rapidly until I woke up at 4 a.m., still incoherent and reeking of alcohol. I had experienced another blackout from drinking too much. I had no recollection of what happened in those four hours. I had no idea how I got home. I went outside to check to see if my car was there, the first car I had ever bought for myself. As I stepped into the driveway in front of my house, I was shocked to see my car, but even more shocked by the fact that the right side of the front of the car was completely smashed in. *Oh, my god! What the heck happened and why can't I remember anything?*

You would think that something like this happening would have shaken me to my senses and made me change my life forever. Well, it didn't. What did happen was that I felt guilty, ashamed, and embarrassed. So, of course, to avoid feeling those feelings, I continued to drink and make bad decisions. *Feeling* my emotions was too much to handle. I couldn't face the person I was becoming, but I didn't know how to escape. It was always easier to just numb the pain instead.

After five years of being in and out of school, making terrible decisions, and living in the warzone of my head, a familiar urge overcame me. It was time to move again, to run away. Maybe this new beginning and the thrill of living in a new city would make me feel better, I thought. Every time I traveled, I felt amazing. There were only small hints of loneliness at times. The experience of seeing a new place gave me the rush of endorphins that I so much needed. So maybe this was the answer I needed, a way to end my misery. Making up my mind, I packed my bags and moved to San Diego, knowing only one person who lived there—someone I had dated, who at the time didn't see any value in me. Again, another confirmation that I was not good enough.

In the beginning, San Diego was all I ever dreamed of. I had always wanted to live in California, ever since I was a teenager. And here I was, a dream come true! But it was not what I expected. For some reason, I still was not happy. Here I was in a new city and getting a fresh start, but the reality hit me that I was alone again. None of my issues had been resolved, whether it was career, finances, or having a healthy relationship with myself or others. I was at a standstill, again stuck questioning my own existence.

Two years passed and I remember spending days in my bed, not being able to leave because I was so depressed. Depression came in waves for me, starting in my teenage years. But this time, it lasted an entire two years. There were days and nights where I cried myself to sleep, isolating myself from the world. During this depression, I often thought, *Would anyone even care if I left this world*? No one knew the pain I suffered secretly, because I kept up an incredible front. I masked myself so no one could notice the sadness and emptiness I hid deep down.

In fact, I became quite good at putting on a mask, creating a facade of this picture-perfect girl. I became the prime example of the "girl who had it all." I was driving a nice BMW living in UTC San Diego, a nice neighborhood that was booming. I had designer bags and a closet full of nice clothing. I was always well-kempt, showing up to events dressed flawlessly. I perfected my look to the tee—full make-up, beautiful hair, and an outfit to kill. I rocked a beautiful smile for everyone to see. At least that's what everyone thought. The truth was, I was a really good actress and it was all a scripted show. I felt incredibly empty inside. I had no genuine love for myself or anyone else.

I was sad and depressed. I had deep feelings of unhappiness. My life felt like a mess and I was constantly stressed out on a day to day basis. During this time, I felt lucky to meet my boyfriend. When we met, I was swept away, drawn away from my own feelings of sorrow. He was the answer I was looking for, a "Prince Charming" coming to save me. He helped me in so many ways, but he also challenged me in just as many ways. Our relationship was toxic, not because he was a bad person, but because we were both so damaged. We hardly knew what love was. It's often said that relationships teach you a lot about yourself and it's true. We brought out the worst in each other. He triggered me in every single way possible. He reminded me of my own feelings of rejection, reinforcing my false belief that someone else could fix my problems, and revealing a terribly dark side of my personality. I was already unhappy when we met, so naturally, it carried into our relationship once our honeymoon phase ended. Our relationship forced me to realize that two broken people cannot fix each other. They can only be abrasive toward each other and it resulted in a very explosive relationship. After some time, we ended up breaking up.

Life was throwing me around like a toy. At this point in my life, I was at another all-time low constantly wondering *Why is it that I can never get anything right? Why is my life still a disaster*? If you've ever heard of Murphy's Law, you know it states that, "Whatever can go wrong will go wrong." That law was basically my life, and I kept attracting disasters, not knowing all along that I was the one who was creating this reality. It was another year before I discovered the Law of Attraction[4], and I started to wonder if maybe I was bringing some of these problems upon myself.

Like they say, I was at rock bottom, at an all-time low. I was desperate to get out of this misery but did not know how. One day, I decided that enough was enough. I was going to figure out a way to free myself from this pain. I began searching for answers. My desperation fueled the vigor that led me on my incredible Hero's Journey.

At the start of my journey, I had no one to rely on but myself. I would have given anything for some wise and caring person to take me aside and show me the ropes. I needed help getting my life back together. Well, the next best thing to having a personal guide was books. I started by putting my hands on as many self-development books as possible. I would head to the local Barnes and Nobles store and grace the self-help section. The first book I read that had a huge impact on me was *The Power of Now* by Eckhart Tolle. Eckhart's book really resonated with me because of his own story. If you haven't read it, Eckhart was on the verge of committing suicide when he had his spiritual awakening and realized that his suffering could end[5]. I thought to myself, *If he was at the point of almost committing suicide and, somehow, he figured a way out, surely there must be a way for me to pull myself out of this depression.*

After consuming that first eye-opening book, I decided to continue reading self-development books and soon learned about meditating. I had been convinced that there had to be a way to fix my depression and unhappiness without pills. I refused to be another person numbed by psychiatric medications. Besides, psychiatric medications only address the symptoms and not the problem. I wanted to get to the root of my depression and rip it out of my mind! I was tired of being tormented. Meditating was a healthy start.

This overall beginning stage of the Hero's Journey is what they call the "dark night of the soul." You may be experiencing something similar and that is why you picked up this book. You are dissatisfied with your life right now. You feel trapped. Don't give up before you start moving forward.

Read on to learn how to take the next step...

"I don't need to look for happiness in anyone or anything else. My key to happiness was already inside me! At that moment, I knew that everything would be okay and that it will only continue to get better from there on out."

~ *Julia*

Chapter 2:

The Awakening

My Call to Adventure

THE ACTIVE PHASE of *The Hero's Journey* really begins with the "Call to Adventure." The Hero, who feels extremely unsatisfied in his or her ordinary world, is faced with a life-changing decision calling him or her to a bigger and better future. Are you up for the challenge? Joseph Campbell described two paths we can take in life:

◇ the right-hand path

◇ or the left-hand path.[1]

The *right-hand path* is the path of the "ego." It's the path that most of us begin with because of how we grew up and what society taught us about norms. This path is much more practical. It usually lines up with societal expectations and keeps us in a bubble. It's limited with its means, keeping you confined in a reality that does not push your boundaries. It's the traditional path of growing up and getting an education, going to college, and getting a career. It's likely one that you probably do not really enjoy, however, it is honorable, according to other people. It's climbing the success ladder, except that this climb does not lead you to true fulfillment.

The *left-hand path* is the opposite of the right-hand path. It's the path of the soul, a riskier journey. It's the path of truly following your dreams instead of living according to societal expectations. This path has no order. It might take you into dangerous territories, but, towards the end, there will be rewards and riches to take back home—most importantly, that of a fulfilling life. This path enables you to live a greater life filled with creativity. It's the path of freedom of expression. This path takes you on *The Hero's Journey*.

My Call to Adventure

I continued practicing meditation and reading self-development books over the next year or so while I slowly made progress. Then on one winter day in sunny San Diego as I was driving in my car after the breakup with my boyfriend, I was listening to "Hey Jude" by the Beatles[2] and some of the lyrics started hitting home:

Hey Jude, don't make it bad

Take a sad song and make it better

Remember to let her into your heart

Then you can start to make it better

Hey Jude, don't be afraid

You were made to go out and get her

The minute you let her under your skin

Then you begin to make it better

And anytime you feel the pain

...

Hey Jude, don't let me down

You have found her, now go and get her

Remember to let her into your heart

Then you can start to make it better

So let it out and let it in

Hey Jude, begin

You're waiting for someone to perform with

And don't you know that it's just you.

I was driving my convertible BMW with the top down, feeling the gentle breeze and cool air as the lyrics resonated with me: *Don't you know that it's just you . . . It's just you . . .* echoed in my head, and I suddenly had this moment of grace, a spark of revelation where I clearly understood everything. I was wonder-struck by this profound understanding *that the person who I've been looking for my entire life was right in front of me. It was me!*

Now, that might sound crazy to you, but it took me many years of suffering before I came to this realization. I didn't need to look for happiness in anyone or anything else. My key to happiness was already inside me! At that moment, I knew

that everything would be okay and that it will only continue to get better from there on out.

At that moment, I experienced what Stephen Levine calls "the presence of what is called the Great Desire, the will toward mystery, the longing for deeper knowing, the draw toward the sacred heart, redefines life. A gradual upwelling of the still small voice within is heard. . . It is an insistent grace that draws us to the edge and beckons us to surrender safe territory and enter our enormity."[3]

**I had finally found my place of safety.
Now I could move forward.**

This was my "Call to Adventure!" It marked the beginning of a period where I had massive growth and transformation. It was time for me to embark on this expedition, a path to healing and overcoming my darkness, and a way toward transformation. This was a huge step in my self-discovery journey! It was not only the beginning of my Spiritual Awakening but also the beginning of when I began to question everything about my existence. I began to evaluate the path that I had taken that led me to where I was that day. What I realized was that I had stuck to the right-hand path for quite a while. I did what most people did—I went to school, became a nurse, got a job and helped someone else fulfill their dreams instead of fulfilling my own. Maybe this was the time to try the left-hand path...

TAKING RESPONSIBILITY

Listening to that song gave me a sudden revelation. But the most important revelation I received came later on when I realized that I needed to take responsibility for my own life. For years, I blamed my dad, various ex-boyfriends, family, and friends for the demise that I created. However, if I wanted to transform my life, I needed to realize that my life is 100% my responsibility. I came across this revelation as I read Jack Canfield's *The Success Principles*.

Before that day, I had struggled with one of Canfield's concepts: "Coming into my power."[4] According to Canfield, "Coming into my power" meant that I am the one in charge of my life. This can initially be a hard concept to understand or to accept because oftentimes we blame our problems on the external world. I'm not saying that taking responsibility means that everything that ever happened to you is your fault. I mean that "taking responsibility" for your reactions involves understanding what happens to you externally and how you react internally. If you continue to blame other people for what happens in your life, then you will always be the victim. The victim will never have power, but you can decide to take responsibility and take this power back.

Being responsible means knowing that you are the co-creator of your life, and you can choose to forge a new path for yourself. Making the choice may be difficult at first, but this choice will lead you to a life beyond your wildest imagination.

As I learned to take responsibility for my life, I had to look at my locus of control. "Locus of control"[5] is a concept in psychology that defines a person's belief system regarding the causes of his or her experiences and how they can contribute to that person's successes or failures. There are two categories: *internal* and *external*.

People with an *external locus of control* believe that they are *not* in control of their lives and they believe that external circumstances create their reality. When you operate from an external locus of control, you might not make the effort to fix a difficult event in your life because you feel like it is out of your hands and cannot be changed.

People with an *internal locus of control* believe that they can use their own abilities to create their success in the world around them. They believe that even when things go wrong, they can influence and change the outcomes of the situation or their life. These people believe that they can influence the future with their own hands. They take charge of their lives by taking the necessary actions to change their lives so that they can begin to reach their goals.

When I first began my self-development journey, I operated from an external locus of control. I did not believe that I had the power to change my life because I felt that external conditions were controlling my life. Each negative event that had happened to me caused me to further believe that I am a victim of these conditions, that I could not change my life because I was not lucky enough. However, as I continued my growth, I began to believe in my own power to take responsibility, to change and to create my destiny.

EXERCISE E2-1: LOCUS OF CONTROL

◇ Think about your own life. Do you tend to blame others for your circumstances? Or do you take responsibility and know that your future is determined by your own efforts?

◇ Take a look at the chart that follows and see what locus of control you are currently operating from.

◇ Decide which column you most identify with and if you can make any small changes to improve your perspective and your overall life.

INTERNAL LOCUS OF CONTROL	EXTERNAL LOCUS OF CONTROL
TAKES RESPONSIBILITY	BLAMES EXTERNAL EVENTS FOR CIRCUMSTANCES
LESS INFLUENCED BY OTHERS	BELIEVES THAT SUCCESS RESULTS FROM CHANCES OR LUCK
STRONG SELF-EFFICACY	DOESN'T BELIEVE IN THEIR ABILITY TO CHANGE THEIR LIFE
HAPPIER & INDEPENDENT	FEELS HOPELESS AND POWERLESS
INDEPENDENT	EXPERIENCES LEARNED HELPLESSNESS

LEARNED HELPLESSNESS

Many of us fall prey to a "victim mentality" because we were conditioned this way. However, instead of identifying with this victim role, we can "switch gears" and use past experiences as catalysts to trigger our change and growth—the way our car takes off when we switch gears from neutral to drive. Growing up as a kid, this victim mentality was extremely prevalent in my family. The belief that you are a victim of your circumstances can be more than simple conditioning; it can become a rigid mindset ingrained in you by situations that occur in your life.

Sometimes it's because we were never taught to rely on our own personal power. Maybe we were never shown that we do have the ability to change our lives, that we don't need someone else or something else to do it. My mother was a single mom taking care of four kids. She worked hard to support our family, but that meant she could not be there much of the time to provide emotional support or teach us coping mechanisms. She also didn't know them too well due to her own upbringing in Vietnam. It is uncommon for Asian families to openly express their feelings and communicate to resolve problems. Oftentimes, feelings and emotions are suppressed and dealt with individually. Because I spent a lot of time on my own as a child, I learned independence and self-reliance, both seemingly positive skills. However, consistently facing day-to-day struggles alone conditioned me to default to always carrying the weight of life's challenges myself instead of asking others for help.

My mother was oblivious to how our home situation was affecting me. I never indicated that it was. This is a common scenario for people who suffer from depression. They equate sharing their feelings and problems with burdening their loved ones. Over time, my beliefs became more and more concrete in my mind: I cannot ask for help. There is no way out. This will forever be my reality. Looking back now, I realized I could have asked for help, but being a teenage girl, that was not the way that I thought. The victim mentality can also manifest as "learned helplessness."

Learned helplessness is a state that people experience when they continually face difficulties and they begin to believe that they cannot control the outcome of the situation. A symptom of learned helplessness is feeling trapped by circumstances. Once individuals have this belief, they do not even attempt to fix the outcome because they believe that their efforts do not matter.

During the mid-1960s Martin E.P. Seligman did a research project on dogs where he discovered the phenomenon of learned helplessness.[6] His research project adapted Pavlovian classical conditioning with dogs to study how they would respond to electric shock. He realized that these dogs soon developed "learned helplessness."

After this experiment, he broadened his experiments to see if learned helplessness also affected humans. With further research, Seligman concluded that there was a correlation between learned helplessness and the degree of optimism toward life. An *explanatory style* is a way in which individuals habitually respond and react to events that occur. He theorized that people have two typical explanatory styles: *optimistic* and *pessimistic*.

He found that people who were more *optimistic* had higher levels of motivation and achievement, and they believed that their circumstances were temporary and external. Because of this optimism, they would not develop helplessness.

In contrast, people who tended to be *pessimistic*, always focusing on negative outcomes and seeing problems as permanent and pervasive, would easily develop helplessness and this would affect all other aspects of their life.[7]

The main difference between the two personality styles is that people who are optimistic believe their actions can control their lives while, inversely, pessimistic people believe that their actions will not create positive outcomes, their efforts will be undermined, and they have little or no control over their lives.

When I continued to face stress as a teenager without any help or resources, I was often paralyzed by the belief that "nothing I do matters." I was convinced that no matter how much time and effort I put into something, the result I wanted would not be satisfactory. This led to learned helplessness, which contributed to my depression. Many people who suffer from mental health disorders resort to the mechanism of learned helplessness. It usually develops in childhood when an event happens repeatedly and, because we have no coping skills, we learn that there is nothing we can do to change the situation.

For example, being shy can lead to "learned helplessness." If you are shy by nature and have bad experiences whenever you are in social situations, you may begin to feel that there is nothing you can do to overcome this shyness. Over time, instead of interacting with people, you avoid them instead, because you believe that this will always be the case. When I had to face traumatic events in my life all alone and lacked the skills to cope with and process the events, I became helpless and hopeless. This affected me for many years until adulthood when I discovered how to develop my coping skills and my personal power.

The combination of shifting your locus of control, building self-efficacy, and developing an optimistic personality will all help you on your journey to becoming your best self and overcoming any challenges ahead. You have the ability to change your locus of control if you want to. It will gradually shift as you learn to love yourself, rely on yourself, and tap into your own personal power.

Shifting your locus of control is the beginning of what is called "self-efficacy," which is "an individual's belief in his or her capacity to execute behaviors necessary to produce specific performance attainments."[8] Self-efficacy means that you have confident control over your motivations and the behaviors and actions you take to obtain the life that you desire. It is the ability to rise to the occasion and do what's necessary to reach a goal, a self-regulatory mechanism that helps you adapt and flourish even in the harshest conditions. People with high self-efficacy have belief in themselves and in their abilities. They look at challenging problems as a way to learn and increase their skills. They have a stronger sense of commitment to their interests and goals. They also recover quickly from setbacks and disappointments.

On the opposite end, when you have low self-efficacy, you may avoid challenging situations because you might feel that you cannot handle them. You might also tend to focus on negative outcomes, and you might not have confidence in yourself and your abilities. Don't worry if you feel like you are on the lower end of the self-efficacy spectrum. I was also once there, too. As you travel along your Hero's Journey, I will teach you the skills that will make self-efficacy a natural and empowering part of your life!

"Understanding my ego was a critical part of my journey as I sought to connect to my higher self and the truth of who I am."

~ *Julia*

CHAPTER 3:

REFUSAL OF THE CALL

∽♾️∾

FTER MY SPIRITUAL AWAKENING, life was amazing! I got a glimpse of what seemed like heaven on earth. I was excited to embark on this new journey and create a life worth living. Everything in my life now made sense and seemed so crystal clear. I felt like I was ALIVE and AWAKE for the first time in my life. It was like waking up from a really bad dream and realizing that I had been asleep the entire time. I was filled with awe and amazement again, just like I once was as a little toddler. The happy little girl in me had woken up. The universe was filled with endless possibilities and there was so much for me to see. I became enticed by the wonders of the world. Everywhere I looked seemed to hold a spark of magic.

I remember looking at the trees and feeling so full of hope as I saw the komorebi (when sunlight shines through trees) filter between the leaves. I felt connected with the earth and the universe, taking in the truth that the universe has been around for billions of years, and there I was, on a tiny planet that's floating in space. I mean, how incredible is that? I began to see the magic of life and the spark of creation, for the very first time. It was like taking a breath of fresh air for the first time after suffocating for so long. As I sat there and observed the trees, I looked up at the sky filled with fluffy clouds and birds flying freely. I focused in on a seagull gliding through the air, and I could not believe how miraculous it was to see this creature floating through the air as the wind picked up beneath its wings. I finally understood what it meant to feel the *aliveness* of being free and in the present moment. It was then that I concluded that there was so much more to life than suffering.

These moments of bliss graced my life from time to time and I began to appreciate the small things in life. I would wake up feeling grateful for being alive, for having fresh air, for having a roof over my head, and something as small as being able to breathe. There was a newfound happiness in my life. There were days when I felt as if I could take on the world. I was filled with so much love and happiness as my heart continued to expand and become weightless. I was swimming in an abyss of joy, and life finally felt good.

THE EGO

I was lucky to have these experiences that lifted me up because soon after, my ego decided to kick in. I'm sure you've heard of the term "ego" before, but you might not have realized the power it really has in our lives. The word "ego" can have different definitions and meanings depending on the perception of the individual. In this book, I am referring to the ego as the voice of the negative mind—this voice that is constantly nagging and creating limiting beliefs in your mind. When talking about the ego, I'm not referring to the overinflated sense of self. The ego is much more than that. The ego, also known as your "conscious mind," is the voice in your head that keeps you in pain and suffering. In a way, the ego believes it is helping you.

When you were a child, the ego was developed as a way to protect you, because you were so young and could not manage life all on your own. However, as you merge into adulthood, this voice remains present, forming into a protection mechanism to ensure your survival. So, it constantly talks to you in a way to ensure your safety and security. It's an ever-present voice that creates incessant chatter in your mind.

Unfortunately, the ego can also show up in thoughts and feelings that make you feel inferior or cause self-hatred, preventing you from tapping into your truest potential. The ego is the compulsive voice you hear when you are feeling negative emotions, such as sadness, anger, fear, or jealousy. Part of the human experience is being attached to our ego. The ego gives us our sense of identity. It remembers everything that we have accepted to be true about ourselves and replays it over and over—especially the lies we have come to believe about ourselves. That is why when we attempt new changes, the voice of the ego kicks in, invading our minds and holding us back. *Understanding my ego was a critical part of my journey as I sought to connect to my higher self and the truth of who I am.*

Because the ego had such a strong presence, it fought me as I tried to change and become the best version of myself. It has a mesmerizing quality to it, easily persuading the individual of its truth. It kept me in a state of ultimate fear and negativity. It attempted to work as a protective barrier, holding onto habits of the past, because the uncertainty of the unknown was even more paralyzing to it. From time to time, I would hear its voice creeping back into my life and trying to prevent me from coming into my power. Coming into my own power meant the voice of the ego would become eradicated, and, of course, the ego didn't like that.

You see, change is extremely difficult for all individuals. So, be prepared: this battle is going to be one for the books! It is much easier to cling to the past, to cling to a story that we have accepted as true, than to enact change within our lives. In some dysfunctional way, we are all addicted to this drama. However, like nature, if you do not change, you will die. Change is the only constant in the world. Another aspect of this that kept me from growing was the ego's need to stick to what's familiar. For more than 10 years of my life, I was the person suffering from depression. My body and mind were running on an automatic program that I was conditioned to. So, when I began to become happier, the ego did not like this. I was treading through unfamiliar and unknown territory, which caused me deep angst and fear. The ego wanted to hold me back by keeping me glued to familiarity, reintroducing the thoughts that had kept me down and depressed for so long.

The ego's force is powerful. It heavily resisted me as I tried to outgrow it. It was like a powerful magnet pulling me back to my old behaviors. But I refused to let the ego take over my life again. It had already taken so much away from me. Besides, I had experienced happiness and joy beyond my imagination, and I had become addicted to that eternal bliss. I knew that there were parts of me that were ready to move on and that I was ready to tap into my fullest potential, but the old version of me was scared and held tightly to what was familiar.

The truth was that it was easier to revert back to old patterns and conditioning because that was what I was accustomed to. It was literally hard-wired in me. I had spent those ten years reinforcing the thoughts and behaviors of an insecure and depressed person, so I knew it would take time before I could break those neural connections that were so strongly bonded. This just meant that I had to put in additional effort to really overcome the outdated version of myself.

Neural connections that are used over and over again become *habits* and they can be hard to break. Let's say you developed a bad habit of eating sugary foods all the time without noticing the impact on your body. You started by eating a sugary snack every day in the afternoon as a "pick-me-up." What's so bad about that? Then you start grabbing a Danish with your coffee every morning. It's very satisfying because sugar is extremely addicting. You are now eating extra sugar twice a day. After a month, this has become a habit. Before long, you can eat sugar without consciously being aware that you are doing it. As soon as you see a piece of candy lying around, you pick it up. You start stopping by the vending machine after work each day for another snack. Soon you are eating sweets regularly four times a day. One day three months later, you notice your reflection as you pass by a store window and you are shocked at how you look. Over three months, you have gained a noticeable amount of weight—all because of this habit.

Now you are on a mission to lose that weight. But, because most people like to have quick fixes, you think that you can quickly lose this weight in a couple of weeks. You set crazy goals for yourself and go to extremes to try to get the weight off, but to no avail. Realistically, it took you three months to build and reinforce your sweet-eating habit, but you think you can lose the weight much faster than you put it on? Be realistic. Not only do you have to worry about calories, but you are also up against a brick wall called a "habit." When you are trying to break past habits and develop new ones, remember that it takes time to build a new habit. Plus, it takes the same amount of effort to break a habit as to create a new one.

There are no shortcuts here. Change does not happen overnight, but little by little, step by step, you will continue to make progress until one day, you will not be a victim of your habit. It takes time to implement changes and keep them going. This won't happen overnight, but with each change made and each step forward, you are winning.

It works the same way with our mindset. This is something that I learned the hard way from experience. If we have allowed our ego to make us view ourselves as a victim of our circumstances, this mindset becomes a habit (a neural connection) that controls us. Just like craving a piece of candy every afternoon, our mind and our mood hinge on this victim mentality and urge us to act in line with that mentality. Once we discover how to break that habit, we will no longer primarily operate from a victim mentality or succumb to the voice of our ego.

In the beginning, when you are learning to overcome your negative thoughts, feelings, and behaviors, it is going to be difficult. It is human nature's natural disposition to resist change, and you will do it fighting and screaming. Part of you will want to stay where you are comfortable while the other part is waiting to be fully embraced. As you learn to overcome your own feelings of depression or your own negative belief systems, I want to remind you that it takes time and effort and that this is just part of the journey. There will be moments when you make progress and there will be moments when you feel like you are taking one step forward and two steps backwards. However, any progress means you are moving forward, and the only way to get to a state of happiness is by working at it.

Understanding the voice of the *ego* will help you as you embark on your self-discovery journey. Being able to identify its voice is necessary if you are determined to continue your process of transformation. Recognizing the voice of your ego helps you navigate as you are faced with challenges because the voice of the ego will always try to keep you in a negative state and prevent you from moving forward in your journey. It is important to develop an awareness of the voice of the ego so that you can discern the "truth" versus the voice of the ego. Listen closely to hear the voice of the ego, as it will usually present itself in the ways described below.

THE DYSFUNCTIONS

While reading *Playing Big: Practical Wisdom for Women Who Want to Speak Up, Create, and Lead*, written by Tara Mohr, I learned that my ego does not always function properly or for my benefit. Who knew? Below are some eye-opening truths she shared about the ego[1]:

◇ **The ego is typically negative**. The ego constantly focuses on the negatives and never sees the positive in any situation. It continually complains. It always thinks of the worst-case scenarios.

◇ **The ego likes to compare**. The ego constantly forces you to compare yourself to others, fostering the false belief that you are not good enough.

◇ **The ego constantly judges**. The ego constantly judges everyone and everything including itself. Judgment strokes the ego and makes it feel safe.

◇ **The ego is never satisfied**. The ego is on an endless search for material goods, status, money, and happiness. It is never satisfied with what it has and will seek out external validations.

◇ **The ego personalizes everything**. The ego thinks everything is about *the ego*. Whenever something happens, it creates a personalized story, thinking that the world is "attacking it."

Accept the fact that the fight with your ego will be an ongoing battle, but you can overcome anything if you put your mind to it. Don't let your ego's pesky voice keep you intimidated or hold you back from your calling as the "hero" of your life, because once you master your ego, you will begin to experience amazing shifts in your life that will lead to massive growth and open up possibilities you never dreamed of.

EXERCISE E3-1: HOW DOES THE EGO SHOW UP IN YOUR LIFE?

1. How does the voice of *the ego* show up in your life?

2. Can you identify the voice of *the ego* according to the descriptions above?

3. Grab a pen and paper or journal and write down a few different ways the ego voice shows up in your life.

4. Hold on to this paper so you can refer back to it in later exercises.

"Your mentors and the people you meet along your journey are reflections of you. They are there to guide you and show you the answers that you hold within yourself."

~Julia

CHAPTER 4:

MEETING THE MENTOR

⌒⌒⌒

MY JOURNEY to overcoming my depression was a combination of will and effort, but it would not have been possible without the help of my mentors. I did not have physical mentors, but I found many spiritual teachers who helped guide me along the way. To name a few, I followed:

◇ Abraham Hicks,

◇ Eckhart Tolle,

◇ Jack Canfield,

◇ and Gabrielle Bernstein.

When I was feeling lost or unsure, I would look to my mentors to find answers. There are plenty of free resources out there, so find books or DVDs by mentors that you resonate with and start to study their teachings. We are lucky to live in an era where information is totally accessible and you can find answers within seconds on the Internet; do a simple research online to find inspirational speakers and see who you resonate with. Your mentor might not come in the form of a spiritual teacher but it does not matter. The point here is to find someone you can relate to, someone who inspires you, and someone who motivates you to become the best version of yourself. You can seek out a mentor through online groups, local communities, or perhaps reaching out to friends and family who are willing to take on the role.

Having a mentor is a wonderful thing! Mentors can help guide you along your journey and push you to the greatest heights. Mentors help you clarify and enlarge your vision as well as nourish you as you grow and transform into who you are meant to be. Mentors are wise, knowledgeable, and already have life experiences to help you gain new perspectives and fresh ideas. Everyone needs to connect with others in order to grow. It is through mentors, and the support, insight and feedback they give you, that you are able to see another side within yourself—the true and authentic "you" that has been there all along. They see your truth and remind you of the reason for your journey. They affirm that you are here to light up the world with your brilliance. Not only do they keep you aligned and on purpose, but they motivate and challenge you to step into your superhero suit.

If you can, of course, find someone who is willing to mentor you in person. This will help you through the process. Although I do have to say that the lack of a physical mentor forced me to rely on my own abilities to create change and have breakthroughs within myself.

After finding a mentor, really dig into the thinking of this amazing person. You may even find two or three people whose life experience connects somehow with your own struggles. You need to study how all your mentors talk, how they behave, and the actions that they take on a daily basis. Study the methods they use to help them succeed and live a fulfilling life. Studying your mentors is not enough. At some point, you have to begin to model your mentors. Walk their walk and talk their talk. This will give you a preview of what it is like to be them and will help you expand your perception of yourself. The best way to get to where you want to be is to model someone who is successful and has already made it.

Another option is to find a therapist or coach to work with. A therapist or coach can help you see a different perspective and push you towards fulfillment. Most of us tend to rely on ourselves and avoid asking for help, but asking for help does not make you weak. In a sense, admitting that you need help is proof that you are stronger than you think. So, don't hesitate to ask for help. We all need additional resources to guide us along the way, so don't be afraid to ask.

YOUR INNER MENTOR

Your mentors and the people you meet along your journey are reflections of you. They are there to guide you and show you the answers that you hold within yourself. Oftentimes we seek out help from other people when we have a question or are struggling with a question. Internally, we already know the right answer; we just seek this validation from others to confirm our own feelings.

Don't forget, within each of us is an inner mentor. Your inner mentor is the "Hero" within you, a powerful internal resource. You always have access to this inner mentor. You might want to think about your inner mentor as your intuition. You can connect with this inner guidance system at any time you want. Many of us forget that we have this powerful source within us and we always search for help from the external world, but sometimes, the answer you are looking for is right there within you.

The voice of the inner mentor is basically an older and wiser part of yourself. This voice can help guide you along the way of your transformational journey. It can help you make the right decisions when you're feeling confused. It can navigate through troubled waters and help you find a stillness within the chaos. Just as the deep waters of the ocean are not disturbed by a hurricane on the surface of the water, you can find the stillness deep inside yourself—no matter what turbulence is going on in your life. The inner mentor is filled with creative solutions and can help you remain aligned to your path, giving you the wisdom you need.

When you first connect with your *inner mentor*, you might struggle with identifying the voice within you. When you hear the inner mentor's voice, it will be soft and soothing, giving you a sense of peace. The inner mentor does not shout like the "inner critic's" voice, and sometimes it will give you very basic answers. The voice of your inner mentor can be obscure at times, so it's up to you to listen and to figure out the message that voice is trying to give you. However, this is how the inner mentor's voice works. It will give you the solutions necessary for the highest good. So, listen closely.

EXERCISE E4-1: "MEETING THE INNER MENTOR" MEDITATION

1. Have a pen and paper or journal handy to answer the questions after your meditation.

2. Find a comfortable place to sit or lie down.

3. Close your eyes and take three, deep, cleansing breaths—slow, long and deep inhales and exhales. With each breath, let the stress of the day and the worries around you melt away. Tune into your breath. Feel the flow of oxygen filling up your lungs as your chest rises and then falls. Feel the oxygen rejuvenating your body and filling you up with life. Begin to feel absolutely relaxed as you go deeper within yourself, connecting with your essence—with the core of who you are.

4. Now imagine a path leading down to the ocean. With each step you take, you will relax even more. As you walk this path, you take in the incredible and majestic views around you. You can see the incredible ocean, clear blue and pristine, and you feel a gentle breeze brush up against your face. You feel happy and grateful for such a beautiful moment.

5. As you get closer to the ocean, you can see your inner mentor in the distance. You feel your mentor's grace, a sense of calmness, a sense of wisdom. You walk up to him or her with a hug, feeling your mentor's inner radiance connect with you. Ask the inner mentor any questions you might have and listen for the answers.

It's important for you to have a *dialogue* with your inner mentor. Remember, mentors are there to serve you and to help you reach your highest potential. Get to know them. They will provide the answers you need if you just listen closely.

Think about your experience with your inner mentor:

◇ What did his or her presence feel like?

◇ How did he or she look?

◇ How can your mentor help you live your life on purpose?

◇ What wisdom can he or she offer you?

THE HERO'S JOURNEY...

PART TWO:
INITIATION

"You see, most of us believe that our negative traits will forever be a part of us and that we cannot change who we are or how we react. I am living proof that change is possible and that our personalities are completely malleable."

~ *Julia*

CHAPTER 5:
CROSSING THE FIRST
THRESHOLD

Taking the Leap

*A*n old Cherokee is teaching his grandson about life. "A
fight is going on inside me," he said to the boy. "It is a
terrible fight and it is between two wolves. One is evil –
he is anger, envy, sorrow, regret, greed, arrogance, self-pity,
guilt, resentment, inferiority, lies, false pride, superiority, and
ego."

He continued, "The other is good – he is joy, peace, love,
hope, serenity, humility, kindness, benevolence, empathy,
generosity, truth, compassion, and faith. The same fight is going
on inside you – and inside every other person, too."

The grandson thought about it for a minute and then asked his grandfather, "Which wolf will win?"

The old Cherokee simply replied, "The one you feed."

A S I MADE the commitment to go on this journey of transformation, I had to face the darkest parts of myself. It was time to face my depression and the beliefs I had formed over the years. I believed that I wasn't good enough, that I was not worthy of love or success. I believed that happiness was not available to me and that life would always be a struggle. I believed that the world was not safe and that I couldn't trust anyone. This was, of course, scary because doing the internal work is challenging. I had to break down all the parts of me that had kept me chained to my depression and stuck in unhappiness. Sometimes we might not realize it, but the darkness can be mesmerizing; it's an addiction that draws us into its enticing nature. It keeps us trapped unless we find a way to break free from it.

The most important part of me that I had to face was the jealousy I felt. I remember as a teenager always being jealous of all the people who seemed to have it all—a happy, complete family; money; or the ability to travel and do whatever they wished. Meanwhile, I let this torment torture me because of my deep feelings of jealousy. As I grew older, this condition only worsened. I played it off coolly, but deep down I continued to have horribly envious feelings toward others. In my relationship with my boyfriend from "my ordinary world" subchapter that sparked my spiritual awakening, my biggest problem was again jealousy.

JEALOUSY

Jealousy ate at me and permeated throughout my soul. I was a jealous monster and was completely unhappy with myself. I was jealous and constantly worried he was cheating on me, worried that he would meet someone who he thought was better than me. I was jealous, even, of him spending time with his friends because I felt like I should be the only person in his life. I would get jealous if we were out walking and there was a pretty girl around us. I was constantly on the lookout for the next occasion to become upset and triggered by the jealousy. I was in a dark place and felt emotionally heavy, imprisoned by these negative feelings.

Jealousy had become a part of my personality. I believed that I had no way of escaping it. It was not until I noticed patterns repeating themselves in my relationships that I decided it was finally time to resolve these feelings. I took an honest look at all my relationships shortly after a particularly rough breakup—how they failed, and what I could have done better. I began to see that my jealousy had a huge part in causing my relationships to fail.

You see, most of us believe that our negative traits will forever be a part of us and that we cannot change who we are or how we react. I am living proof that change is possible and that our personalities are completely malleable. In order for us to change, however, we have to first become aware of exactly what we want to change in ourselves, be absolutely sure that we want this change, and then believe that it is possible.

Before we can start changing, we have to distance ourselves from our ego. *The ego resists change*. It says, "You are stuck this way, so live with it." So, when you're attached to the ego, like I was, you will just tell yourself, "This is the truth about me and there is no other way." For me, I would often tell myself, "This is just who I am." I spent a lot of my time believing that I could not change the parts of myself that I was unhappy with and that other people needed to accept it because that was who I was. But I came to realize that I actually do have the power to change this aspect of myself that makes me so miserable. Moreover, it was not fair to me or to the other people in my life to give them the power to make me happy. In reality, I am the only one who can do that.

To continue on my journey meant that I had to face these feelings and understand why they were taking over my life. What I found, as I mentioned earlier, was that I did not feel like I was good enough. In fact, I never felt like I was good enough— to do anything right, to be successful, to be worthy of anyone's approval. These feelings arose from the constant familial conditioning of a highly critical family, and that's who I blamed for a long time. My family constantly criticized me about my weight and the way I looked, and because this was repeated daily, it eventually became molded into my personality.

I remember being 13 years old at my grandmother's home and asking to use her scale. Her first response was, "You are not skinny, so why do you need to weigh yourself?" I began to believe that there was something wrong with me. When you are a child or even a teenager, you rely on your family and those who are closest to you to support you and make you feel good. I had the opposite. I am not saying that they didn't care about me because I know they did, but they had a different way of showing it. I know this is a cultural thing. Asian families tend to be critical and have high expectations for their children. I could have gone on blaming my family for messing up my life but the truth is, it was time for me to take responsibility. Despite the way I was raised, I had to take responsibility for my own feelings, reactions, and actions.

As I learned to overcome my jealousy, one of the most important things I learned was that it is necessary for me to adopt a "Win-Win Mentality"[1] (see Jack Canfield's *The Success Principles*). The "Win-Win Mentality" is the belief that everyone has a chance to succeed and, just because another person may succeed, that does not mean that you are not good enough. There is enough room for everyone to find love, to succeed, and to be happy. You do not need to live in constant fear that another person's success is taking away from your own. This mentality gave me a fresh perspective on jealousy and competition. There can be healthy competition, but if it is destroying your life, you must evaluate it further to see how you developed these feelings and why you respond the way that you do.

Charles Darwin created the evolutionary theory of survival of the fittest and the "struggle for existence."[2] Now, this may appear true in biological evolutionary terms, but it does not work the same way with our neighbors, coworkers, and friends. There does not have to be a bloody battle in which we compete and fight for our life. In fact, the evolution of another person's existence has nothing to do with you. Everyone is on his or her own journey and has a separate path. You would not compare an apple to an orange because they are two completely different fruits. They each have a distinct genetic purpose and are appreciated for what they are. So, keep this in mind when you are tempted to have feelings of jealousy or fear that someone might take away your spotlight. Of course, we're all humans and this will happen from time to time, but jealousy is an extremely poisonous emotion. Take it from me, who has experienced it first-hand. When another person succeeds, what does that take away from you? That's right... the answer is nothing, because it was not yours in the first place. Neither will your success interfere with someone else's. So, there is no reason to fear or be jealous.

You see, the jealousy was only a surface layer symptom of a deeper belief that I held onto tightly. When I understood this truth, I realized that my identity had been shaped by so many negative beliefs that I had been forced into depression. Sometimes we might not understand the depression or negative beliefs and where they come from, but if we're brave enough and we look a little harder, we might find the answers we are looking for within us.

It was time for me to do some spring cleaning and reevaluate all the thoughts and beliefs I had up until this point in my life. Boy, was I in for a surprise! It was necessary for me to confront my innermost demons and the outdated beliefs and behavior patterns that had ruled my life thus far:

At the root of all my behaviors were the beliefs that:

◇ I'm not enough.

◇ I'm not worthy.

◇ I'm not deserving of love.

When I was able to identify these core beliefs, I knew that I had the power to change them. In order for us to change our beliefs, we have to take a look at how they were formed while adopting a new set of beliefs.

COGNITIVE BEHAVIORAL THERAPY (CBT)

Cognitive Behavioral Therapy—a talking therapy in which therapists help patients analyze their thoughts and belief systems to help them create positive change—has a huge influence on changing behavior for people who are anxious or depressed. Although I never went to therapy for CBT specifically along my own journey, I have learned a lot of tools from CBT that have helped me create change in my life and modify my behaviors for better outcomes. CBT is not only effective for people who are suffering from anxiety and depression, but I believe it helps anyone who wants to change in general.

Cognitive Behavioral Therapy combines:

◇ our cognitions (how we think),

◇ our emotions (how we feel),

◇ and our behavior (how we act).

CBT starts with the premise that our thoughts create our behaviors. The key to CBT is helping patients become aware of what is behind their behavioral patterns. Once they are able to identify them, they can begin to create change and alter their behaviors. According to Aaron Beck, one of the pioneers in this field, CBT is based on the "hypothesis that people's emotions and behaviors are influenced by their perceptions of events. It is not a situation in and of itself that determines what people feel but rather the way in which they construe a situation."[3]

Understanding how our thoughts and beliefs influence our reality is the basis from which we can cultivate change through awareness. CBT helps individuals develop new thinking styles so that they can adapt a healthier operating system from which they are able to reduce anxiety and depression as well as adopt a healthier thinking system.

Martin Seligman believed that cognitive therapy works because it helps an individual shift from a pessimistic explanatory style to an optimistic explanatory style. Cognitive therapy works because "it gives the self a set of techniques for changing itself. The self chooses to do this work out of self-interest, to make itself feel better."[4]

As we continue this book, we will be using some Cognitive Behavioral Therapy techniques to help you become aware of your core beliefs, dysfunctional assumptions, and negative automatic thoughts. As you internalize these skills, you will be able to see the world in a different light and begin the deep work necessary for your Hero's Journey.

If our thoughts really do create our behaviors, then, in order to change our behaviors, we have to understand more about our thoughts.

THOUGHTS

So, how do thoughts affect our lives? Well, in more ways than you can imagine:

Thoughts are the basis of our reality.

Our reality is a *construct* our minds create based on past experiences. This means that your thoughts result from the interpretation you have of events that happened in the past. How you perceive your reality depends on whether you have a *pessimistic explanatory style* or an *optimistic explanatory style* when trying to interpret your reality. Your style determines what thoughts will be attached to that reality.

Before you can deal with your reality, you have to deconstruct it. Ask yourself, "What is the truth about my reality? Why is it that one person can survive a tough situation and another person can't? It really comes down to how the individual interprets the event. In order for you to create a reality that leads you to happiness and fulfillment, you have to look at how you interpret different situations and the meanings you attach to these events.

◇ Think about the living cells of an organism. If a cell is placed in a toxic environment, the cell could shrink and die, or swell and burst. Now think about the environment your mind lives in, the positive and negative thoughts that fill up your mind daily. Are the conditions in your mind livable, or are your thoughts creating a toxic environment within you? The kinds of thoughts that constantly swirl around in your mind taint your perspective on reality for the better or for the worse. How does a *pessimistic explanatory style* affect your thoughts about an event? What about an *optimistic explanatory style*?

Did you also know that when you think a thought you are actually creating a physical reaction in your body? Think about when you are feeling happy, sad, anxious, or fearful. What are the normal reactions that tend to happen in your body? When you are thinking happy thoughts, you release the "feel good" hormones such as dopamine, serotonin, oxytocin, and endorphins. This can cause an increase in positive emotions, motivation, and an overall sense of wellbeing.

On the other hand, when you are thinking a negative thought, this creates stress and you will have an increase in hormones such as cortisol and adrenaline surging through your bloodstream. These "fight or flight" hormones immediately put you on edge because this stress response is hard-wired in you to protect you from potential threats. This "fight or flight" response is a physiological reaction in your body that occurs when your nervous system is engaged in preparation for anticipated danger. It enhances your awareness and sharpens your senses, causes your heart-rate to go up, speeds up respiration, and gives you superhuman potential.

This mechanism is necessary when you need protection, but if it continues to be triggered by a non-stop flood of negative thoughts, it can cause chronic stress, which will alter your brain chemistry in real life. If you are in this mode every single day, it can also have extremely detrimental effects on your body's ability to function. When you are constantly stressed-out for months or even years, it wreaks havoc on your mind and body. You then become vulnerable to illnesses and diseases. Body aches, fatigue, a compromised immune system, depression, and anxiety are all signs that you are experiencing chronic stress.

Stress hormones decrease how effectively your immune system works, and that is why it can lead to physical illnesses. In recent years, there has been an uptick in the number of studies about the mind and body connection.[5] This research suggests that your mind and body are interconnected and that, in order to achieve overall health, you need to have a balance between them. In the field of psychoneuroimmunology, research has shown that the mechanisms triggered by stressful emotions can alter white blood cell functions. The white blood cell is the most crucial cell to the immune system, so we can see that if we are constantly stressed out, we negatively affect our white blood cells.[6]

So, how does this relate back to your thoughts? Well, your thoughts create physical responses in your body. If you continue to think negative thoughts, you are putting your body into overdrive, and this can cause detrimental responses. What this means is that it is time for you to evaluate your thoughts and see whether they are physically helping or hurting you. Think about it as if you were taking care of a plant. If you water it, bathe it in sunlight, give it lots of attention and care, then it will grow and develop into a healthy plant. If, on the other hand, you neglect the plant, forget to water it, and leave it in the dark, it will most likely wilt and die. Apply this concept to the thoughts that you feed yourself every day: The more frequently you think negative thoughts, the more you damage your mind, body and sense of self.

Psychologists have labeled the negative thoughts that we constantly think as "automatic negative thoughts." They suggest that the reason we predominantly have automated negative thoughts is because our ancestors used to use this type of thinking as a way of anticipating potential threats and dangers. In other words, it was crucial for them to analyze everything in a negative light because they lived in dangerous environments. Believe it or not, we still operate from this fear-based instinct that our ancestors have passed down to us. True, this can be helpful in dangerous situations, but fortunately, most of us are not faced with a potential crisis in everyday life. Today's crisis is the *crisis in our minds*.

CHALLENGING YOUR THOUGHTS

Now we can't completely get rid of our negative thoughts, but we can learn how to challenge them. First, we need to cultivate self-awareness: We have to notice when these negative thoughts seem to dominate our mind. Once we are aware of these thoughts, then we can learn to challenge them, to dispute their right to occupy our mind. How? By simply arguing with ourselves! This tool is extremely effective in reframing our thoughts especially when we are faced with a difficult situation. This is often referred to as *learned optimism*, a concept explained in Martin Seligman's book, *Learned Optimism: How to Change Your Mind and Your Life*.[7]

Here is an example of how to use the *learned optimism* tool. When I first became a nurse, I faced many challenges and uncertainty. I worked at a high-demand nursing facility where I had more than 25 patients. This added tremendous pressure since I was a novice nurse. There were moments when I felt like a complete failure and like maybe I should never have become a nurse. So, let's analyze my thoughts and beliefs and reframe them in a way that is more beneficial:

⬦ **Situation**: I was working as a temp for a nursing facility with 25 patients. I was a brand-new nurse and a bit inexperienced in dealing with that many patients. As I was working my shift, another nurse commented, "You're taking a really long time to pass out the medications."

⬦ **Thought/Belief**: She's right. I am taking a long time. There are still 15 patients and I'm running way behind. Maybe I'm not right for this job. I'm incompetent compared to the other nurses.

⬦ **Consequence**: I put myself down and I feel bad about myself and my abilities as a nurse. I feel guilty for not doing the job well. I feel like quitting my nursing career because I'm not good at it.

◇ **Reframe**: I am a new nurse and I am still learning. I have to be patient with myself. Not everyone starts off amazing at their career. Besides, the other nurses have more experience than I do and have been doing this job for many years. Having 25 patients to myself is a lot, so I need to be kind to myself. I am doing the best that I can do with the resources that I have.

Notice what I was doing when I was *reframing*. I affirmed my value and my knowledge, while recognizing that I didn't have as much experience as other nurses on the floor. I let myself off the hook for not being as fast as the more experienced nurses, telling myself that I was doing the best job possible under the circumstances. And that I will be faster and more efficient as I gain more experience.

Reframing is a great tool for reversing negativity, guilt, and self-condemnation that comes from comparing yourself to everyone else. By confirming the positive truths about yourself and the situation, your thoughts become more positive and lead to long-lasting positive beliefs about yourself. *Once you finish reframing, you will feel more capable and less overwhelmed about whatever situation you might be in.*

Another way to handle this situation is by *disputing* the wrong thoughts and beliefs. With *learned optimism*,[7] there are four ways to challenge negative thoughts:

1. **Evidence**: Isolate the thought or belief. What evidence actually supports your belief? Is there evidence to disregard this belief?

2. **Alternatives**: Is there another explanation for this thought or belief? What's an alternative way to look at

it? Once you have a list of alternatives, check for evidence of these alternatives.

3. **Implications**: What if your thought or belief is true? Is it the end of the world? Does this mean that everything will really not work out?

4. **Usefulness**: How useful is this thought or belief? If you continue to believe this thought or belief, does it help you in some way?

This is how to apply these approaches to my example:

Evidence:

◇ I am behind schedule so there is evidence that I am slow.

◇ Being slow does not mean that I am terrible at my job and should quit.

◇ The nurse working on the other floor is also behind schedule.

Alternatives:

◇ I am slow because I am new and still learning.

◇ I am behind schedule because the workload is extreme and demanding.

Implications:

◇ Yes, maybe I am slow right now. However, that doesn't mean I will be slow forever. I will get better with time and practice. Being slow does not make me a bad nurse. Being slow does not mean I will get fired from my job.

Usefulness:

◇ If I keep thinking that I am not a good nurse and quit my job, I will not benefit in the long term.

◇ Feeling guilty and frustrated in the moment does not help me work more efficiently.

EXERCISE E5-1: CHALLENGING YOUR THOUGHTS

Once we are aware of sabotaging thoughts, then we can learn to dispute and challenge them by arguing with ourselves! This tool is extremely effective in reframing your thoughts when you are faced with difficult situations.

1. Write out a situation that you are facing and what negative thoughts and beliefs it has triggered about yourself.

2. Challenge your thoughts and beliefs by asking yourself the following questions. Write out your answers:

   a. **Evidence**: What is the thought or belief that you have? What's the evidence to support the belief? What's the evidence to disregard the belief?

   b. **Alternatives**: Is there another explanation for your thought or belief? What's an alternative way to look at it? Once you have a list of alternatives, check for evidence of these alternatives.

    c. **Implications**: What if your thought or belief is true? Is it the end of the world? Does this mean that everything will really not work out?

    d. **Usefulness**: How useful is this thought or belief? If you continue to believe this thought or belief, does it help you in some way?

3. Now *reframe* your thoughts and beliefs so that they reflect positively on your abilities to handle this situation and others like it.

BELIEFS

Did you know that *repetitive thoughts* can become *beliefs* that embed into your subconscious mind? A belief is "an acceptance that something exists or is true, especially one without proof."[8] Suppose that while you were growing up, your parent or grandparent kept telling you that you would never amount to anything. Whenever you made a mistake, you repeated that thought to yourself. At some point, that thought grew deep into your subconscious and you began to believe it as the truth.

How many beliefs do you hold that actually have no evidence supporting them? These beliefs are just thoughts that you have repeated to yourself for years. Starting the day each of us is born, we continuously develop neural connections in our brain and body that are based on our experiences. Throughout our life, we continue to build these connections. They are reinforced by our habits, behaviors, and thought processes. Some of these are bad habits and behaviors. These cause us to form deeply rooted misinformed beliefs within ourselves about the reality of the world.

Where do our beliefs come from? Well, the answer is simple. Our beliefs generally come from the outside world. The beliefs could have originated from your family surroundings, environment, life experiences, or society. Usually, these beliefs are introduced to you without you even realizing it. Have you ever examined your thoughts and beliefs to truly consider where they came from? Or have you wondered if they are even true? Well, many of your beliefs and strongly-held convictions can be untrue. Usually, untrue beliefs are programmed into us through a negative experience.

For example, when you were younger, you may have had a teacher who treated you as if you were not as smart as other students. This false message—if there was nothing to counteract it—could have easily formed a false belief, a warped understanding of your true identity. As a result, as an adult, you may have been avoiding pursuing great opportunities because you feel underqualified. You have come to believe that you are not smart enough to succeed at these new opportunities.

There is no room in your life for holding onto feelings that cause you pain. It's time to escape the mental limitations of your mind. Refuse to be imprisoned by a belief system that will limit your potential and prevent you from becoming the hero in your story. Milton Erikson once posed the question, "If someone gives you a present you don't like, will you keep it?"[9] The same holds for the beliefs that people around you might have pushed onto you.

The good news is that we can 100% alter these neural connections and beliefs that do not support us in a positive way! How? *By developing new behaviors and habits.* You can create an internal dialogue that is encouraging and positive through a rewiring process similar to the process you learned earlier about questioning your thoughts and beliefs, and then challenging them. This dialogue is something new that you say to yourself to counteract the old negative voice in your mind that keeps repeating those false beliefs. You have been listening to it for years. Today is the day to change that voice! Start saying positive things to yourself that affirm your strengths, abilities, and uniqueness. Drown out that old voice. As you learn new ways of thinking in this book, they are becoming embedded in your mind, giving you a shift in perception, and helping you make the changes that are necessary for you to overcome your limiting beliefs.

The more you repeat these positive truths about yourself, the more easily you will be able to believe that they *are* true. And they are true! This will positively affect your actions and reactions to whatever life throws at you. Even when you face major challenges, you will be able to face them with ease and grace.

Do not get discouraged if you keep falling back into your old ways of thinking. Building new beliefs and habits takes time, effort, and dedication. But no one said this self-development journey would be easy. The fact that you are reading this book right now means that you are ready to make targeted changes so that you can begin to live the uncompromised life that you deserve to live.

Have you ever heard the term, "self-fulfilling prophecy"? You just learned that beliefs are formed by the conditioning of repeated thoughts. Science has proven that what we truly believe about ourselves eventually comes true—it is a self-fulfilling prophecy! That's why people who believe that they are a failure, end up failing at whatever they try to do. A self-fulfilling prophecy is often referred to as the *Pygmalion Effect*.

In the 1960s, a psychologist named Robert Rosenthal experimented on several groups of elementary school children to see if they would live up to the expectations that their teachers had for them. Secretly, he told the teachers that certain students were "intellectual bloomers," meaning that they were very smart and just needed a little encouragement to reach their potential. He selected them randomly, which meant that some were better students and others were struggling students. By the end of the semester, to everyone's surprise, all of the students who had been secretly identified as "intellectual bloomers" had performed better. Why? Because the teachers believed in them. Later studies showed that the teachers unwittingly gave more positive attention, feedback, and learning opportunities to the students they thought had more potential. In short, teachers were biased and able to "nonverbally" communicate their positive expectations for academic success to these students."[10]

The *Pygmalion Effect* could be one of your secret weapons in your Self-Discovery Journey! The test children in the above experiment were expected to do well in class—whether they were great students or not. They actually lived up to that expectation because they had the positive encouragement of their teachers, which helped them to develop *belief* in themselves and their capabilities. Think about the thoughts you are feeding yourself daily: Is it, "I'm not good enough," "I'll never be happy," "I can never find love," or "I'm too old/too young/too fat/too skinny?" If you're like most people out there, myself included, you are bombarded by these thoughts every single day.

As I mentioned earlier, if we continue to repeat the same thoughts that we've been saying to ourselves for years, we are forming stronger neural connections, and this causes us to believe that these thoughts are true when, in fact, they are absolute nonsense.

Thoughts like this are what I call "limiting beliefs." Limiting beliefs are thoughts that we think are true and that we identify with. Unfortunately, these are the very thoughts that hold us back from achieving and accomplishing everything that we aspire to do.

SELF-AWARENESS

How do we fix this? We have to re-wire our brain. No, you don't need an operation! Re-wiring is just part of your Self-Discovery Journey. The first step to rewiring your brain is practicing self-awareness. Self-awareness is the key to shifting us from being limited by our beliefs to being free to move ahead in our journey. Self-awareness means not only recognizing your strengths but also admitting to your weaknesses. Like it or not, a big part of your weakness is your limiting beliefs. In order to deal with them, you have to be able to identify them.

EXERCISE E5-2: IDENTIFYING LIMITING BELIEFS

1. Take a minute to identify the limiting beliefs you have about yourself. Use the statements from the box below to create your list.

2. Then cross out these limiting beliefs with a red pen.

3. Rewrite each of your limiting beliefs to be something more positive.

Example:

◇ **Limiting Belief**: There will never be enough money.

◇ **Reframe**: My life is abundant and money is on its way to me.

"THERE WILL NEVER BE ENOUGH_____."

"IF ONLY. I WISH I WOULD HAVE_____."

"I CAN'T BELIEVE _____ HAPPENED TO ME."

"I'M FAT."

"I HATE MY _____."

"I DON'T DESERVE _____."

"I LACK WHAT IT TAKES."

"I DON'T KNOW HOW."

"I HAVE NO CHOICE."

"I'M TOO _____."

"I CAN NEVER _____."

Do any of the above limiting beliefs keep bouncing around in your head, holding you back from your potential? Limiting beliefs shape our perception of the world, and our perception of the world shapes our reality. So, in a way, these are "reality statements" for us because they shape our reality.

By paying attention to your reality statements, you can get clues into what is holding you back from creating your dream life. Feel free to add more to this list.

Now that you've identified your beliefs, we can begin to shift your beliefs, thoughts, and actions, so that you can begin to live your dream life. The way to do this is by replacing your old false beliefs about yourself with new, true beliefs.

NEUROPLASTICITY

It is time to eradicate every false belief out of your life! I want you to reread each of your limiting beliefs and then read out loud the new positive statements that you replaced them with. Use these statements as affirmations to read out loud to yourself every day. This will help you begin to rewire your brain. Doctors call this process "neuroplasticity," which is when the brain creates new neural patterns from new experiences.

Your brain is not set in stone. It is pliable. You can change how you think, which changes what you believe, which changes how you act and react. Remember, too, that for neuroplasticity to happen, there needs to be repetition. Your brain is like a muscle. Just as you need to exercise your muscles to increase tone and strength, you also have to work out your brain muscle! So, make saying these affirmations something that you work at each day. You will begin to notice subtle changes in your life as your thinking and belief system changes.

MORE ABOUT FALSE THOUGHTS AND BELIEFS

Before I embarked on my self-development journey, I did not realize that the thoughts I was thinking could actually be false.

In my reality, they were absolutely true. Learning about common cognitive distortions helped free me from the associations I had with these thoughts and beliefs. Being able to identify these distorted thoughts in the moment will really empower you because you can reframe them as soon as you are aware of what these thoughts are. Think about it like this: We all live in a reality that we create and which we believe is true based on our formative imprints. However, if you really take the time to evaluate these thoughts and beliefs, you might come to realize that in fact, they weren't true in the first place.

When you're beginning to analyze your thoughts and beliefs, I want you to put on your lab coat and channel the scientist within. Look at everything from an analytical perspective, without bias, and study the details to see if the conclusion you've drawn from your thoughts and beliefs that have been in your mind this whole time are true or can be proven. Like the scientific method, follow these steps: Make an observation, ask a question, form a hypothesis, or testable explanation, make a prediction based on the hypothesis, test the prediction, and iterate, or use the results to make new hypotheses or predictions.

Counselors and psychiatrists refer to false thoughts and beliefs as "cognitive distortions," which are biased perspectives we have about ourselves and the world around us. They are irrational thoughts and beliefs that we unknowingly reinforce over time."[11] Very often they come from a misconception that is internalized and believed. These distorted thoughts tend to lie beneath the surface of our rational thinking. They are often hidden from us, so we may never realize that they are responsible for tainting our perspectives. Unless we pay close attention to what we are thinking, we will continue to be oblivious to these thoughts, letting them take control of our lives.

Below are 16 of the most common *cognitive distortions* that people experience. The first eleven come straight from David Burns' *Feeling Good Handbook* (1989).[12] Read through this list and see which ones have been making your life a living hell:

1. All-or-Nothing Thinking / Polarized Thinking

This distortion identifies everything that happens in life as either fantastic or terrible. Called "black and white thinking," there is no room for shades of gray. Thus, the person has to be "perfect" or else he or she is a "total failure."

2. Overgeneralization

People with this distortion tend to latch on to one negative event or experience and make the gross assumption that it is indicative of a pattern that will always be true. Failing one test and then being absolutely sure that you will fail every test after that is an example of overgeneralization. People who overgeneralize are frequently plagued with negative thoughts about themselves and their life. The generalization becomes pervasive. Eventually the student who fails the test comes to believe that he or she is stupid and will never succeed at anything.

3. Mental Filter

The *mental filter* distortion is similar to overgeneralization. It super-focuses on one negative word or event and misses all the positive ones. Suppose a person with this distortion is in a long-term relationship that is generally happy. One negative or even a joking comment by his or her partner will become the filter by which he judges the whole relationship. He immediately assumes that this one remark is proof that his partner no longer loves him. He can't see past the one negative comment and see how many positive and loving conversations they have had.

4. Disqualifying the Positive

The "disqualifying the positive" distortion recognizes positive experiences but refuses to believe them. When this person receives a compliment, he immediately finds a reason as to why that compliment can't possibly be true or valid. In his mind he even comes up with logical reasons as to why someone might be complimenting him, such as, she's just being polite, or she says nice things to everybody. This distortion holds people back from their potential because it reinforces negative thought patterns, even when there is plenty of evidence that the person has actually done something worthwhile.

5. Jumping to Conclusions – Mind Reading

This distortion convinces the person that he can know what others are thinking—without there ever being a way to know it. "Jumping to conclusions" is a reactive distortion that makes the person so sure of his negative interpretation of someone's facial expression or a snippet of a conversation that he never bothers to confirm his assumptions. He just reacts, muttering a negative remark or impulsively responding out of proportion to the situation.

6. Jumping to Conclusions – Fortune Telling

Like jumping to conclusions, "fortune telling," is "the tendency to make conclusions and predictions based on little to no evidence and holding them as gospel truth." A great "example of *fortune-telling* is a young, single woman predicting that she will never find love or have a committed and happy relationship based only on the fact that she has not found it yet." Because she refuses to even imagine any other possibilities, she creates a self-fulfilling prophecy for herself and then makes sure that it comes true.

7. Magnification (Catastrophizing) or Minimization

Magnification and minimization are two sides of the same coin: Imagine that you are looking through binoculars. Small things appear very large. The *magnification distortion* magnifies the importance and significance of an experience. For example, an office assistant who makes a tiny error on a document may be mortified by it and believe that her career is over.

The *minimization distortion* does the opposite: minimizes them, as if you were holding the wrong end of the binoculars up to your eyes. A person with this distortion may earn an Employee-of-the-Year Award, but may feel that it doesn't prove anything and that he will never measure up to his supervisor's expectations.

8. Emotional Reasoning

This distortion is very common, but not recognized by most people as a problem. Yet, it needs to be stopped in its tracks. *Emotional reasoning* confuses fact with emotion. In other words, the person believes that "if I feel it, it must be true." This leads to distorted thoughts, misunderstandings and false beliefs.

9. "Should" Statements

"Should" statements act like a ball and chain, keeping you imprisoned. These are statements that confine you emotionally and psychologically because they dictate what you "should" do, what you "ought" to do, and what you "must" do. As you race around trying to do all the things this distortion says you have to, you end up living in a constant state of guilt. Most often "should" statements also extend to the people around you, making you expect certain behaviors from them even if you have never told them so. This leads to disappointment, anger and resentment when they don't live up to those unspoken expectations.

10. Labeling and Mislabeling

Labeling and mislabeling come from being in the habit of constantly overgeneralizing. It results in us placing a label on ourselves or on others based on only one instance or experience. Chances are that that one experience doesn't give us the entire picture and we usually mislabel. We probably will use emotionally-charged language to express our feelings. A homeowner who hears his neighbor's dog growl one time, may mislabel the animal as dangerous or mean, not knowing that that one particular time a child was teasing the dog and that the dog is normally gentle and friendly.

Another example is seeing a homeless woman walking along the street. An onlooker with this distortion might label her as pitiful, dirty—a moocher on society. The truth may be that she is homeless because her husband suddenly died and she was evicted because she couldn't find a job that paid enough to cover the rent.

11. Personalization

"As the name implies, this distortion involves taking everything personally or assigning blame to yourself for no logical reason to believe you are to blame."

Personalization makes you feel responsible for things that are out of your control and often aren't even directly connected to you. This distortion makes you automatically blame yourself even if you know you didn't have anything to do with the situation. For example, personalization makes you feel that your friends have a right to be mad at you when you cancelled a cookout because of rain. Or, you believe that it's somehow your fault if your husband or wife is in a bad mood after work.

The following cognitive distortions are identified by Ackerman:[13]

12. Control Fallacies

A *control fallacy* expresses itself as one of two damaging and equally inaccurate beliefs:

(1) that people are victims of fate and have no way to control their lives, or

(2) that people have complete control of their lives and situations, and therefore are responsible for the feeling of the people around them.

In examining this fallacy, we need to remember that no one can ever be in complete control of what happens to them. At the same time everyone can have at least some control over their own situation. Even when it seems like individuals have no choices as to what to do

or say, they do have control of how they think about
and process their situation—that's some control.

13. Fallacy of Fairness

Life is not fair. We all know this, but people with the
fallacy of fairness can't move past their perception of
what is fair, which of course, differs from person to
person. A person with this distortion will constantly be
disappointed and frustrated when life repeatedly
proves itself to be unfair. They are angered when the
people around them don't behave fairly and may act
out against them. These negative feelings can lead to
resentment and despair.

14. Fallacy of Change

The *fallacy of change* distortion hinges on the belief that
our happiness and success depend on other people
changing their behavior. People with this distortion
expect that if they nag or pressure their spouse,
children, co-workers, neighbors, etc., enough, these
people will eventually change and life will be so much
better. Unfortunately, this can lead to some devious
actions on the part of the person who thinks that his or
her happiness is at stake unless that person changes.

15. Always Being Right

If you have to always be right or perfect, and being wrong
is just not acceptable, then you are suffering from this
cognitive distortion. And it is a distortion because no
one can ever always be right. Perfectionists know what
it feels like to miss the mark of perfection that they
have set for themselves. It's devastating. It's a never-
ending daily struggle to make sure that you are right
while making sure that everyone around you

recognizes that you are right. And even if you are wrong, you will still argue to prove that you are right. This distortion has become noticeably widespread with the popularity of social media. People have their own opinions, and if they will spend endless hours online trying to tear down anyone who disagrees with them, then they most likely have this distortion.

16. Heaven's Reward Fallacy

The *heaven's reward fallacy* distortion is what we call belief in a "happy ending." It says that all life's hard work, struggles and suffering will result in a just reward for the person. The criminal gets caught and the victim gets justice—a happy ending. But this fallacy also expects that the reward will be a tangible one, where the person has success or at least is finally recognized by everyone around him for his risk, pain and sacrifices.

It is obvious why this type of thinking is a distortion. How many examples can you think of, just within the realm of your personal acquaintances, where hard work and sacrifice did not pay off? Where they are still struggling to get ahead or they are still suffering?

Sometimes no matter how hard we work or how much we sacrifice, we will not achieve what we hope to achieve. To think otherwise is a potentially damaging pattern of thought that can result in disappointment, frustration, anger, and even depression when the awaited reward does not materialize.

Please note that the *heaven's reward* distortion is totally separate from having spiritual faith in God. The "just reward" aspect of this distortion refers to expecting to be eventually recognized by co-workers or your boss for your hard work or expecting that your suffering will end because of your efforts. This is unrealistic. Many people who have deep faith in God know better than to expect a reward or some kind of justice from other people. Their hope hinges on a relationship with God, rather than dependency on how others react to their efforts.

Now that you understand a little more about the common cognitive distortions, you will be able to identify them as they pop up in your mind. However, it is not enough to just know and learn this material. The key to getting real results is taking action and using what you've learned.

EXERCISE E5-3: DISCOVERING COGNITIVE DISTORTIONS

Try this exercise to identify the cognitive distortions that have been affecting your life:

1. Think about a negative emotion or judgmental thought that could be distorting your view of your abilities or your situation.

2. Write it down on a piece of paper and see if you can identify which cognitive distortion it is.

3. After identifying the cognitive distortion, let's reframe that distortion and write down the truth.

Example:

When I started working on my business, I hit a roadblock. I began to think thoughts like "I'm such a failure," "I can never get things right," and "This will never work for me because I'm not good enough." These thoughts were extremely strong and pre-occupied my mind. I could not see anything else but these thoughts as my truth.

Can you identify which of the cognitive distortions I was struggling against?

It was the *mental filter* distortion. I was so focused on the roadblock that I did not see all the progress I had made up until that point. When I began to review my successes over the previous year, I realized that I had been focusing only on that one roadblock instead of honoring myself for how far I had gotten. I had filtered out all the positive things and focused on the one negative situation that had swallowed my attention.

Now, you try:

1. Write down a negative emotion or judgmental thought that you suspect is warping your view of your abilities or your situation.

Example: Roadblock = "failure," "not good enough," "destined to fail."

2. Identify the cognitive distortion from the above list.

Example: Mental Filter = Focusing on single negative event and filtering out positive events.

3. Reframe the cognitive distortion into a new reality statement.

Example: "Yes, I did hit a roadblock, but look at all I accomplished in spite of it!"

4. Now, identify all your successes and failures over the last year.

My Failures:

- Hit a roadblock in my business

My Successes:

(List the things you did successfully during that time.)

- Created a workbook

- Developed my own website

- Made an inspirational video

- Pushed my boundaries

We all have dreams that we want to make happen, but sometimes negative beliefs and fear hold us back from accessing our potential. The truth is, the time will never be right. You just have to take that leap. Think about it: In twenty years' time, will you look back and be proud of yourself for making the decision to chase after what you wanted? Or will you be full of regret because you were too afraid to try? Do you really want to fall into this deathbed fallacy? Bonnie Ware was a palliative care nurse treating terminal patients. She created a list of the most common regrets people had on their deathbeds. A few items on that list are as follows:

◇ "I wish I'd had the courage to live a life true to myself, not the life others expected of me."

◇ "I wish I didn't work so hard."

◇ "I wish I'd had the courage to express my feelings."

◇ "I wish I had stayed in touch with my friends."

◇ "I wish that I had let myself be happier."[14]

Do you want to be one of those people with these regrets? I am positive that you don't. So, whatever it is that you want, no matter how scared you are, go after it anyway! Slowly, step-by-step, build your way to those dreams, and one day you will realize them.

"The most important thing I want you to realize about fear is that it is a normal part of life! Having fear, doubt, and insecurity is absolutely normal. So, get used to it."

~ Julia

CHAPTER 6:

TESTS, ALLIES, & ENEMIES

I F YOU ASK yourself what really keeps you from moving forward and chasing the life of your dreams, it really comes down to one thing: *fear.*

I have lived most of my life in fear. Fear of being alone. Fear of being rejected. Fear of letting other people in. Fear of judgment from others. Fear of being seen even though deep down that was what I craved. This fear paralyzed me. It kept me feeling small and prevented me from doing the things that I really wanted to do. It kept me isolated from other people so I could not be hurt. But I was hurting anyways, all on my own. This manifested into depression and took over my life. When I finally freed myself from my fears, I was able to become who I was meant to be.

It was a beautiful moonlit night at the Los Angeles Convention Center where I was surrounded by thousands of people, ready to face their fears and overcome anything that was holding them back. There was a sense of camaraderie and unity as we all lined up to walk across hot coals, a signature of the "Unleash the Power Within" event. Walking across hot coals with bare feet was a challenge to show us that our fear is just a figment of our imagination. Once we walked over the hot coals, we would learn to overcome our fears and realize that we no longer had to succumb to fear. On the other side of the hot coals was a lifelong lesson, a freedom from the mind, a paradigm shift that would show us that we are capable of doing anything.

As I took my place in line, I gazed up at the clear open skies, the brilliant moon shining and glistening over the crowd. I could hear the sound of the beating drums in the background synchronizing with the rhythm of my heart. I was lost in this sacred ritual that would show me my true powers. My heart rate began to rise as the crowd was chanting, "Yes! Yes! Yes!" Anxiety filled my entire body and I felt the fear coming over me, a wave of hormones began signaling me to get ready for fight or flight.

I breathed deeply trying to remain calm, but the fear had already taken over my body putting me in full panic mode. In my mind, I kept repeating the mantra, "Mind over matter... I got this!" As the person ahead of me got ready to walk across the hot coals, my anxiety magnified, knowing that it was my turn next.

I stepped up and took my place, standing in front of the hot coals. I looked up to the open skies of the universe. "I got this!" I told the universe, and I stormed across the hot coals. As I stepped off the hot coals, the people who had already completed the challenge cheered me on and congratulated me. "Wow! I did it! I walked across hot coals!" I thought to myself. I felt a sense of relief and gratitude for making it to the other side uninjured. I felt a sense of accomplishment that I never felt before. "Wow, I'm amazing! I cannot believe I just did that!" I stood there embracing that moment where I felt my power. In that moment, I understood that I could do anything I put my mind to. This marked the beginning of another major paradigm shift in my view of myself and my life.

Fear is the capacity to respond to a threat. It is both a biological and a psychological response triggered when a person perceives danger. Once activated, the fear stimuli send a signal to the amygdala to release adrenaline, which activates the sympathetic nervous system and causes the fight-or-flight response. Although fear is basically biological, it is also a concept the mind creates to protect us from danger. In some situations, fear is necessary, but in other cases it can be exaggerated by the thoughts and beliefs that we associate with it. This biochemical chain reaction caused by fear leads to an emotional response, and that is why we can be crippled by fear. Our emotional response to the fear is extremely personal because it is based on our previous life experiences. Thus, it is why we believe that fear may harm us.

Fear can be debilitating because it freezes us. Fear is the only thing that constantly stops us from taking action in the direction of our dreams. Fear works as a protection mechanism—and that's a good thing in dangerous circumstances. However, if we are constantly operating in protection mode, we will be unable to grow. Worse yet, it causes long-term, damaging stress to our bodies and minds. Fear is a necessary aspect of human nature, but many people hide behind their fear. They utilize fear in a way that shields them from doing things that are out of their comfort zone. When we hide behind fear, we let it hinder our progress and prevent us from reaching our fullest potential. Fear can be a huge barrier, preventing us from moving forward in our journey toward self-mastery.

The most common fears that humans have are:

◇ The fear of rejection

◇ The fear of failure

◇ The fear of success

◇ The fear of love or lack of

◇ The fear of being alone

◇ The fear of the unknown[1]

EXERCISE E6-1: IDENTIFYING FEARS

Are you struggling with any of these fears? They can infiltrate our thinking, our view of ourselves. They are so pervasive that it's no wonder that they can paralyze us in our tracks and limit what we accomplish.

◇ What are some of your fears?

◇ When did they develop?

◇ What can you do to overcome these fears?

EXERCISE E6-2: DEFINING AND CONTROLLING YOUR FEAR

1. **Define your fear**. Think about your fear and imagine the worst nightmare you can imagine. What would happen? What doubt, fears, and "what-ifs" come up as you think about the big changes you can—or need—to

make associated with your fear? Imagine it in painstaking detail.

2. After describing your worst nightmare, **answer the questions below**.

   - Would it be the end of your life?
   - What permanent impact would it have in your life?
   - On a scale of 1–10, how horrible would this scenario be?
   - Are these things really permanent?
   - How likely do you think it is that they would actually happen?

3. If this "nightmare" happens, **what steps could you take** to repair the damage even if temporarily? How could you get things back under control?

4. Now that you've defined the nightmare, **define the opposite**. What is the more likely positive outcome?

5. After describing your positive outcome, **answer the questions below**:

   - What are the more likely positive outcomes, it could be internal (confidence, self-esteem, etc.) or external?

- What would the impact of these more likely outcomes be on a scale of 1–10?

- How likely is it that you could produce at least a moderately good outcome?

- Have less intelligent people done this before and pulled it off?

6. Additionally, **answer these questions** about your fear.

- What is the cost of the inaction?

- What is it costing you—financially, emotionally, and physically—to postpone action?

- If you don't pursue those things that excite you, where will you be in one year, five years, and ten years?

- How will you feel if you allow ten more years of your life to pass hiding behind fear and not doing things that will fulfill you?

What are you putting off out of *fear*? Usually, what we most fear doing is what we most need to do. That phone call, that conversation, whatever the action might be—it is the fear of the unknown that prevents us from doing what we need to do. Define the worst case scenario, analyze its truth and the possibility of it really happening, then look at alternative outcomes. Don't let it prevent you from taking action. *Sometimes the most amazing things happen on the other side of fear, if you're willing to overcome it and do what you're afraid of.*

Dancing with Fear!

If there's one thing I have learned about fear, it's that you can never totally get rid of it! So, what can you do instead? You can dance with it! Sounds crazy, right? But I am serious! Fear will always be present because it is a natural response hard-wired into our psyches. Designed to protect us, it unfortunately can take us over if we let it. When facing fear head-on, you have to recognize that the fear will always be there, so you just have to keep it in its place and get better at dealing with it. Besides, you can use fear as your biggest motivator!

Think about when you were a kid learning to ride a bicycle for the very first time. I'm sure you felt anxious and extremely scared. However, over time with practice and experience, you learned how to ride your bike and maybe even loved it! Whenever you feel fearful, you just have to remember your bike-riding experience. In the beginning, when you start something new, of course you will feel those normal feelings of fright. However, if you continue to persist and practice, eventually it gets easier and easier—and that's all you can really ask of yourself, to show up and keep at it. One day you will have mastered the skill (whether it's learning to ride a bike or overcoming the fear of learning to do it) and you will forget that fear was there in the first place.

Think about another time when you were really excited to try something new. For me, it was skydiving. The first time I went skydiving, I felt extremely nervous but excited at the same time. You see, your body creates the same response whether you are feeling *scared* or *excited*. So, the next time when you're feeling nervous, think about channeling all that nervous energy into excitement. Your body is creating the same response anyway—so, why not use it to help you?

The most important thing I want you to realize about fear is that it is a normal part of life! Having fear, doubt, and insecurity is absolutely normal. So, get used to it.

The second thing that you have to understand about fear is that it's not necessary to get rid of it. You just have to learn how to manage it and be strategic about it. You cannot always control how you feel, but you can always choose what you think and do! YOUR power actually comes from not always controlling your feelings, but controlling the thoughts that are linked to those feelings. Because, if you can manage your thoughts and prevent yourself from succumbing to them, then the fear does not win!

You will often feel waves of fear, doubt, and anxiety, but you don't have to let yourself be drowned by them. Instead, you can learn to ride the wave! The key to happiness is refusing to let fear direct your actions. This is the battle we're going to fight.

So whatever fear you have, don't let it stop you. Be brave and face it. One of the most transforming lessons that I've learned in life is that the time will never be right. The time to act will never be perfect, so waiting for that perfect moment will not get you anywhere. Whatever it is that you want to do or to create, start now. Be brave and courageous and just take the leap. Napoleon Hill once said:

"Don't wait. The time will never be just right. Start where you stand, and work with whatever tools you may have at your command and better tools will be found as you go along."[2]

So many people are limiting themselves because they are waiting for certain things to happen first in order for them to start doing what they really want. They end up waiting their entire lives. Is this what you want to happen to you? My guess is most likely not...

Maybe these are some of the things you are waiting for:

◇ "I want to date a terrific person like that, but first I've got to . . ."

◇ "That's my dream job, but first I have to get a lot more experience. It might take me 10 years . . ."

◇ "I want my dream body, but first I have to focus on my career."

◇ "I want to make an impact, but no one cares about who I am now, so let me become rich, famous, and powerful first."

It's easy to say that we will pursue our dreams in the future. We think that we will have so much time to get there, so we don't make it a priority. It's easy to not face the challenges and put ourselves out there because it's more comfortable to imagine that it will just happen someday. But that "someday" has to be "today" or it might be "never." Make that choice NOW because if you avoid it, one day you will run out of time. Life is too short to not pursue your dreams now. It's okay to be nervous. *If your goals don't scare you, they're not big enough.*

When you push your boundaries, you will have the most growth. A boundary is just a partition keeping you where you are instead of letting you grow into who you are meant to be. It is necessary for you to do what makes you uncomfortable because exponential growth happens when you are willing to push your fear aside and surpass your boundaries.

In my life, I have always pushed my boundaries to go as far as I could, whether it was jumping out of a plane, climbing to the highest peak of a mountain, moving to a new city all alone, or even public speaking. Now, of course there were moments when the fear prevented me from doing what I wanted to do, but the key is that I will keep trying no matter what. This repeated exposure to my attempts of trying helps me acclimate to the fears I face.

It is important for you to learn that if you want to change your life, you have to be willing to do the things that make you uncomfortable every single day. You have to practice pushing these boundaries, because once you do, tremendous growth will follow. Overcoming your fears is truly a process of acclimation. Acclimation is when you have repeated exposure to the source of your fear. The more you face that fear, the less fear you will feel. Once you become acclimated, it will not be as scary as it was before because you will be familiar with it. Remember that learned behaviors can be unlearned and that if you have learned a certain fear, it is not the end of the world. Life does not have to always remain the way it is today. You can unlearn your fears if you put in the effort.

Of course, when it comes to deeply-rooted fears, they are harder to tackle. The secret to dealing with these fears is understanding the reasons behind them. Once we are aware of why we are afraid in certain circumstances, we will be better able to deal with the fears when they reveal themselves in our lives.

Marianne Williamson puts fear in another light. She says, "Our deepest fear is not that we are inadequate. Our deepest fear is that we are powerful beyond measure. It is our light, not our darkness that most frightens us. We ask ourselves, *Who am I to be brilliant, gorgeous, talented, fabulous*? Actually, who are you not to be? You are a child of God. Playing small does not serve the world. There is nothing enlightened about shrinking so that other people won't feel insecure around you. We are all meant to shine, as children do. We were born to make manifest the glory of God that is within us. It's not just in some of us; it's in everyone. And as we let our own light shine, we unconsciously give other people permission to do the same. As we are liberated from our own fear, our presence automatically liberates others."[3]

Yes, *fear of success* is a real thing!

It may sound like such a bizarre claim because most people strive for success, but striving for success does not mean that they are ready to accept it. This fear can develop from many different things, but for most people it's because they are afraid of what will happen when they reach success. They are afraid of losing the people closest to them, they are afraid of being criticized, they are afraid of jealousy, and others not being happy for them. They may be afraid of failing after they succeed and being embarrassed. Sometimes this fear is more deeply rooted and has to do with conditioning that occurred in childhood because of their parents.

Recently, I worked with a client who came to me for a hypnotherapy session to find out why she was unable to lose 10 pounds. She had been able to lose weight in the past. She was eating healthily and working out regularly. However, for some reason, at this time in her life she was unable to lose the excess weight. She thought it had to do with self-sabotaging and overanalyzing, but she was not exactly sure. As we went through our session, she realized that she was holding onto the weight because her father was struggling with his finances and she felt that if she were to succeed, she would make him unhappy and she would not feel loved by him. We found out that her dad's financial struggles were literally "weighing her down." When people have physical symptoms, usually there is an underlying psychological cause. So, a fear of success might appear superficial, but if you examine how this fear surfaced, you can see that there is so much more than meets the eye.

TESTS, ALLIES, & ENEMIES

As I continued my adventure to uncover the depths of my mind and belief systems, I continued to be faced with many challenges along the way. There were moments where I felt alone and abandoned, but I continued to face the challenges that life threw at me. It was not easy. I struggled with deep pangs of loneliness and sadness as I learned to heal my wounds.

Everything that happens in your life is a lesson for you to learn. When I was operating from a "victim mentality," there were periods when I questioned my existence deeply and I just did not understand the point of life at all. If there were a God, why was he punishing me with all of these challenges? I just could not comprehend the bigger picture. I was too focused on myself, the little problems of my mind, the things that were affecting me, making me miserable. Anything else was too much for me to understand. What I learned when I overcame this victim mentality was that life is like a school and contains a world full of enlightening life lessons. I discovered that I could break out of my victim mentality by looking for the lesson to be learned in each experience. You can break free, too. By learning these lessons, you can reprogram yourself to be the *best* version of who you are.

When you experience difficulties, mistakes or challenges in your life, remember that the universe is simply teaching you a lesson. Some lessons are harder than others, but they are in no way a form of punishment. The hardest lessons to learn are the ones that involve overcoming the ego, the mind, and victimization, so that we can be free to live a life filled with love and happiness.

Even more, our greatest lessons come from the people we interact with. Some may be acquaintances, some may be those that are dearest to our hearts and some may be our enemies. These people each carry with them an important lesson, a teaching of wisdom, whether you realize it or not. Some people will be there to support you along your journey, some people will be there to break you down or trigger you. Whatever their role is, there is a purpose to it. Look for the reason they are in your life at this particular time. What can you learn as you interact with them?

Part of my experience led me to evaluate the people that I surrounded myself with. I had to question the meaning they had in my life. Were they there to help me? Did they fully accept and support me? Or, were they there constantly causing me pain? When I took a closer look, I saw some things that didn't make sense: People whom I thought were my friends had turned against me because of their own internal suffering. Although I learned from them, I knew that at some point I would have to release the people who were no longer helping me on this journey. Because my established beliefs continually challenged me as I wrestled with them, I had to dissociate myself from the outside world at times in order to fix what was on the inside of me. Those ingrained beliefs tested my commitment to rise to the occasion of my Hero's Journey.

What is life without its challenges, right? How you look at what's ahead makes all the difference: After embarking on your journey to self-realization (and battling with your past behaviors and your stubborn ego), of course you will face more obstacles. So, start thinking of your journey as a life adventure filled with trials and tribulations mixed with great strides forward!

Tests, allies, and enemies can come in many forms, but the most important thing to remember is that they each hold within them a powerful lesson to be learned.-Everything in your life, every situation, every interaction, and every circumstance in your life is meant to teach you something. And when you learn your lesson, you will not have to repeat the lesson. However, if you don't learn the lesson, you will continue to face the same challenges until you learn what is necessary for your growth. *Listen and observe closely. The universe is always speaking to you in small hints and gestures.* If you are suffering from something, whether it's a difficulty of the mind or some type of physical malfunction, remember that the symptom is just a sign that there is something more, something deeper that needs to be healed. There is always an underlying reason you can't see or feel behind the symptom. Only if you look deeper, will you truly find the root cause or the hidden message.

These tests, allies and enemies are meant to give you a clue, a hint, or a small sense of direction as to where you need to go and what you need to do next. Remember, "like all heroes, the Buddha doesn't show you the truth, the illumination; he shows you the way to it."[4] These lessons will guide you on your journey, and the guide will be there to help you along the way. Ultimately, however, it is up to you to create the change you need in order to become the best version of yourself.

Tests can come as failures along your journey. You might face a failure and feel defeated and want to give up. However, you have to remember that the road to transformation is never a straight one, it's one filled with many twists and turns.

Enemies can be friends that you have now. Shocked? Anyone who is not helping you or urging you to reach your highest potential is an enemy. If you have friends who are dragging you down, it's time to let them go. There are friends who sap away all your energy, complain, and keep you where you are. Those are not the friends that you need. Upgrade your friends to people who inspire you, motivate you, and fully support your dreams and visions. In all honesty, most people will not understand your dream or your chase for a bigger and better life. Let them play small and safe. You do not need them. Instead, surround yourself with those who dream big! Because these are the people that will accelerate your growth and potential.

Sometimes people you thought were your enemies actually turn out to be your allies. The enemy's role is to challenge you, to alter your perspective, and to force you to grow, learn, and prevail. If someone is challenging you to re-evaluate some aspect of your life or thinking, stop thinking of that person as the enemy. Start considering these enemies as allies in your self-discovery journey. Maybe taking their advice will get you over an obstacle.

There are also internal enemies that fight us—such as, bad habits, addictions, and self-condemnation. Overcoming these internal demons helps you build strength and character along your journey, so that when you face more adversity, you can handle it with guts and grace.

Humans thrive off of love and acceptance from each other, so if we are not accepted by society, it affects us at a deeply emotional level. If you are disconnected socially and have no one you can rely on, this can cause you unfathomable pain and unhappiness. So, you have to evaluate your world and see the connections you have that are reliable and safe. Do the people you surround yourself with make you feel safe and at home? If you answered no to this, it's time to find people who can support you and help you grow.

The best types of people to surround yourself with are:

◇ those who show interest in your success

◇ those who are invested in your success

◇ those who have your best interest in mind

◇ those who focuses on helping you be the best you can be

◇ those who complement you by being supportive when you need help

◇ those who inspire and motivate you

EXERCISE E6-3: SUPPORT SYSTEM

1. Create a list of the people you surround yourself with.

2. Ask yourself: Are these people supportive and positively impacting you? Or are they having a negative influence on you.

3. Think about the value of the friendship or relationship. Is it one you should continue?

"When you can identify where your wounds
came from, you can then begin to heal them."

~ *Julia*

Chapter 7:

The Innermost Cave

"When you can accept yourself as you are, in the present, then you will no longer have to chase a future destination to feel fulfilled."

—Julia

W HEN I WAS YOUNGER, I thought traveling was amazing. Every time I explored a new place, I got this rush that was so incredible, so magical. It woke up the spirit within me. It felt right, like I was home. It was my escape. Every time I felt sad, lost, or confused, I sought out a new place to explore. After so many years, I came to realize that I was actually running away from my reality. Traveling gave me a new perspective. It opened my eyes up to new sights and for brief moments it helped me forget my current reality and the deep sadness I felt within.

The more I traveled, the more I realized that I was chasing after a dream, chasing after a destination, but still feeling empty on the inside. In the beginning, the "high" of new places would overtake me. It felt like bliss and an end to my misery. However, as soon as the "high" faded away, I was left with this loneliness and emptiness that persisted. Even so, I continued to seek out happiness from the external world.

As many places as I've been to, I finally came to the realization that *it does not matter where you go—your problems will follow you. You might be distracted for a while, but when the high of the experience fades, you will be faced with your eternal longing and need to search for something more.*

Travel far enough and you might just meet yourself.[1]

—David Mitchell, *Cloud Atlas*

You see, many of us seek out ways in the external environment to fill ourselves up, make us happy, and make us feel whole. The truth is, you can have everything in the world and still feel empty inside. That's why it is extremely important for us to look within ourselves for this source of happiness, because if we do not feel complete on the inside, nothing in the world will ever make us feel better. We might think that money, fame, recognition, and the illusion of reality will bring us happiness. But very often, people who seem to have it all— money or fame—aren't fully happy. In fact, very often the people who seem to have very little are actually the happiest. Through my travels I was able to visit third-world countries such as Vietnam, Bali, India, and Mexico. Some of my favorite places to visit were the small villages where the people had so little but greeted you with such warm and genuine smiles. You could tell they were happy with the simple lives they were living.

Think about Marilyn Monroe. She was labeled one of the most beautiful women in history and she seemed to have it all when it came to success, fame, and money. Unfortunately, she ended her life by overdosing on barbiturates.

Stories like these show us that having all of the "things" in the world or external successes does not mean that deep down you will feel good about yourself and who you are. I understand this well, and that is why I continue on my self-development journey.

My personal journey eventually led me to becoming a Transformational Coach. In my work, I have met quite a few people who have achieved worldly success, but who are still deeply unhappy.

One client came to me because he had lost his sense of motivation and drive in life. He had done it all—created an extremely successful business for himself, had all the money and material wealth that one could ask for, and yet he still felt incomplete. Through his therapy sessions, he realized that he had lost himself trying to chase the dream of what society deemed as "successful." He had it all, the money, the status, the recognition, but he was still unhappy because deep down he still did not feel like he was ever good enough. (Sound familiar?) I am sharing his story to show you the importance of building a relationship with yourself first. The rest will follow.

In all honesty, when you can be happy with having nothing, you will discover a newfound freedom that you can take with you through all of eternity! Having complete bliss and happiness even when you don't have all the external things will give you an internal power that you've never experienced before.

As I traveled through my conscious mind to the world of the subconscious, I learned a lot about myself. I did not know that the emptiness I felt inside had manifested itself as depression. One of the most difficult parts of my journey was trying to heal from old trauma that had deeply wounded me. All this time I had been wondering where my depression could possibly be coming from. I continued to search for the answer to this burning question. Through *Rapid Transformational Therapy*, a modality combining hypnotherapy, *neuro-linguistic programming* (NLP), and regression, I was able to recall memories from my past and piece together how it all led to my depression. As I explored my subconscious, I went back in time, traveling through the depths of my memories, many of which I had blocked out.

I floated back to my childhood and began to remember my first day in preschool. It was a traumatic scene for this little 5-year-old girl. I saw my mom dropping me off at school and leaving me there for the very first time. I was so attached to her that when she left me there alone, I cried my eyes out. My teacher decided to lock me in the bathroom because I was crying so much. At 5 years old, I did not know any better and I was confused at what was going on. *Why am I being punished for crying and why is the adult figure putting me in this room?*

I did not feel safe and my teacher thought it was inappropriate for me to express my emotions. This was the point in my life where I learned that it was not safe to share my emotions. After leaving that memory, I floated to another scene that came to my mind. I was a child and I remembered waking up in a hospital room, with no one around me. I felt scared, alone, and sad. My mom and sister had gone to get food, but because I woke up and no one was there, I felt alone, and again, thought that no one cared for me. These two scenarios were the first of many that made me feel like I was not safe or cared for in this world.

Flash forward to my teenage years. When I was 14 years old, I met my first love. The beginning of our relationship was magical. There was a naiveté and sweetness to the innocence of being in love for the first time. However, that sweetness was easily robbed as our relationship progressed. My boyfriend at the time was much older than I was. We met when he was 19. As a young teenager, being in love for the first time, I did not know any better. I had no idea that I was crazy in love with an alcoholic. In the throes of so much passion and surging hormones as a teenager in love, it was a madness, and I could not see anything but the good things.

I remember being at a party with him and asking him if we could leave, but he refused. I continued to beg him to leave, but he continued to deny my request. I could not remember what was said next, but the argument escalated. I can remember the shame and embarrassment I felt when he pushed me to the floor in front of all his friends. I can still remember it as if it had happened yesterday. I was mortified as everyone watched and did nothing. Being a young teenager, I was confused as to why no one had helped me. I was even accused of being "crazy."

Flash forward to another memory where my boyfriend and I were sitting at his house arguing in front of another friend. My boyfriend suddenly grabbed me violently by the throat. I was in shock from fear and felt completely helpless. Tears rolled down my face, but his friend did absolutely nothing. Flash to the scene of another heated argument where he grabbed me by the throat again in a drunken stupor. He laughed as I cried and trembled in fear. He taunted me, saying, "Don't be afraid, I'm not going to hit you."

The trauma of the physical abuse was not the worst thing for me. What really damaged me was the "bystander effect"—seeing how other people witnessed what he did but did not bother to intervene and help me.

These events left powerful psychological scars that shaped my behaviors and beliefs as I matured into adulthood. These memories led me to believe that the world is not a safe place and that no one really cares, because if they did, they would have done something to help me. Because of this, I always felt unsafe and I had to figure out a way to protect myself. That's when depression decided to root itself in me. This was a subconscious part of myself that emerged to help me. Depression kept me isolated and alone, because the world was scary, and if I was alone, I could not be hurt. Although this made me feel sad and isolated, I felt like, somehow, it kept me protected.

You see, when we are faced with traumatic experiences in our early years, it can cause irreparable damage—until we are brave enough to face it again and unmask it.

When you can identify where your wounds came from, you can then begin to heal them.

In order for us to finally overcome persistent feelings of sadness or emptiness, insecurities, and belief patterns that keep us from reaching our full potential, we have to look at where these emotional negatives reside. *They reside in our mind.*

As you dive deep into the *innermost cave*, it's time to break the cycle that has kept you stuck in the past. A key to your freedom and to tapping into your limitless potential is stopping the cycle of negative beliefs, limitations, fears—of anything that is keeping you stuck where you are right now. Look at your life now and notice any emotions, behaviors, or patterns that you continue to repeat, whether it's in your relationships, business, or personal life.

Where does this cycle lead you? Are you getting the end results that you want? Or, are you creating an outcome that continues to be further away from your dreams? Cycles in our lives are important because they give us clues as to what behavior or patterns we need to break. If a cycle continues to persist in your life, observe it closely because this is a tell-tale sign that there is a huge lesson for you to learn. If you keep doing what you're doing, you will keep getting the same results. So, if you're looking to create a life beyond your wildest imagination, you must learn the lesson and break the cycle.

THE INNERMOST CAVE

The cave you fear to enter holds the treasure you seek.[2]

—Joseph Campbell

I can tell you that before we rise, we must fall. We must be broken down into tiny pieces so that when we rebuild ourselves, we are 1,000 times stronger. Times can be tough, but do not worry because once you hit rock bottom, the only way to go is up. When you are weak and frail, look deep within yourself. And when you face who you really are, you can realize that you are an incredible person, beautiful on the inside and outside, and whole in every single way. You were born to be amazing! You're alive to go on a journey where the end goal is returning back to you. To return back to the stars. To return back to the universe. You are magic. Every single inch of you. Don't forget that. And when you do, look in the mirror and stare at the perfection that is you. And love yourself. Embrace yourself. Because that's who you are, *pure love*.

As you approach "The Innermost Cave," it is time to review the old concepts, ideals, and emotional patterns that are no longer useful in your life. It is the place where you can dive deep and revisit past traumatic events in order to discover the sources of your pain. It is also where you start to discover how your mind works to create your identity. Your identity and your view of how the world operates can be shaped and even warped by trauma. Trauma is any significant negative incident that happened to you, whether in your early childhood years or through time as you became an adult. Trauma can generate intense emotions and if you do not process these emotions at the time of the event, the trauma becomes stuck in your mind and body. It will remain in your life even through adulthood unless you attempt to resolve it. It does not matter whether a trauma is big or small, life-altering or seemingly insignificant, it still can create a lasting impact on you. (This statement is not meant to minimize any trauma or the depth of the trauma. It is simply stating that any trauma is considered trauma, no matter what it means to a person.)

We must explore the landscape of our mind and fix what's necessary in order for us to stop being "the wounded child" and morph into "the Hero Within." The mind is an incredibly powerful tool and most of us do not use it to our advantage. We think over 70,000 thoughts a day, and if you really evaluated these thoughts, you would discover to your horror that they tend to be negative ones. Yes, thinking mostly negative thoughts may be common, but it is not beneficial in any way. Negative thoughts will never take you to positive results.

Let's analyze those thoughts. You might be surprised that some of them come from other people; other times they are your own thoughts. These thoughts usually focus on things you dislike about yourself, things you wish you could change, and even worse, things you hate about yourself.

We were gifted with this incredible tool so that we can use it to achieve and grow—not to tear ourselves down. So how can you change your thought patterns so that they can help you become the magnificent human being that you are meant to be?

WHY CHANGING YOUR THOUGHTS CAN CHANGE YOUR LIFE.

First let's take a look at this model[3] and the cycle of thoughts and beliefs that create our ever-present reality.

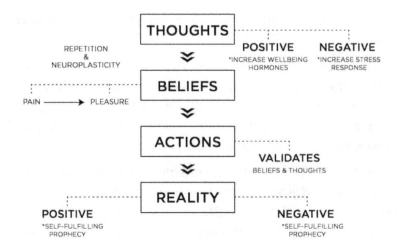

Exploring the depths of your mind and rewiring it takes time, so welcome to the University of Adversity, where we will understand how our wiring was imprinted and left a mark on our lives! A Hero's Journey is marked by the hero's ability to overcome adversity. When you're doing internal healing work, you have to dive deeper where there will be a lot to work through. It's similar to peeling back the layers of an onion; there are many layers that you have to go through to get to the core of who you really are.

A Map of the Human Mind: Parts and Archetypes

Understanding the mind meant I had to take a deeper internal look at myself. This is when I realized that there are many parts of who I am: There is the part of me that is the dreamer. There is the part of me that is the go-getter. On the other hand, there is the part of me who lives in fear and a part of me who remains depressed. What I did not know at the time was that all these parts worked together to protect me. Realizing that there are many parts to who I am, I began to study Carl Jung and his concept that we are comprised of a collection of archetypes, which are the different parts of our self. Later, during my therapy work, I learned how to work with the various parts of myself to bring out the Hero Within.

Psychologist Jay Earley said, "The human mind isn't a unitary thing that sometimes has irrational feelings. It is a complex system of interacting parts, each with a mind of its own."[4] Facing my inner demons and internal struggles helped me identify these parts. You see, our identity is made up of many little parts interconnected to create a whole. Like Steven Johnson said, "Your mind is more like an orchestra than a soloist."[5] In truth, we are multifaceted beings composed of many different parts. Think of "parts" and "archetypes" as sub-personalities that make up your whole personality. It's like a pizza that has been cut into twelve slices. Each slice contributes to the entire pizza, but they are all individual and unique in their own way. Another way to look at it is to think about a mosaic made of beautifully colored tiles. The individual tiles of the mosaic combine together to create a whole picture. This is how parts and archetypes function. They form different sides of your personality that express themselves at different times, depending on the situation you are facing.

"Parts" are by definition different from "archetypes," although they may have similar qualities. We'll start with the archetypes and explore the parts a little later. As I take you through this, I will be referring to Carl Jung's 12 Archetypes to help me explain the roles they perform in our lives.

Archetypes

An ***archetype*** is a typical character that embodies universal patterns of human nature. It is typically not something you are aware of until you learn about archetypes and how they can influence your behavior. Archetypes are essentially your inner guidance system. Once you identify them, you will better understand yourself and why you respond and behave the way you do. Imagine that your mind is a conference room. All of your archetypes are sitting there waiting to take their turn in the discussion. Carl Jung, a Swiss psychologist, believed that archetypes represent our collective unconsciousness. I am using archetypes to help you understand how the parts of you interact and affect your thinking and behavior. As you discover what each archetype represents for you, you will be able to decipher your own behavior patterns.

You are already familiar with archetypes. Think of all the children's stories and heroic tales that you've heard and read growing up. There are typical archetypes, such as the hero, the villain and the advisor in Shakespeare's plays, for example. These archetypes are just parts of the whole story, each bringing its own significance to the story. These archetypes are characters that personify a specific role. Archetypes in stories express patterns. For our purposes, we are looking at behavioral patterns that show up with each archetype relating to your life story and identity. Archetypes influence our behaviors when we are being emotionally triggered. In other words, when we are triggered, we have an emotional response that is based on the patterns of behavior that relate to a specific archetype.

You can look at these archetypes as characters wearing different hats, each contributing to the whole of your personality, or the *self*. The self is a combination of all the archetypes, the unified consciousness of an individual. Archetypes provide depth for each of our individual personas. Each archetype serves its own purpose and can either work for you or against you.

There is a unique dynamic that goes on among your archetypes. It's like an intense negotiation (picture a conference room packed with opinionated co-workers). The *archetypes* are each tugging and pulling at you to get you to behave in accordance with their particular pattern. Your job is to listen to each *negotiator's* argument and decide how you will act. For most of your life, since you didn't know about the archetypes, you just acted in alignment with the loudest or strongest one. Often this made you behave differently than if you had really thought things through. Since these archetypes or negotiators are so deeply ingrained in you, they often make you act impulsively and illogically. Sometimes they can even make you sabotage your own goals in life.

Here is a list of some of your mind's *inner negotiators* based on The 12 Jungian Archetypes[6]:

THE SAGE	THE MAGICIAN
THE INNOCENT	THE HERO
THE EXPLORER	THE REBEL
THE RULER	THE LOVER
THE CREATOR	THE JESTER
THE CAREGIVER	THE ORPHAN

THE SAGE

This is your intellectual or thinking self. The Sage is intelligent and loves to learn. It is always seeking intellectual stimulation and engagement. It's the part of you that thinks logically and analytically, and can rationalize. It wants to comprehend the world around it and the meaning of life.

THE INNOCENT

The Innocent is inexperienced and naïve, trusting and dependent like a child. It is eager to please others and to belong. Vulnerable, it has to rely on others for safety. Very hopeful, it is an eternal optimist. The Innocent is fascinated by the world and is on an irrepressible search for happiness. It's the part of you that is always positive, seeing the brighter side of life.

THE EXPLORER

The Explorer has an insatiable desire for adventure and exploration. It loves to travel and is always on the verge of discovery! Not only does it want to see new places, but it also wants to uncover new things about itself and the world. In the process, the Explorer begins to experience a sense of freedom within itself.

THE RULER/EVERYMAN/REALIST

The Ruler is the part of you that is the leader. It has an innate desire to take charge, so it will jump at any opportunity to volunteer. Its mission is to stabilize the person, so it works hard to maintain order, and to regulate and contain emotions, excitement, creativity, and spontaneity. Consequently, in the process of leading, it often imposes its will on others.

THE CREATOR

The Creator, true to its name, loves to design and create new things, exercising the person's imagination and innovation whenever possible. It has a deep appreciation of art, music, and poetry. This part of us loves being true to our nature as original and unique as we are, and seeks opportunities to create masterpieces of its own. The reward that the Creator desires is to inspire others through its creations.

THE CAREGIVER

The Caregiver is both the mother and the defender. Altruistic, it is naturally compassionate and feels led to take care of others. It is also generous and loves to give to others, even strangers. It provides emotional and spiritual support as well as guidance when the person isn't sure what to do next. As the defender, the Caregiver protects those that are in its inner circle. It notices potential threats and knows how to restore peace and safety.

THE MAGICIAN

"The Magician is the transformative archetype." This is the part that is never satisfied with the status quo. It has a deep connection with the universe and knows that we can become more. So, it never stops trying to "improve, change, and grow." Its intensity for transformation comes from the belief that it can create its own dream.

THE HERO

The Hero is the archetype with all the power and determination. Unwavering, it never loses touch with its role and has the strength and the will to complete its purpose no matter what. Courageous and ambitious in a good way, it toils tirelessly toward making its dreams a reality. The hero is the embodiment of everything that is good and righteousness, and "always seeks to restore justice to society."

THE REBEL/OUTLAW

Rebellious to the core, the Rebel revels in its right to rebel against expectations, against the opinions of others, against whatever is infringing on its freedom at the moment. It enjoys doing things just because it can, and sometimes its behavior is unhealthy or dangerous. It hates being corrected and refuses to be pressured or influenced to change its ways.

THE LOVER

The Lover loves everything about LOVE. Love is its essence and purpose. It appreciates life and what life has to offer, enjoying the world's beauty. The Lover shares love, emotions, feelings and sensuality naturally and freely with others. Its greatest joy is when it connects in a moment of happiness with the ones it loves.

THE JESTER

The Jester is the clown, who "is filled with an insatiable desire for fun and its main goal is to make the most of each day and enjoy life as much as possible." Think of the Jester archetype as yourself when you were five years old—without a care in the world, acting silly and laughing about everything. The Jester sees the world as a comedy act, so there is no reason to ever be serious or solemn or grown up. The Jester expresses the joyful freedom of the child inside you and allows you to have fun.

THE ORPHAN/EVERYMAN

The Orphan is the part of you that is wounded by the past. It's the damaged child within you that clings desperately to the only thing it can remember—the pain from its past. The orphan has no joy. It doesn't laugh. It only knows disappointment, fear and abandonment. No wonder that it sometimes plays the victim.

These 12 archetypes are the driving force behind your behaviors at an unconscious level. You might not be aware of them, but they are present in our daily lives through symbolism, religion, fairy tales, legends, etc. Every one of us inherently has all 12 archetypes within our personality.

Although Carl Jung used a number of Freud's main ideas in his work, he was considered a Neo-Freudian, branching away from Freud's teachings because he felt they were too hyper-sexualized. He instead built his archetypes around common personality traits that interact with the ego.

Jung also grouped the above 12 archetypes into the Four Cardinal Orientations.[7] According to Jung, the Four Cardinal Orientations are categories of the archetypes that show how the archetypes work together to serve a greater purpose.

1. Ego

This group of archetypes seeks to make the world a better place, making an impact, and leaving a legacy for future generations.

- Hero
- Magician
- Outlaw

2. Order

This group of archetypes seeks to provide a structure and order for the world.

- Creator
- Ruler
- Caregiver

3. Social

This group of archetypes strives to make connections with others and form lasting bonds.

- Everyman
- Jester
- Lover

4. Freedom

This group of archetypes seeks to realize its own sense of paradise.

- Innocent

- Sage

- Explorer

We need to be aware of which Archetypes and Negotiators have the greatest influence on us. Besides orientations, Jung also identifies specific characteristics that the archetypes share.

There are three Types:

1. Ego,

2. Soul,

3. and Self.

Knowing the characteristics of each of Jung's three types will make it easier for you to recognize them in yourself and get them to work with you—not against you—in the future.

Here are the characteristics of each of the Archetypes that are classified as "Ego Types"[8]:

1. The Innocent

- Motto: "Free to be you and me!"

- Core desire: to get to paradise

- Goal: to be happy

- Greatest fear: to be punished for doing something bad or wrong

- Strategy: to do things right

- Weakness: boring for all their naive innocence

- Talent: faith and optimism

- The Innocent is also known as utopian, traditionalist, naive, mystic, saint, romantic, dreamer

2. **The Everyman**

- Motto: "All men and women are created equal"

- Core Desire: connecting with others

- Goal: to belong

- Greatest fear: to be left out or to stand out from the crowd

- Strategy: develop ordinary solid virtues, be down to earth, the common touch

- Weakness: losing one's own self in an effort to blend in or for the sake of superficial relationships

- Talent: realism, empathy, lack of pretense

- The Everyman is also known as the good old boy, regular guy/girl, the person next door, the realist, the working stiff, the solid citizen, the good neighbor, the silent majority

3. The Hero

- Motto: "Where there's a will, there's a way"
- Core desire: to prove one's worth through courageous acts
- Goal: expert mastery in a way that improves the world
- Greatest fear: weakness, vulnerability, being a "chicken" (slang)
- Strategy: to be as strong and competent as possible
- Weakness: arrogance, always needing another battle to fight
- Talent: competence and courage
- The Hero is also known as the warrior, crusader, rescuer, superhero, the soldier, dragon slayer, the winner and the team player

4. The Caregiver

- Motto: "Love your neighbor as yourself"
- Core desire: to protect and care for others
- Goal: to help others
- Greatest fear: selfishness and ingratitude
- Strategy: doing things for others
- Weakness: martyrdom and being exploited
- Talent: compassion, generosity
- The Caregiver is also known as the saint, altruist, parent, helper, supporter

These are the characteristics of "The Soul Types"[9]:

5. **The Explorer**

   - Motto: "Don't fence me in"
   - Core desire: the freedom to find out who you are through exploring the world
   - Goal: to experience a better, more authentic, more fulfilling life
   - Biggest fear: getting trapped, conformity, and inner emptiness
   - Strategy: journey, seeking out and experiencing new things, escape from boredom
   - Weakness: aimless wandering, becoming a misfit
   - Talent: autonomy, ambition, being true to one's soul
   - The explorer is also known as the seeker, iconoclast, wanderer, individualist, pilgrim

6. **The Rebel**

   - Motto: "Rules are made to be broken"
   - Core desire: revenge or revolution
   - Goal: to overturn what isn't working
   - Greatest fear: to be powerless or ineffectual
   - Strategy: disrupt, destroy, or shock
   - Weakness: crossing over to the dark side, crime
   - Talent: outrageousness, radical freedom

- The Outlaw is also known as the rebel, revolutionary, wild man, the misfit, or iconoclast

7. The Lover

- Motto: "You're the only one"
- Core desire: intimacy and experience
- Goal: being in a relationship with the people, work and surroundings they love
- Greatest fear: being alone, a wallflower, unwanted, unloved
- Strategy: to become more and more physically and emotionally attractive
- Weakness: outward-directed desire to please others at risk of losing own identity
- Talent: passion, gratitude, appreciation, and commitment
- The Lover is also known as the partner, friend, intimate, enthusiast, sensualist, spouse, team-builder

8. The Creator/Artist

- Motto: "If you can imagine it, it can be done"
- Core desire: to create things of enduring value
- Goal: to realize a vision
- Greatest fear: mediocre vision or execution
- Strategy: develop artistic control and skill

- Task: to create culture, express own vision

- Weakness: perfectionism, bad solutions

- Talent: creativity and imagination

- The Creator is also known as the artist, inventor, innovator, musician, writer or dreamer

These are the characteristics of "The Self Types"[10]:

9. The Jester

- Motto: "You only live once"

- Core desire: to live in the moment with full enjoyment

- Goal: to have a great time and lighten up the world

- Greatest fear: being bored or boring others

- Strategy: play, make jokes, be funny

- Weakness: frivolity, wasting time

- Talent: joy

- The Jester is also known as the fool, trickster, joker, practical joker or comedian

10. The Sage

- Motto: "The truth will set you free"

- Core desire: to find the truth

- Goal: to use intelligence and analysis to understand the world

- Biggest fear: being duped, misled—or ignorance

- Strategy: seeking out information and knowledge; self-reflection and understanding thought processes

- Weakness: can study details forever and never act

- Talent: wisdom, intelligence

- The Sage is also known as the expert, scholar, detective, advisor, thinker, philosopher, academic, researcher, thinker, planner, professional, mentor, teacher, contemplative

11. The Magician

- Motto: "I make things happen"

- Core desire: understanding the fundamental laws of the universe

- Goal: to make dreams come true

- Greatest fear: unintended negative consequences

- Strategy: develop a vision and live by it

- Weakness: becoming manipulative

- Talent: finding win-win solutions

- The Magician is also known as the visionary, catalyst, inventor, charismatic leader, shaman, healer, medicine man

12. The Ruler

- Motto: "Power isn't everything, it's the only thing"

- Core desire: control

- Goal: create a prosperous, successful family or community

- Strategy: exercise power

- Greatest fear: chaos, being overthrown

- Weakness: being authoritarian, unable to delegate

- Talent: responsibility, leadership

- The Ruler is also known as the boss, leader, aristocrat, king, queen, politician, role model, manager or administrator

Psychologists have identified a number of archetypes beyond Jungians main 12 listed here. Later, I will mention a few additional archetypes that are typically present within every human's psyche.

All of us have many archetypes that present themselves throughout our lifetime, and they seem to appear and disappear depending on the situation. This is your chance to learn to work with your archetypes so that you can weave them into the healthy, happy "Self" you've always wanted to be!

When you look at all these archetypes, they seem to be separate, but in reality, they are fractions of who you are. Together they create the Self, which is all aspects of your identity. YOU are the hero, the sage, the orphan, the creator—you are all of these. They just work together to help you when you need assistance. When you realize that all of these archetypes contribute to who you are, you can begin to understand them. This understanding will help you discover a new sense of ease and clarity within your life.

Which Archetype describes YOU most of the time?

Think back to several scenarios that have occurred in your life. Can you match up most of your actions with one or more of these archetypes? Everyone demonstrates some characteristics of each of the archetypes, but there is typically one archetypal role that will be dominant in your life. *Your most dominant archetype has grown out of your unique personal life experiences.*

PARTS

Parts are a little different from archetypes. While archetypes are part of the collective unconscious, *parts* are formed on an individual basis. Typically, these parts of our identity develop as a coping mechanism to trauma. So, these parts form fragments of your true Self, the essence of who you really are. These parts of you work as protectors and become engaged when you are triggered. They are usually triggered and associated with the *pain body*.

The *pain body* is any past emotional trauma you might have experienced and is stored in your nervous system. Because it is linked permanently to your nervous system, it can cause extreme reactions once the part (or coping mechanism) is triggered and will usually result in fear, anger, frustration, or sadness. When the part is triggered, we tend to identify with the *pain body* and lose our sense of self, mistakenly undertaking their role as our own.

We have to not only learn to identify our parts, but also learn to observe them from an outside perspective, not letting them take us over. For example, one of my biggest fears was the fear of abandonment. I developed this fear after my parents got divorced. As I began to start having romantic relationships, every time my partner would leave me to hang out with his friends, it triggered this response in me—the fear of abandonment (the part). Once this part was triggered, I would lose complete control and have an extreme meltdown. I became so identified with this part that I lost my sense of self. This tends to happen when we are triggered and have emotional responses, which are harder to control. Now, not all cases relating to the parts cause a reaction to this degree; however, this was my personal case because the fear ran very deep.

When dealing with triggers, we have to be aware of how we respond to them. A key component to working with our triggers is learning to consciously respond and not simply to react. This may take some time and effort, but once you learn to avoid becoming emotionally charged when you are triggered, you will be better able to cope with adverse situations.

So how can you respond instead of reacting? When you are triggered, it is easy to get consumed by negative thoughts in your mind. But this is the moment when you need to take a step back. It's like practicing mindfulness, but in an extreme situation. This is the ultimate test. The more often you refuse to be triggered when pressured, the more effectively you will be able to self-regulate your responses in any situation. Of course, when you first learn this technique, it's not as easy as it sounds. However, over time, you will be able to transmute your habitual emotional reaction into a proactive response. When you are triggered, it's important to focus on taking long, deep breaths because the trigger is not only a psychological response but it also becomes a physical response.

When I was triggered in the above scenario, I remember exactly how it felt. My heart rate began to rise rapidly, my body trembled with a rush of adrenaline, and I was in full fear and panic mode. I could feel myself getting hot as my sympathetic nervous system engaged and the all-too familiar sense of doom took over my body. I was filled with anxiety and frustration. It was a full-on fight-or-flight reaction—me ready to take on any enemy that came my way! The reaction made the threat of the situation seem real, but in retrospect, I can see that the scenario had blown way out of proportion in my mind. When you're at the peak of an adrenaline rush, it's easy to go into overdrive and do or say things you later regret; but if you can recognize the sensations as they develop in your body, this is the time to focus on deep breathing and help settle down your perceived threat.

There is a way to control your *fight-or-flight* responses. Neurofeedback studies have demonstrated that people can override overreactions to stimuli. During a number of studies, patients were hooked up to biofeedback machines and shown how to interact with the machine to regulate their own breathing and responses. People who panic or over-react can learn to tamp down their *fight-or-flight* responses. You don't actually need a machine to do the biofeedback technique, just use your slow, deep breathing to calm yourself whenever you feel triggered. This way you can control your responses to triggers rather than being a victim to your own reactions to them. Mastering this technique gives the power back to you even in the worst circumstances!

We will discuss breathing exercises in a later chapter so you can practice regulating your body in stressful situations.

UNDERSTANDING PARTS MORE DEEPLY

For our purposes here, a "part" is defined as a piece of you that you personally identify with. It is often modeled after one of the archetypes mentioned earlier. No matter what the role of the part is, it behaves the way it does because it believes that it is helping and protecting you in one way or another. The parts of your mind will take on different roles, depending on what is needed at the time.

Okay. So, you might be thinking, if there are many different parts to my personality and identity, does this mean that I'm like a person who has *dissociative identity disorder* or *schizophrenia*? Let me put you at ease—absolutely not! EVERYBODY has all these parts! We are just breaking down the parts of your personality so that you can understand yourself better. There has been quite a lot of research about "archetypes" and "parts" and how they relate to human behavior. Dr. Richard Schwartz, a specialist in family therapy, came up with a modality called *Internal Family Systems*. Internal Family Systems is a therapeutic model that engages the multiplicity of the mind, looking at the different parts of the mind and how we can dialogue with them to free us from misguided and/or self-destructive beliefs that we might have. During his therapy practice, he recognized that his patients continued to identify different parts within themselves, and thus he created this therapy to work with the "parts."[11]

Think about it: Have you ever had to make a decision and started using the language of parts without realizing it? Most people have, at some point or another. For example, let's say that you are on the brink of a breakup and you cannot decide what to do. You decide to discuss it with a friend to gain some perspective and you start saying "a part of me feels like I should stay with Bryan, but another part of me feels like I should leave him." This is a prime example of identifying the parts. So, one part of you, maybe the lover archetype, loves being in a relationship because it fulfills you and makes you feel happy. The other part of you might be the sage archetype who knows that this relationship will not work in the long run because there are many unhealthy aspects to it. Learning to identify our parts and the related archetypes helps us uncover our personality and understand why we behave the way that we do. It also lets us lock into the truth about our situation, which can guide us to make better decisions in the future.

Through my experience as a *rapid transformational therapist*, I have used "parts therapy" as a part of my practice and have had major success with it. I have noticed that in most cases, the parts typically embed in the psyche after a traumatic event—usually when people are much younger. Because the part is embedded, it will show up when triggered, leading to a chain of reactions. Typically, the part is an unwanted behavior that serves as a protective mechanism, although this may not always be the case and it can vary from person to person.

For example, I had a client who, strangely enough, wanted to explore his relationship with money. He was always able to make money, but it seemed impossible for him to keep the money for very long. As soon as he got it, he spent it. During our therapy sessions, we recovered a memory from when he was a child. He was sitting in the back seat of his grandmother's car, wanting to eat some ice cream. He saw his grandmother's purse and stole a quarter from it. He recalled his grandmother telling him that "money will burn a hole in your pocket." This belief became ingrained in his mind and became his reality even through adulthood. When we began the parts therapy section, where we dialogued with the part, we found out that the part of him that continued to make him spend the money did it because he felt that he was "not worthy" of having it since he once stole from his grandmother when he was younger.

Exercise E7-1: Trigger Visualization

Past events and memories can trigger unexpected or unwanted reactions in us. If you find yourself believing something negative about yourself whenever confronted by a specific trigger, try this exercise to sort out the cause and create a healthier way to respond:

◇ When you are triggered, take a few deep breaths and close your eyes.

◇ Begin to focus on your breathing as you take long, deep inhales and exhales.

◇ As you are breathing deeply, imagine the scene that is causing the trigger. As you see this scene in your mind, begin to zoom out from the scene. Take a step back as if you are watching the scene on a TV screen in your mind.

◇ Take a look at the scene from a 2nd person perspective so you can detach from the emotions that are coming up. Watch and observe closely. See what thoughts you have now as you are taking yourself out of the scene.

◇ The act of detaching from the trigger should help you look at it from different perspectives. Try to analyze from as many different perspectives as possible. What can you see as the truth? What is just a figment of your imagination that you are creating?

◇ After you feel you have explored the scene and trigger enough, take 3 additional cleansing breaths. As you exhale, release a loud "ahhhhh" so you can release the tension and negative feelings from your body. You can do this as long as you need to.

◇ When you feel ready, open up your eyes. If you want to, you can journal about this experience afterwards to further explore the trigger.

EXERCISE E7-2: FINDING YOUR DOMINANT ARCHETYPE

Before working with your archetypes, it is critical that you build a relationship with the parts of yourself. It's not hard and you do not need a therapist to help you build a relationship with your parts. All you need is awareness.

1. Take a look at the list of the archetypes and their characteristics described earlier in this chapter. Decide which Archetype you identify with most often.

2. Grab a paper and pen and write it down. Then, ask yourself:

   • How does this archetype show up in my life?

   • How do I identify with this archetype?

   • What situations trigger this archetype to affect how I respond?

   • What is the opposite archetype?

   • How can I switch my perspective to that of the opposite archetype so that I can feel at ease?

If you find that you are having difficulty coming up with answers to these questions, it's okay. Go to the visualization and dialoguing exercises below. You can do these exercises with any of the archetypes. These exercises will help you understand all aspects of the archetypes within you more fully.

EXERCISE E7-3: ARCHETYPE
VISUALIZATION EXERCISE

1. Close your eyes and imagine an archetype or part of you that you want to connect with.

2. Feel where that part is in your body or visualize an image of what that part looks like, and if you struggle, it's totally okay.

3. Just ask the part or archetype to simply show itself to you. Identifying the part or archetype may feel different for everyone based on their learning styles, whether they are visual, audio, or kinesthetic learners, etc. Maybe you hear something or see a symbol that connects with you. Maybe you feel a sensation somewhere in your body. Just tune in and pay attention.

4. Then, get curious about the part or archetype and ask it:

   • What do you look like?

   • How old are you?

   • What situations bring you out?

   • What is your role in my life?

   • What is your approach to the world?

- What do you want and need?

- What is your purpose for being there?

- What can you offer me?

- What are your blocks?

- When did you first decide to come into my life? What was going on?

- What helps you grow?

- How can you help me in a way that does not hold me back?

- How do you relate to women, men, and children?

- What can I do to deactivate the Archetypes that have been holding me back?

- What can I do to activate the opposite Archetype that will let me move forward in my life?

Side note: When you are practicing the visualization exercise, try it a few times. Some people may not experience the part immediately, however, if you are patient with the process, you will eventually experience it. It may be easier to practice simple meditation in the beginning before you start trying to work with the part.

After being able to identify your parts and archetypes, we can do some exercises to work with them. When working with the archetypes, it's an exploration of the depths of your mind. You want to ask, "What can I do to deactivate the archetypes that have been holding me back? What can I do to activate the opposite ones that will let me move forward in my life?"

Archetypes have both a light side and a shadowy side.

In this chapter we are focusing on the shadow side of the archetypes. These are the ones that keep you in the dark. In a later chapter we will work with the light side of the archetypes. Always remember this: When an archetype is working against you, you want to channel (connect) with the opposite archetype. For example, if you are operating from a wounded child perspective, you need to parent the wounded child part of you. This flips you to the opposite version of that archetype—one that is supportive and nurturing instead of a wounded child that lives in fear and does not feel safe. We will learn more about this later as we work with the wounded child.

Exercise E7-4: Channeling the Opposite Archetype

For this exercise, picture yourself as a victim and then as a hero. The descriptions below will help you identify with each role.

Victim: Before I took back control of my life, I often felt like a victim—like the world was happening to me and I couldn't do anything to change it. I was a victim and subservient to the negative voices in my mind, never once believing in my own power or abilities.

Hero: When I operated from this victim mentality, it was not helping me. What I had to do to switch out of the "victim role" was to channel the "hero role." I had to ask myself, what does the "victim in me" need right now? I needed kindness but also needed to be in a dominant role like the hero's role to pull myself out of this victim space. Instead of identifying with the victim, I can learn to channel the energy of the hero—by realizing that I am the creator of my destiny.

1. Visualize the victim (archetype).

2. Feel its emotions, honor the emotions, and sit with it.

3. Then imagine that you are the (opposite archetype), the Hero, empowering that victim and supporting the victim with strength, courage, and bravery.

INNER CRITIC, INNER CHILD

Aside from the Jungian Archetypes, there are two other parts that are extremely important in your life:

◇ *inner critic*

◇ *inner child.*

Of all the parts within you, the most important part you have to work with is the "inner critic." The inner critic is the voice of self-doubt. This voice permeates through your mind, is constantly on replay, always keeping you at a distance from achieving your goals. It feeds off fear, reminds you that you're not good enough, and keeps you feeling small. This background noise in your head is quite irrational, yet it easily persuades you to believe what it's telling you. We are so used to hearing this voice every day that we do not realize there could be an alternative. So, we listen to its harsh words and let it convince us that we're not good enough. It's the silent killer of hopes and dreams because this critic prevents you from taking up all of the opportunities that come your way.

The voice of the inner critic sounds like this:

◇ "You're not smart enough."

◇ "People won't listen to what you have to say."

◇ "You need more experience."

◇ "You can't ever succeed."

Let's be real. We're all too familiar with that nagging voice inside our heads that prevents us from realizing our dreams. That voice is the "inner critic" or the "thinker." On one hand, the inner critic's role is to keep you safe and protected. On the other hand, the inner critic prevents you from doing the things that you really want to do. It plays a contradicting role. So how can you negotiate with this inner critic so that you can be safe and still achieve your biggest desires?

EXERCISE E7-5: DIALOGUING EXERCISE - THE INNER CRITIC

1. Imagine that this part of you—in this case, the *inner critic*—is sitting right in front of you.

2. Ask that part, how can you protect me while letting me accomplish my dreams?

3. Sometimes it's as simple as assigning that part a new role. Tell that part about its new role. "I would like to give you a new role: "I want you to (encourage me, give me confidence, motivate me)." Give it whatever role you find helpful.

Another way to work with the *inner critic* is by shifting your focus. Sometimes, when we are inside of our heads, we are sucked into its drama and then we end up going down a rabbit hole. An effective way to interrupt this inner critic is to shout, "Stop!" in your mind (or out loud if you do not mind looking a little crazy—this can be fun sometimes). This interruption breaks the cycle you are in and frees you from the thinking loop that you have been trapped in. Another thing you can tell this voice is, "I will not allow or accept what you're telling me." When you are dialoging with the inner critic this way, its voice will fade and you can take back your power. Once you're out of the loop, immediately find something else you can focus on— something that grabs your attention. This could be a few minutes of being "present" with your environment and enjoying what's around you: the beauty of nature, the trees, the sky, a sunset, a child laughing and playing. You can also shift focus to the sensations you feel in your body. Pay close attention to your body. What are you feeling at this exact moment? What slight changes can you notice in your body, in your breathing? Because, let's face it, most of us are so stressed that sometimes we forget to even breathe.

We cannot fully get rid of the voice of the inner critic because it serves a purpose in our lives, most importantly as a safety instinct. However, we can learn to keep that voice quiet and refuse to take direction from it.

EXERCISE E7-6: SHIFTING YOUR FOCUS— THE INNER CRITIC

1. When you hear the voice of the inner critic, shout "stop" out loud or in your mind. You can also tell the voice, "I will not allow or accept what you're telling me."

2. After doing number 1, try shifting your focus. Focus on the sensations you are feeling in your body.

3. Take note of everything you are feeling in your body and be present in the moment. This will help you break the cycle.

THE INNER CHILD—THE 7-YEAR-OLD WHO LIVES WITHIN US

Understanding Dysfunctional Family Roles

When children grow up in healthy situations, they are able to rely on their parents and other adults to ensure their survival and safety. However, often we are born into dysfunctional families and thus, our ego develops protective mechanisms to help us survive. Understanding dysfunctional families and the role you have assumed will help you figure out how and why the child within you remains in protective mode even though you are a functioning adult.

A dysfunctional family can have many different attributes. It is usually a "family plagued by mental illness, trauma from tragedy, or simply by being headed by individuals with very poor parenting skills."[13] Most of us are affected by this in one way or another because although most parents do the best that they can do for us, a lot still have unresolved issues from their own parents that affect the way they raise us. These dysfunctional families tend to carry an array of problems from conflict, neglect, shame, substance-abuse problems, and much more. Dysfunctional family dynamics can have profound effects on the children growing up in these conditions and cause the children to adopt certain sabotaging behaviors.

If we examine family "roles," we can gain an understanding of why we might have certain behaviors and attitudes towards a situation. Most of us grow up in dysfunctional families and do not even realize it. Our parents may constantly argue, be unhappy, or be divorced. We go through traumatic experiences, whether it is something small or something extreme, such as verbal or physical abuse. These events in our childhood can leave an imprint that we carry on with us into adulthood. As kids, we don't understand that this can form self-sabotaging beliefs that we identify with for the rest of our lives. Since we do not know any better, we accept this as our reality and we adopt dysfunctional family roles in order to survive

These are the four main dysfunctional family roles that children tend to adopt[14]:

The Hero: The Over-Responsible and Self-Sufficient One

The Scapegoat: The Problem Child

The Clown: The Comedian of the Family

The Lost Child: The Quiet One of the Family

Read over the descriptions of these roles on the following chart and think about the traumas that plagued your childhood and teen years. Did you adopt one or more of these dysfunctional roles in order to survive your own situation?

Recognizing these roles can help you break the cycle now so that your past does not spill into your present and future and affect your children or others that you care about. Once you've identified the roles you picked up from your family, it's time to think about how you can unmask yourself so that you can heal.

Next page: Chart of Dysfunctional Family Roles
https://www.wiseword.org/pg/dysfunctional_family_roles.[12]

Dysfunctional Family Role	What's on the Outside	What You Don't See	What They Do For the Family and Why They Play Along	Without Help This is Very Possible	What is Possible with Help
Hero	Perfect, can't be wrong, gets positive attention, awards, degrees.	Fear of failing, over-controlled.	Family feels we are not so bad because this person is so good. The hero likes the extra power and attention.	Workaholic, physical illness, controlling, not much fun, pride, shameless.	Achievement-oriented vs. success, has learned to say no, and not be so perfect. Can get in touch with the "bad" stuff.
Scapegoat	Bad, angry, impulsive, never good enough, "black sheep" of the family, doesn't fit in.	Hurt, rejection, full of shame, feels like a loser.	Marriage is brought together to "fix" the scapegoat. Hero feels "good" because scapegoat is "bad." We can avoid the "bad" stuff by downloading it onto the scapegoat.	Addictive, trouble with the law, promiscuous, "chip on shoulder." Continuing to play the role in jobs and future relationships. Constantly in trouble.	Can learn to be good and feel good. Learns to take appropriate risks. Business owners, missionary types.
Lost Child	Ignored, quiet, invisible. Loves animals, material possessions. Artistic. Sometimes has learning disabilities.	Frozen feelings—Can't express feelings. Lonely.	Family feels, "At least we don't have to worry about this kid."	Doesn't share opinions, doesn't feel needed. Can die early because of this.	Talented and creative, can learn to participate and share wisdom that they achieve by being quieter. Good listeners. Fells needed and connected with time.
Clown or Mascot	Funny, hysterical, anything for a laugh. Cute, immature.	Hides pain with humor. Scared, feels inadequate.	They bring comic relief to the family. Helps the family avoid issues.	Continues to build up pain. Lets others tell them what to do. Too much of a follower. Never grows up.	Can feel range of emotion. Can use laughter in good ways. Learns to take the lead more. Grows up into more responsibility.

165

EXERCISE E7-7A: IDENTIFYING YOUR ROLE

1. First, let yourself feel the emotions related to your role: Take about 15-20 minutes to journal about your role in your family and how it has affected you up until this point in your life.

2. List the behaviors and beliefs that you have developed because of this role: How are you still behaving in ways that relate to that role? How does it make you feel? What are some challenges you have personally with this role? What changes can you make to free you from this role? What have you learned from this role?

3. Learn to parent yourself: We will go further with this a little later through visualization, but for now, write down what you always needed when you were a child. Did you need more love? More support? Did you need your parents to prioritize you? Did you need them to make you feel safe and secure? Whatever you needed, write it down. Next to it, write down possible ways you can do this for yourself.

4. Compare and Contrast: This is the only time I believe it's necessary to compare and contrast! Look at your life as a child and see how much you've changed and grown into the adult you are now. Although you might have been influenced by past events, the truth is that you are no longer a child. A child might not have been

able to process the events at the time it happens, however, you are an adult now. You do not have to live life through the eyes of a child unless it's those times when you are connecting with the happy child inside you.

Example: (I combined all the steps into a single paragraph. Feel free to separate them if it's easier for you.) I grew up in a single-parent family and I picked up the Scapegoat role. I always felt like I did not belong and continued to cause trouble through my teenage years and even during my early adult years. I was often compulsive with shopping and promiscuity. One of my biggest fears was the fear of rejection. Being the scapegoat was a way for me to gain attention because I felt unloved and rejected by my family. Through time, I've learned to manage this Scapegoat role, I've learned how to feel good in a healthy way through reading self-development books and meditating. I also channeled this role to own a business that helps other people. As a child, I needed love and acceptance from my family. Although they tried to give it to me, they were often unsuccessful. Now, as an adult, I can give myself this love and acceptance through building my self-esteem and belief in myself.

Once you've learned about the role you picked up as a child, it's time for us to dive deeper into this Inner Child, the little seven-year-old girl or boy that lives within us. There are two main parts of the Inner Child that we will focus on. One is the wounded child and the other is the happy child.

The "wounded child" is the younger version of ourselves who has been wounded through traumatic experiences. The role you took on from the dysfunctional family roles is a part of the wounded child. It holds on to past memories of neglect and abuse that we endured as a child. The wounded child is the part of you that still acts out of fear and seeks safety due to the imprints that were left on you from past events. The wounded child is highly associated with your relationship with your parents and the impact—intentional or not—that they left on you as a child. The wounded child might harbor feelings of guilt, shame, resentment, fear, and hatred. The wounded child is the basis for the continuation of dysfunctional relationships in your life, recreating the patterns you had with your parents. Left unhealed, the wounded child may prevent you from truly connecting with others due to the fact that it is the part of you that is scared.

Many of us do not realize the imprint that childhood trauma can have on us, even if the traumatic event is something we think is negligible and we write off as insignificant. We need to realize that whether the trauma was large or small, it would have shaped our behavior in the long term anyhow. The term "small" is relative; you might think something that happened in your younger years was so minute that it was not a real trauma. However, from a child's perspective or the younger version of you, that minute event may have shocked you to your core. It left a mark on your development, embedding into your subconscious mind. I truly believe that every single person's problem is real and true no matter how small it might seem. No one else can understand your personal experience and how it affected you. So, do not disregard any event that happened to you—even if you cannot quite understand how it plays a role in your current behaviors and belief systems.

As children, we do not understand trauma. We rely on our parents to provide a safe and protective environment for us, although sometimes they fail to do so. For small children, even something as insignificant as a slight rejection can cause an intense reaction and cause them to see the situation as life-threatening. Children also tend to internalize and blame themselves for any traumatic events that they experience. This is because their brain is not developed like an adult's brain and they are not able to process the event. Once these traumatic events are internalized, they will develop a belief system based on the trauma. They will continue to carry these beliefs and attitudes into their adult lives unless something helps them understand and work through it.

We all have belief systems built on traumatic events. That is why it is so critical that we enter our "Innermost Cave" and start sorting it all out. We need to look at key events that happened in our younger years to see how they might have warped our thinking and are still influencing our life today. Below are a few common childhood traumas that could have been minimized or ignored by the adults in our life at the time. (These are the basics. Of course, there are more extreme cases that are not listed.)

CHILDHOOD TRAUMAS

◇ **Neglected**: You were often left alone by your parents. Beliefs formed: "My parents don't care about me or love me. I'm not lovable."

◇ **Criticism**: Nothing you ever did was "good enough" to your parents and this caused low self-esteem. Beliefs formed: "Nothing I do will be good enough." "I'm not good enough." "Everyone is better than me."

◇ **Gaslighting**: Parents or people close to you denied your reality. This is usually a situation where the other person makes you question your own reality as if it were false. You might have told them what you felt, but instead of listening to you, they respond with "Come on. I never said that," or "You are just being overly sensitive." Beliefs formed: "I can't trust anyone because even my parents don't believe me." "It's not safe." "I have to protect myself."

◇ **Suppression**: You were not allowed to fully express yourself. Beliefs formed: "I can't show my true self because I will be rejected." "Showing who I really am will only cause me pain."

◇ **Invalidated**: You were not being seen, heard, or listened to, your parents did not validate your reality. Beliefs formed: "No one understands me." "What I think, feel and believe don't matter."

◇ **Emotions not allowed**: You were punished for showing your emotions. Beliefs formed: "I can't show my emotions because they are 'bad.' " "Showing my emotions means I'm weak." "I have to always be strong."

EXERCISE E7-7B: HEALING THE WOUNDED CHILD BY JOURNALING

Healing the wounded child means you have to connect with that broken part of yourself. A great way to connect with the wounded child is to do some journaling:

◇ Write down any past pain or resentment you might have held onto from your relationship with your parents.

◇ Think about how that relationship has influenced your beliefs and behaviors today.

◇ Keep this journal entry in mind as you proceed through the book; you will have an opportunity to do a forgiveness exercise to help you release any resentment you feel towards your parents.

◇ Another thing you can do to help the wounded child heal is by having a dialogue with your parents about how they hurt you in the past. You do not have to do this physically. Just write a letter to your parents expressing all of your feelings and emotions. No need to mail it. The act of simply writing the letter allows the damaged part of yourself to start healing. However, if you are able to have a conversation with your parents, of course this wouldn't hurt as long as you know you are in a safe environment.

You can also do the following *visualizations*. The first is to help you connect with the wounded child and see what he or she needs from you.

EXERCISE E7-7C: WOUNDED CHILD VISUALIZATION

Imagine… you're walking along a gorgeous stretch of the beach! Feel your feet as they sink into the sand that gently touches the soles of your feet. Look at the incredible vastness of the ocean beside you, feel the gentle breeze as you hear the gentle waves crashing on the shore.

Look around you and inhale the beauty of life that you see, including a few dolphins swimming in the distance. Let all the worries of the world fade away as you connect with this mesmerizing moment. Feel the warmth of the sun as it embraces your skin.

As you walk along the beach, you see a little girl or boy in the distance sitting alone. This little girl or boy is you. You feel a stronger sense of connection as you inch closer. As you walk towards this child, you know that this is a younger version of you. That little child seems melancholy sitting all alone. You take a seat next to this child and you start up a conversation. You ask, "Why are you all alone?" "What makes you sad?" "What makes you angry?"

Listen closely to what the child, the younger you, has to say. Then you say, "It's going to be okay now. You are safe." "I will take care of you." "I love you very much." "I will always be here for you." Then tell your child-self anything else that you want to say that will help your wounded child heal. Give that child a loving hug, feeling the warmth and closeness. As you say your healing words, you see your child-self begin to light up. You see the sparkle in his or her eyes and a shy smile. Your embrace is so full of love that this sweet child can't help but feel it too. You stand up together and begin to play and run around on the beach. The child feels at peace and supported next to you. You both run off together into the distance, merging into one.

This next visualization is to help you connect with your happy inner child:

> This happy child is the version that is lighthearted and innocent, one who is full of love, happiness, laughter, and joy. It's the younger version of you who does not care about anything in the world except the present moment. We have so much to learn from our younger selves. Sometimes, we're so busy being an adult that we forget to connect with this inner child, this child who is desperately seeking to come out and play. We're so focused on our wounds that we forget that this little child still resides within us.

EXERCISE E7-7D: HAPPY CHILD VISUALIZATION

> Imagine... You're walking through a beautiful rain forest. Feel your feet as you walk through this lush forest, connecting with Mother Earth. Look around you and inhale the beauty of life that you see. Look at the incredible trees that have been there for thousands of years coming to life again this day as a gentle breeze touches and soothes your face. Let all the worries of the world fade away as you connect with this mesmerizing moment, hearing the gentle whispers of the wind and the music of the birds chirping.

Feel the warmth of the sun as it peaks through the leaves of the trees. As you walk through this forest, you come to a clearing that is flooded with radiant, white light. As you leave the forest, you walk into a beautiful open field with gorgeous mountain backdrops. In the middle of the field is a younger version of you. That little you is smiling, laughing, and playing, fully connected with the true essence of who you are. You walk up to this little child, sensing a deep affinity. You reach out your hands and grasp the child's little hands as you spin and dance together. You feel the deep gratitude and bliss that you know has been within you all along. You pick up that child, looking deeply into his/her eyes, and say fervently, "I love you. You are always good enough. You are safe. I will always take care of you." You hug the younger you as you feel the child merging into your heart and life now.

You see, that little child has been inside you all along, waiting to reconnect with you and let you know that eternal bliss is absolutely available to you. So, whenever you feel sad or discouraged, give that little child a visit and remind your child-like self of the countless wonders that life holds for you both.

If you struggle with these visualizations, visit my website: www.thedreamlifefoundation.com/meditations for a guided meditation.

THE ORPHAN OR THE VICTIM

Another important archetype we will look at is the *orphan*, which is more commonly known as the victim. The role of the victim is the one that most people identify with at the start of their transformational journey. The victim does not take any responsibility for its own circumstances; it constantly blames other people for its deficiency. The victim has a tendency to portray itself as always being taken advantage of and that nothing is ever its fault. The victim plays this role because it usually will get positive feedback from other people, reinforcing its behavior.

However, if you always identify with this role, you will not be able to transcend into the hero that you are. Connecting with your Inner Victim will help you learn more about how it plays a role in your life.

EXERCISE E7-8A: THE VICTIM & THE ORPHAN—JOURNALING

1. Grab a pen and paper or journal.

2. Spend 20 minutes journaling and answering the following questions:

   - Do I take responsibility for my life? Or do I blame others?

   - Do I constantly victimize myself when situations do not work out the way I expect them to?

   - Do I feel powerless, or feel like I don't have control of my life?

- Do I envy others because they get what they want out of life?

- Do I wallow in self-pity?

- What do I gain from being the victim?

EXERCISE E7-8B: SHIFTING FROM VICTIM TO VICTOR - JOURNALING

◇ How can I take greater responsibility for my life?

◇ What are some changes I can make to lift me out of this victim role?

◇ What action steps can I take now to claim my power back?

◇ Who have I blamed in the past for my life?

THE SABOTEUR

The Saboteur is another important archetype because many of us tend to take on this role when we are doing something new or learning a new skill. The saboteur will stop you in your tracks and fill you up with fear, creating hesitation and preventing any progress. The saboteur uses excuses and fear to prevent you from an imagined and painful outcome. It assumes the worst outcome, such as rejection, before you even start. It capitalizes on your low self-esteem and causes you to block your own success. It is absolutely essential that you get into the habit of recognizing when your saboteur is coming into play, so that you can make better choices instead of letting it dictate your decisions and sabotage your success. The saboteur will prevent you from taking any risks because it is afraid, and the more you succumb to it, the more it will work to avoid this vulnerability.

EXERCISE E7-9: THE SABOTEUR-JOURNALING

1. Grab a pen and paper or journal.

2. Spend 20 minutes journaling and answering these questions.

   - What role does the saboteur have in my life?

   - What is the saboteur's main purpose?

   - What if I do not listen to the saboteur's voice? How would my actions be different?

What is the best possible outcome of the situation I am in?

THE HERO'S JOURNEY...

PART THREE:
RETURN

"It all sounds cheesy and, yes, maybe so. But the truth is that the process of falling in love with yourself is the key to ultimate happiness."

~ *Julia*

CHAPTER 8:

ORDEAL

Activating Your True Self

ARCHETYPES ARE A GREAT way for us to understand WHY we think, feel, and behave the way that we do, but also how we are not limited to the confines of our archetypes. Think of them as the starting line for the race that is before you. To better understand ourselves and guide us on the journey of change, we need to understand the way our minds work and how we construct realities through the basis of our thoughts, emotions, and belief systems. For a long time, people believed that change was not possible, that people develop their personalities by the age of five and that we are confined to this personality forever. This concept was Freudian. However, over time with research, we have found that change is possible, even though it may be challenging.

We are no longer fixed with certain personality traits or behaviors. Instead, they can be changed through time with effort. This is a breakthrough for many of us, especially those of us who believe that change is impossible. In fact, I am proof that change is 100% possible as long as you make the commitment and put in the time and effort to make it happen.

NEUROPLASTICITY

To understand how change happens in the brain, we have to look at neuroplasticity and how it enables us to create changes in our life for the better. For many years, it was believed that the brain remained the same after childhood and that we were not able to change it. However, in recent years, research has shown that the brain is actually highly malleable. This concept is called *neuroplasticity*. The "Father of Neuroscience," Santiago Ramón y Cajal, believed that the brain could continue to change even after the person becomes an adult.[1] However, it was not until later on that more research proved that there could be neuronal structural changes after a person reached adulthood (Fuchs & Flügge, 2014).[2] Neuroplasticity is the concept that we can rewire our brains through connections with our internal and external environments. As Dr. Celeste Campbell puts it:

"[Neuroplasticity] refers to the physiological changes in the brain that happen as the result of our interactions with our environment. From the time the brain begins to develop in utero until the day we die, the connections among the cells in our brains reorganize in response to our changing needs. This dynamic process allows us to learn from and adapt to different experiences."[3]

Plasticity is what gives us the ability to learn, grow, and adapt to our environments. We are continuously developing our brain as well as brain patterns and neuro-connections throughout our life. This key factor is extremely important because, in order for us to succeed and tap into our potential, we need to be able to disconnect old neural connections and form new pathways that reinforce the behavior we would like to achieve. This is a lot like muscle memory. Suppose I had learned to throw a baseball incorrectly and realized that I was hurting my shoulder muscle every time I threw it. I would need to learn how to move my arm muscles correctly. If I learned a better, more efficient way to throw the ball, I would still need to keep reminding myself during the game to throw it correctly. Otherwise, chances are that my muscle memory would default back to my old, inefficient, and painful way of throwing. Unless I practice the new way consistently, repeatedly, and successfully long enough to make it a new habit, I risk reverting back to my old habit when I am distracted or in a hurry. Our brain's neural connections work the same way when we want to change our behavior.

This mechanism is explained by Hebbian Theory:

"Hebbian Theory is a neuroscientific theory claiming that an increase in synaptic efficacy arises from a presynaptic cell's repeated and persistent stimulation of a postsynaptic cell. It is an attempt to explain synaptic plasticity, the adaptation of brain neurons during the learning process."[4]

To break it down into layman's terms, when we are learning something new, there are many changes that happen in the brain to reinforce the learning. Connections between brain neurons become stronger with repetitive stimulation. With repeated stimulation of the presynaptic neuron to the post synaptic neuron, the synapse strength increases and thus we are reinforcing the pattern of behavior we are learning. In other words, repeating a process or reviewing material *physically changes* our brain chemistry to help the memorization process.

This theory is also known as "cells that fire together wire together."[5]

Neuroplasticity means that we are 100% capable of rewiring our brain to access our real power!

This means that old behaviors that have been wired in our brain can be changed. The first few years of a child's life is a time where the brain is rapidly developing. However, as we age, our number of synapses is reduced by half. The brain does this through synaptic pruning, a process in which the brain eliminates the weak neurons and synaptic connections so that the brain can adapt to the ever-changing environment. This is the reason behind our ability to rewire our brain and create new neural connections.[6] Many of our behaviors are linked to an event that happened in the past and we are operating from a belief triggered by that past event. Whether it's a belief system or traumatic event that happened, we can override this system through time, effort and repetition. We can actually learn to change our responses to the past and not become triggered into an unwanted knee-jerk reaction.

Pioneering neuroscientist and psychology professor, Richard Davidson, Ph.D. is the author of *The Emotional Life of The Brain*. He believes that the brain is "the organ of change" and, if you participate in activities that help you develop positive habits, you will be able to transform your life.[7] Engaging in these positive habits over time leads to the rewiring of the brain's neural pathways and will enable you to focus on more positive feelings versus negative ones.

I went through this process myself and I am a living example of the effectiveness of changing one's mindset from a negative to a positive one. As I learned new behaviors and changed the way I thought about my reactions, I began to rewire my brain in a different way. I could feel the depression lift over time like a cloud floating away. When the depression came back, the duration was progressively shorter each time. I was able to deal with difficult situations much more easily. This was due to the fact that I continued to rewire my brain to focus on the positives rather than the negatives. It was also because I learned new coping skills, which I have detailed in this book. This process of neuroplasticity has helped my baseline become a more contented person compared to how I was in the past, always depressed and focusing on negative things.

The exercises provided in this book incorporate a combination of skills and tools that I learned through my personal experience. I also did further research that shows how these exercises help you create changes in your life. While researching, I discovered that I had already been practicing a powerful technique called *self-directed neuroplasticity*. The "self-directed neuroplasticity" model came from researcher Jeffrey Schwartz and his book, *The Mind & The Brain*. He argues that humans are capable of taking on the driver-seat role when it comes to creating changes in our lives.[8] This means that instead of being a passenger and sitting in the backseat, we can take on the primary role of the driver when it comes to using our mind and consciously change our brain for the better. *Self-directed neuroplasticity* specifically focuses on creating changes through awareness and focusing attention in desirable ways that will help us lead the life that we want to live. Self-directed neuroplasticity (SDN) is the mind's ability to change brain function through the power of thought and can alter brain structure in potentially beneficial ways, overcoming habituated and maladaptive responses.[9]

Neuroplasticity changes the development of the brain as individuals learn new habits, behaviors, and traits. As they learn something new, they form neural networks as neurotransmitters are being passed from one neuron to another. As these neurotransmitters are being passed, important changes occur at the synapses. When we think the same thoughts over and over again, do the same behaviors, and repeat things from the past, we are actually increasing the strength of the synaptic junctions, reinforcing those neural pathways. Later research revealed that there is a link between positive and negative thoughts and how they affect the growth and development of these neurons at their synaptic junctions.

As mentioned previously, our thoughts release hormones based on whether they are positive or negative thoughts. With positive thoughts and emotions, the brain produces serotonin which helps us increase our sense of well-being. With heightened levels of serotonin, we will feel happier and more at peace. On the other hand, negative feelings and thoughts, reduce the levels of serotonin being produced and increase the stress hormone cortisol.

As we learn new thought processes, behaviors, and ways of reacting, we are forming new pathways in the brain, which prevent our brain from operating in its default mode. This opens the door for us to create new positive pathways for ourselves.

SELF-DIRECTED NEUROPLASTICITY INVOLVES FIVE CRUCIAL STEPS:

1. **Attention**: Awareness to one's own thoughts, feelings, behaviors, actions

2. **Mindfulness**: Taking oneself out of the scenario and separating from the ego aspect of ourselves or self-defeating behaviors; being non-judgmental

3. **Volition**: Operating from a free-will perspective instead of operating from automatic programming or past habitual thinking

4. **Redirection**: Deciding which thoughts to focus on and redirecting from negative thoughts to positive thoughts

5. **Consistency**: Making a consistent effort to change oneself

Remember that the key to creating life-long changes that can support your personal goals is consistency. You have to work at this every day, multiple times a day, if needed, to break away from your old ways and solidify the new neural patterns.

Repeated neural activity leaves lasting changes in neural structure which is also known as experience-dependent neuroplasticity. By taking deliberate steps to develop your brain in positive ways through CBT, positive psychology, and meditation, research actually suggests that you'll be more successful in all areas of your life.[10]

Forming new neural pathways requires us to learn, adapt, and repeat. When we learn something new, we create new neural pathways. Once we have learned the material, it takes repetition in order to reinforce the new neural connection. In the beginning, as you are learning new behaviors, it will take time and effort. You will need to keep reminding yourself of how you want to respond. With practice, your new behavior will become automatic.

Learning follows four specific stages:

The Four Stages of Learning[11]

1. Unconscious Incompetence

2. Conscious Incompetence

3. Conscious Competence

4. Unconscious Competence

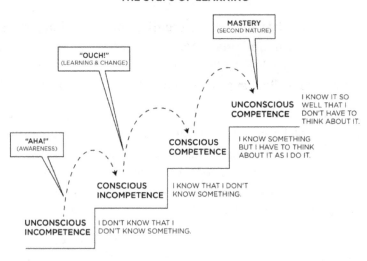

THE STEPS OF LEARNING

*Image © https://fka.com/four-stages-learning-retention-factors/ &
https://www.reddit.com/r/GetMotivated/comments/7m3f2y/image_the_4_stages
_of_learning_keep_practicing/*

UNCONSCIOUS INCOMPETENCE

The first stage of learning is when you do not have a certain skill or knowledge yet. You're not even aware that you need this skill or knowledge. You are blissfully ignorant.

Conscious Incompetence

The second stage of learning is when you realize that it's necessary for you to obtain a certain skill because it is beneficial to you. This is when you start the learning process, whether it's picking up a new book or attending a class to learn about your topic of choice. In this case, it's learning new behaviors that will help you tap into your superhero within. Many people may want to give up at this stage because learning a new skill can be difficult. However, if you persist, it will become easier over time. During this stage, it is important to focus on self-compassion, discipline, and taking action.

Conscious Competence

The third stage is when you've learned a skill, but you have not mastered it yet. You have developed the basic skills necessary. This stage is easier than the last as the grunt work is over. Now you just have to continue to implement the skills in order to master them.

Unconscious Competence

The final stage is when you've mastered a certain skill and can do it automatically. You do not even have to think about it, it just comes naturally to you. The skill is second nature at this point and you can do it easily.

Think back to when you first started trying to ride a bike. While it still had the training wheels attached you were in the *unconscious incompetence* stage. You did not worry about falling over because the training wheels kept you upright. When your dad removed the training wheels, however, you moved into the Conscious Incompetence stage. You were very conscious of your extreme incompetence as you wobbled the front wheel hoping that your dad would not let go of your seat. After several tumbles and lots of attempts, you finally felt like you were getting the hang of this bike-riding thing. You could ride all by yourself as long as you concentrated on keeping your balance. You have reached the Conscious Competence stage.

After months of riding your bike, you could then jump on your bike and take off at top speed while yelling "Race you!" to your sister. You are finally in the Unconscious Competence stage.

Believing that you can accomplish something is just half the battle. It is essential that you adopt the attitude of believing that you are capable of learning the skills necessary to achieve what you want. Learning is not easy for many of us, especially because it often involves unlearning old habits and learning new behaviors. However, there are stages for everything in life. So, keep that in mind as you use these new tools to help you. Be patient with yourself and give yourself time to grow.

The mind is not only powerful in its plasticity, but it also has the power to create miraculous results through the power of belief. If you still do not believe how powerful your thoughts are, let's examine "The Placebo Effect" and the miraculous things that have resulted from it.

As you know, The Placebo Effect is a concept that proves the mind can trick you into believing a treatment has therapeutic results, even if the treatment does not utilize the actual medications or the full method of treatment. Even the harshest skeptics cannot argue that the *placebo effect* has validity. This marvelous mystery in medicine is probably one of the most fascinating. The truth is, we don't really know the reason why this phenomenon works and how we are able to fool the mind into believing what we tell it to be true, but what we do know is that it works!

In all new studies regarding medications, the FDA requires a Placebo Group, a group of subjects who receive a sugar pill instead of the test drug. The purpose of this is to determine whether or not the medication being tested is effective. The results of the test group are compared to those of the placebo group. Surprisingly there have been many cases in which patients are given "sugar pills" to fix a disease or illness without knowing it, and, because they believed the treatment would work, it did! This shows us the reality that the ability to heal oneself relies on the power of the brain and its beliefs.

The brain is the master controller of your body, regulating many biological processes. It's no wonder how powerful it is, even when it comes to healing the mind and body. This phenomenal brain power gives us hope that change is accessible and available for anyone willing to try it. One of the most fascinating cases is the research conducted by Dr. Bruce Mosley. Dr. Bruce Mosley was an orthopedic surgeon who decided to conduct a research experiment where he performed surgery on more than 180 patients who had osteoarthritis. These patients were randomly selected for arthroscopic debridement, arthroscopic lavage, or placebo surgery. The patients who were in the placebo group did not actually receive surgery. Instead, they just received skin incisions and underwent a simulated debridement without insertion of the arthroscope.[12]

Can you guess the outcome? That's right! The outcomes for the patients who had the actual surgery and the placebo surgery were the same! The patients who had the real surgery did not have better results than the placebo group. You can see from this experiment that the mind is incredibly malleable and can create the reality that it believes in.

What this really means is: *Whatever you believe in becomes your reality.*

Henry Ford was well aware of this and once said, "Whether you think you can, or you think you can't—you're right."[13] How would your life be different—happier, more fulfilling—if you believed the best of yourself and it became your reality?

The Placebo Effect demonstrates that this psychological phenomenon has true healing potential, and thus if you believe in the power of your mind, anything is possible. Beyond its powerful uses in medicine, The Placebo Effect also works miraculously for cognitive performance.

THE MIND AND BODY CONNECTION

If you think back to what I talked about earlier, that our thoughts in fact create physical reactions in our body, then you can understand how interconnected the mind and body really are. The conscious and subconscious minds work together to regulate your body and keep you in a state of homeostasis. There are many unconscious processes going on in the background that we are unaware of. The subconscious and unconscious parts of our mind are much more powerful than the conscious mind because they run on automatic, driving our behaviors. The unconscious mind, according to Freud, is out of the reach of our conscious mind. The subconscious mind is where all of our deep-rooted beliefs, behaviors, habits, and protective mechanisms lie. Thus, if we want to be in control of our actions and reactions, it is critical that we understand how the mind and the body are inter-connected.

Candice Pert, a scientist studying the mind and body connection, came up with the conclusion that our conscious mind is capable of creating molecules of emotion which can actually program our bodies to feel better.[14] This suggests that maybe we have more control over ourselves and our lives than we thought!

So now, let's tie it all together!

1. Our thoughts:

   - Become our beliefs through repetition, (i.e., neuroplasticity).

   - Cause physical reactions in our body. They can cause hormones to be released related to stress or happiness.

   - Our thoughts and beliefs are intertwined, causing happiness or stress.

   - The happiness or stress that we experience can affect our body in a positive or negative way.

   - If we constantly have stressful thoughts, we can:
     - decrease our immune system's ability to function
     - develop illnesses
     - develop mental health disorders

   - If we constantly have positive thoughts, we can:
     - increase our immune system's ability to function

- o increase our motivation

- o increase our self-confidence

- o increase our overall well-being

2. Our beliefs cause us to take action. They can move us towards pleasure and away from pain. Our beliefs can also help us chase our dreams and goals or they can prevent us from achieving the things that we really want.

3. When we take action, this in turn validates or invalidates our thoughts and beliefs.

4. This "belief-action" cycle will repeat itself and create a positive or negative self-fulfilling prophecy, thus creating our ever-present reality and identity.

THE IDENTITY-GAP

Getting from where you are to where you want to be!

Once we go through the Belief-Action Cycle, at the end we form an identity based on those beliefs we have and the actions that we take. As I mentioned earlier, the beliefs that we operate from guide the actions we take, and, in essence, create a self-fulfilling prophecy. This "self-fulfilling prophecy" is the basis of your identity. Humans tend to cling to their identity so tightly because it's all that they know to be true. This is also why most of us resist change because change is hard and scary. When you believe that your identity will always be the same, you will continue to have the same beliefs and repeat the same actions to reinforce that identity.

Until you are able to cultivate a sense of awareness and realize that you have the power to change your identity, you will be stuck.

Awareness is the first step, but at the same time, you have to be willing and open to change. That is where growth happens. It's when you decide that you want to make a change and you consistently put effort into it that you make it happen. Unfortunately, there is a gap between where we are now and where we are meant to be.

We all have the need to reach our potential, and when there is a gap between who we are and who we think we could be, we feel disconnected and become unhappy. Our personality seems to contradict itself: On the one hand, we want happiness, love, and connection. On the other hand, we have a deep-rooted belief that we are not worthy of what we think we deserve to have. We struggle with this internal battle because they are two sides of the same coin. Part of the human experience is learning to tap into our potential power and the infinite resources that reside within us so that we can feel connected and inspired in life.

So, what can we do to close the gap? Well, we have to train our mind to operate differently. This is why the Belief-Action Cycle is so vital. We can use it to analyze our beliefs, thoughts, and behaviors and see where the gap lies. Once we identify the gap, we can begin to make small changes that will lead to a life-changing shift in our reality.

A great example of this is one of Milton Erikson's patients. Milton Erikson was a famous psychotherapist who was also an amazing hypnotherapist. He had a patient, a young girl, who came in for therapy. She told him, "I'm depressed. I've got a good job, but I don't think anybody can like me. I decided I'm going to try psychotherapy but I know it isn't going to work." The patient had a gap between her teeth and was extremely self-conscious about it. She avoided interactions with men because she felt embarrassed by it.[15]

Let's see if we can identify her reality by going through the Belief-Action Cycle:

◇ **Thoughts**: I don't think anybody can like me.

◇ **Beliefs**: The gap between my teeth makes me look ugly and therefore I don't deserve love.

◇ **Actions**: I will avoid interaction with men to prevent myself from being rejected (which reinforces that I'm not worthy).

◇ **Reality**: A negative self-fulfilling prophecy: No one will ever like me and I will always be alone. This is my identity and it must be true.

As you can see, this girl had created a "reality" that matched her thoughts and beliefs. She had operated this way for a long time and believed it was set in stone. However, because Milton Erikson was incredible at his job, all he did was "reframe" her belief that she could never get married because no one liked her. He showed her how to change her perspective so that she could allow a different reality to happen for her. Because of this reframing, she ended up getting married to one of her coworkers.

You do not need a therapist to help you identify your own beliefs and behaviors. You can do this by yourself by filling in your own details to this cycle. Going through this exercise will give you a better understanding of the reality you have created for yourself and how you can change it. The key is to reframe the beliefs that have been holding you back. When you change your perspective, you create an alternative outcome instead of sticking to your current identity and reality.

Exercise E8-1: Going Through the Belief-Action Cycle

The Belief-Action Cycle-Identifying Negative Beliefs

1. Start with a negative thought about yourself that has been making you miserable.

2. Identify the beliefs you have formed because of this thought.

3. What actions do you take because of these beliefs? Do they move you towards pleasure and away from pain?

4. Does this create a positive or negative self-fulfilling prophecy for you?

5. What is the "identity" that you associate with this prophecy? Is this the identity that you truly want to have?

The following example will help you evaluate what you are thinking and believing about yourself, as well as the identity and reality that you are ending up with. Create a blank "Thoughts—Beliefs—Actions—Reality" model like the one below and fill it in with your own negative thoughts, beliefs, etc., and see what you discover about yourself:

THOUGHTS

"I WILL NEVER FIND TRUE LOVE"

BELIEFS

I DON'T DESERVE TRUE LOVE.
I'M NOT WORTHY OF TRUE LOVE.

ACTIONS

I WILL AVOID DATING BECAUSE IT NEVER WORKS OUT ANYWAYS.
AVOIDANCE: MOVES ME AWAY FROM PAIN BECAUSE IT PREVENTS ME
FROM BEING DISAPPOINTED AGAIN.

REALITY

I'M CREATING A NEGATIVE SELF-FULFILLING PROPHECY. I CONTINUE
TO REPEAT TO MYSELF THAT I WON'T FIND LOVE AND EVERYTIME I
MEET SOMEONE NEW, I ASSUME THAT THINGS WILL NOT WORK OUT. I
UNCONSCIOUSLY SABOTAGE THE RELATIONSHIP TO VERIFY MY
BELIEF THAT I'M NOT WORTHY OF TRUE LOVE. THIS BECOMES MY
IDENTITY: SOMEONE WHO CAN NEVER FIND LOVE.

Once you have identified your own current reality and identity, it's time to take a look at who you want to become.

EXERCISE E8-2: NEW THOUGHTS, BELIEFS AND ME

Ask yourself:

- Who is the person that I want to become?

- What does the person I want to become embody?

- What kind of thoughts do people like this have?

- What kind of beliefs do they have?

- What actions do they take?

Example:

- I want to become a person who finds and accept true love.

- People who can find love feel happy and excited, knowing that love is on its way.

- They think: "I can find true love; it just might take some time. I'm open to waiting to find my true love."

- "I am worthy of love." "I deserve love."

- "I will go on dates, meet new people, and continue to put myself out there."

To close the gap between the person you are now and the person you want to be, you have to be actively aware of your thoughts and beliefs every day, and act to embody the person that you want to become. Start by adjusting the things you repeatedly tell yourself. Remember, what you repeat in your mind will reinforce the neural connections you have. These repetitive thoughts are those that will sink deep into your core and form your beliefs about yourself. You may have to make more drastic changes to your thinking to head in your new direction. Think of a ship traveling the ocean. How do you make it change direction? The person at the helm turns it, which slightly adjusts the angle of the rudder. The rudder does not have to move much to redirect that ship. That ship can end up hundreds of miles away from its original trajectory. It's the same with your thoughts. One minor change in your thinking and the beliefs formed from them can have a life-changing impact on your reality and your identity.

The actions that you need to take may make you uncomfortable, but that is where you grow. It's a part of your self-evolution. This will definitely take time and effort, because—let's face it—undoing your beliefs is like running a marathon, not a sprint. However, if you stay focused on your end goal, and take small actions in the direction toward your goal, eventually you will reach it. As you practice changing your behaviors, you will naturally and inevitably reach the outcome you are aiming toward. Give yourself some time to go through the process, and one day you will look back and see how this process helped you become the best version of yourself. As you master training your mind, you are recording the pattern for creating success and happiness in your life!

REWIRING YOUR THOUGHTS THROUGH HYPNOSIS

Once you've realized your negative thought patterns, it's time to rewire them through new positive thoughts that will help you to change your mindset.

"Self-hypnosis is a naturally occurring state of mind which can be defined as a heightened state of focused concentration."[16]

Hypnosis has been around in the United States since the mid-1800s. Although there are still many misconceptions and stigmas regarding hypnosis, it is in fact an extremely useful modality in therapy and in the rewiring of negative thoughts and behavior. Hypnosis is today being adapted by medical practitioners to manage pain. It has even successfully replaced anesthesia in certain surgeries.

I had heard about hypnosis in the past, but it was not until I became a hypnotherapist myself that I really understood how powerful this tool really is. For most people who are new to hypnosis, I describe it as an extremely mentally relaxed state where you are in control the entire time. It's similar to a meditative state, if you've ever experienced it.

Hypnosis works by inducing you into a mental state where you are activating the theta waves of the brain.[17] Activating the theta waves puts you into an absolutely relaxed state. Hypnosis works by reducing the activity of the left-brain hemisphere, which is in charge of logical control, deduction, and reasoning. Reducing the left-brain hemisphere allows the brain to release the conscious mind's inhibitory response and this allows the client to be able to process feelings and emotions related to past traumas. Alternatively, it activates the right brain hemisphere which focuses on creativity and imagination and allows the subconscious mind to surface.[18]

Most people have already experienced hypnosis in their everyday lives without even realizing it. They typically experience a light trance when they are hyper-focused on one activity. As you are quietly reading this book now, taking your time, concentrating, absorbing its content fully, you are in some form of light trance state. Most people think hypnosis is a condition where you are oblivious or mentally unresponsive. In actuality, it's a state of mind where your normal awareness of your surroundings is reduced and your attention is directed toward a specific subject. You experience a heightened awareness of the idea, problem, or stimulus that you are interacting with. While you are hypnotized, there is a degree of detachment from reality and external stimuli as you are completely absorbed in the task at hand. When we are in a trance state, our awareness shifts from the external reality to an internal reality. Consequently, we are less focused on what is going on around us—noise, people, or commotion. This allows us to zone into our inner mental state, a place where we can therapeutically create change when we decide to actively work on it.

As you are learning new tools to incorporate into your life and to help you facilitate change, I believe that hypnosis can make this change and your efforts easier. I have created a self-guided hypnosis recording[19] so that you can explore self-hypnosis on your own. This will give you the ability to rewire your thoughts and behaviors to adapt to your new way of life. Find the link to this recording in the Appendix.

Hypnosis works because of the power of your mind, not anyone or anything else. As I mentioned, the mind is the most powerful tool you have and hypnosis is just another tool you can use to assist you as you develop new, positive behaviors.

Now let's practice!

EXERCISE E8-3: USING HYPNOSIS TO CLEAR THE WAY FORWARD

Preparation:

1. Think about what goals you want to accomplish with hypnosis. What kind of outcome would you like? What feelings would you like to feel? Are you doing it for relaxation or to train your brain?

2. Write a list of positive affirmations or suggestions you would like to tell yourself. Make sure you write this list

in the present tense. Below are a few affirmations to help you get started. Make sure you personalize these affirmations according to your needs.

- I am enough
- I am proud of who I am and all that I've accomplished
- I love and accept myself fully and unconditionally
- I am worthy of love and joy
- My life is full of abundance
- I am healthy
- I radiate confidence
- My positive energy is contagious and influences everyone that I meet
- I am in charge of how I feel today and I am choosing happiness
- I am my own superhero
- I can and I will
- I have the power to create change
- I accept love from the universe
- I am me and that is my superpower
- I am at peace with who I am
- I believe in my skills and abilities
- I can easily create a life I love
- I am unique and that is my Gift to the world

Performing Hypnosis on Yourself

1. Find a quiet place, free from distractions. Sit down in a comfortable position.

2. Take a few deep breaths as you let the day fade away. Connect to this moment and feel fully present.

3. Pick a spot on the wall to focus on, ideally somewhere above your head. Continue to stare at this spot as you take long, slow, deep inhalations and exhalations. Try to take about 20 breaths this way. With each breath, feel your body begin to melt as a strong sense of relaxation takes over your body. You feel as if you are floating and your body is weightless.

4. Once you feel deeply relaxed, close your eyes. Imagine that you're standing in front of a flight of stairs. Picture every detail as you go down these steps. With each step, imagine going deeper and deeper within yourself. Count down from 10 to 1. With each step and number, tell yourself to go deeper and deeper. Once you get to the bottom of the stairs, just let a sense of relaxation take over your entire body.

5. Once you are in this deep state of relaxation, think about the affirmations you wrote down earlier and begin repeating them in your mind. Repeat them as many times as you want and really feel those words as you let them resonate and vibrate within your mind.

6. When you feel like you've read the affirmations enough, slowly come back to your full awareness. Begin by feeling your fingers and toes. Then let in the sounds around you. Feel your body begin to return as you wake up to your surroundings.

7. Repeat this process for at least 30 consecutive days and you will begin to notice affirming shifts and changes in your mindset.

PAIN AND PLEASURE – "THE PLEASURE PRINCIPLE"

The Greek philosopher, Aristotle, claimed that everything happens for a reason.[20] This phrase has resonated with me since I was a teenager. As I went through tough times, I always reminded myself of this truth. I always knew that there was a deeper meaning behind my pain.

When you look at life, you know that pain is something that is inevitable. It's an essential part to life and the part that shows us how amazing things are in absence of it. When you are faced with pain, remember that every difficult experience in your life is designed to shape you in one way or another to become the best version of yourself. Although it may not appear this way at the time, there is always a meaningful lesson behind it. Look at your pain (or frustration and despair) as an opportunity for growth instead of a time of pure suffering. Of course, this does not mean that you should avoid grieving and feeling your emotions at the time as you still have to honor your emotions. It just means that once you are done feeling what you need to feel, it's time to examine your pain and see what lies beneath the surface.

To understand how our mind works, we have to review the developments of Freud's psychoanalytic theory of personality, "The Pleasure Principle." The Pleasure Principle is the concept that human beings are constantly seeking pleasure and avoiding pain. It is a mechanism that satisfies our biological and psychological needs.[21] Our psyche is wired to operate this way, and the decisions we make are based on this idea. We naturally seek out ways for instant gratification that fulfill our primitive needs. At the same time, we will go to extreme lengths to avoid pain as much as possible because we often cannot deal with the uncomfortable emotions associated with it. When you realize that this is the basis of your motivations, you can further analyze your thoughts and behaviors and understand them better.

Pain and suffering are part of the human condition. Because we seek to avoid experiencing them whenever possible, this creates an unbalanced relationship with pain. We see pain as something negative. At the first sign of pain, we seek an immediate solution to free us from the pain. Everything we do in life is designed to help us avoid pain. We deny, suppress and reject our pain. We label it as something "horrible." Instead of facing it, we will do things like emotionally-charged eating, distracting ourselves with external pleasures, or keeping ourselves busy so that we do not have to face the pain. The more we seek out ways to avoid the pain, the more suppressed it becomes—until one day it surfaces and slaps us in the face. *Remember, what you resist, persists.*

While pain may be uncomfortable, it does serve a purpose. Pain functions as our teacher, teaching us invaluable lessons as we explore the edges of our pain. Pain prompts us to evaluate our life and explore the depths of our pain. It forces us to look at the unhealed parts of ourselves, so that we can then begin to heal. It connects us with our consciousness, opening up the door to self-awareness and self-discovery. Suffering and pain force us to reevaluate our life and see how we can make it better. Pain leads to expansion and is the catalyst for the alchemy of our life.

The Pleasure Principle urges you to take steps either to decrease pain or to increase pleasure. Sometimes you end up accomplishing both at the same time. For example, let's say that you have an unhealthy eating habit such as emotional eating. Every time you feel stressed, you end up reaching for your favorite unhealthy snacks. In this way, you are avoiding pain (the stress) and seeking pleasure (eating unhealthily because it releases endorphins and gives you a temporary reprieve from the stress). Now, this might work short term, but there are long-term effects such as gaining weight or suppressing stress, which can lead to physical and mental disorders.

Humans are motivated to avoid pain and to obtain pleasure. People prefer instant gratification, so we frequently make decisions based on that. For example, if we are hungry while driving home from work, we often stop at the nearest fast food drive-thru for food. Unfortunately, when it comes to self-development, there are no quick fixes. You have to be committed, consistent, willing to do the work, and keep taking the actions necessary that will carry you toward your goal—even if there is some discomfort and pain involved.

Be aware that every decision you make will lead to one of the following:

1. Short-term pain

2. Short-term pleasure

3. Long-term pain

4. Long-term pleasure

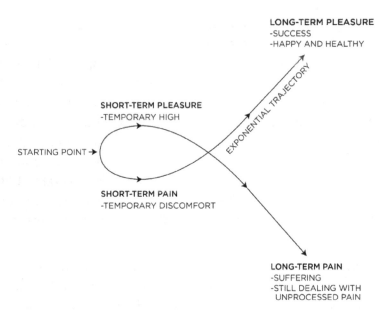

Image © Dr. Kim D'Eramo

As you can see on this diagram, you may be able to experience short-term pleasure by escaping with any number of temporary highs. Unfortunately, this leads to long-term pain because it results in negative impacts upon you. When you operate like this and tell yourself, "I feel bad, so I will do whatever it takes to feel better now," in the end, your negative behaviors and habits will make you susceptible to sabotage due to the way your negative behavior is wired.

If, however, you are willing to face some pain at first, you will have initial discomfort and it can be challenging in the beginning. Soon enough, though, you will feel relief and start to grow exponentially toward the person you want to be and the success you are striving for.

So, be willing to put up with a little discomfort for a while instead of immediately escaping by getting a quick fix for your pain. Keep your eye on your goals as you go through this.

You are the only one who can decide what motivates you and how it will help you now and in the long run. Imagine that you keep thinking negative thoughts for the next twenty years. How will you feel in twenty years' time? Will you become any happier or will you be more depressed? You already know the answer. So, let me ask you this: Is the short-term fix worth another twenty years of pain? I bet not!

EXERCISE E8-4: EFFECTS OF NEGATIVE THOUGHTS, BELIEFS

This exercise is simple but it will help give you some insight into the motivating factors in your life, and how to evaluate what you do and how it helps you.

1. Pick a struggle you are facing, whether it's a negative thought or limiting belief that you would like to work on.

2. Determine what would happen in twenty years' time if you kept up with this behavior, thought, or belief.

3. How would it affect your life?

EXERCISE E8-5: EVALUATING YOUR THOUGHTS, BELIEFS

Take 20 minutes to journal and answer the questions below:

◇ What motivates my decisions each day?

◇ Is this moving me toward pain or pleasure?

◇ What is my temporary solution? How will it affect me in the long run if I continue to use my temporary fix?

◇ Will this lead me to where I want to be? Will it help me reach my life goal? Or will it keep me trapped in my pain?

Remember that pain will push you until you have a vision that pulls you. This is why it's important to have a life's purpose or an overarching goal that you are continually working towards. When you have a goal or direction in mind, this helps to keep you motivated.

THE ROAD BACK

Connecting with the Hero Within

They asked her, "What is the key to saving the world?"

She answered, "You. You are the key. Heal yourself, know yourself, make yourself whole and free. Release all limits so that your love can

flow unconditionally for yourself and the world,
this will open the heaven of your heart
completely and it will guide you without fail."[22]

—Yung Pueblo, *You are the Answer*

The heroic quest of The Hero's Journey is a journey to self-realization, a journey to embrace all that you are, and all that you will become. It's about finding the treasure within you and coming home to your truth—that you are good enough. Slaying the dragon of the illusion that you are not good enough is at the core of this journey. It's about learning to love yourself and igniting the fire from within so that you can live a more abundant life.

With your heroic journey, you will have internalized a newfound truth, that you are complete right now—in this moment . . .

What really defines a hero? The word "hero" comes from the Greek root meaning to protect and serve, the hero is associated with self-sacrifice. He or she is the person who is able to transcend the ego and save the world. Transcending the ego allows the hero to help other people with their gifts of self-revelation.

Aristotle, a famous Greek philosopher, believed that humans should live according to twelve general virtues.[23] As you leave the past behind and connect with the *Hero Within*, it's important to understand which qualities create a Hero. Being a Hero is much more than connecting to your higher self and your full potential. A true hero uses his skills to be an honorable person who helps society. But first, he must master himself so that when he shows up to save the world, he is fully realized and at his peak potential.

THE 12 VIRTUES OF A HERO

1. Courage – bravery and valor
2. Temperance – self-control and restraint
3. Liberality – big-heartedness, charity and generosity
4. Magnificence – radiance, joie de vivre (zest for life)
5. Pride – self-satisfaction
6. Honor – respect, reverence, admiration
7. Good Temper – equanimity, level headedness
8. Friendliness – conviviality and sociability
9. Truthfulness – straightforwardness, frankness and candor
10. Wit – sense of humor, meaninglessness and absurdity
11. Friendship – camaraderie and companionship
12. Justice – impartiality, evenhandedness and fairness

If there is an innate hero within each of us, why have we forgotten that this hero even exists? To understand this, we have to look at where we are disconnected in our life. Only by isolating the places where we have disconnected can we learn how to reconnect. Wherever you are on your journey, whether you are experiencing depression or anxiety, facing an addiction or fear, dealing with feelings of loneliness, or feeling lost in the world, there is always a reason behind it. My depression showed me the disconnections I had within my life.

Reconnecting with Your Essence

Five Disconnections That Keep You from Your Essence

In order to connect with the Hero within, you have to understand disconnections, how they have influenced your life and kept you from who you could be. When you take the Hero's Journey inward, your goal is to eventually connect with your true essence. In order to achieve that goal, you have to explore the disconnections between the "you" of the past and the "you" that you will become.

There are *distinct disconnections* that can interfere with your efforts to reconnect with your authentic self. (If you let them, they can keep you from ever becoming your Inner Hero):

1. DISCONNECTION FROM THE SELF

Humans rely on connection to survive and one of the worst disconnections you can have is a disconnection with yourself. The first connection you have to work on is the connection you have with yourself. You have to learn to build a relationship with yourself. Often people rely on other people to build this connection, however, when you are unable to connect with yourself first, your connection with other people can become dependent. Cultivating this connection with yourself is extremely valuable, as I learned during my own journey. Developing this connection started with learning who I am, what I like, what I don't like, and what my values, goals and dreams are. It's the unfolding and unveiling of the external world—everything I've known to be true in my reality, connecting with the truth of my existence. Fostering this connection with yourself is extremely important because we are all searching for meaning in life, who we are, and what our identity really means.

"Who am I really if I am not me?" This question plagued me as I uncovered my depression and learned that depression was just a part of a reality that I created for myself. For so long, I identified with it. It was my life, so when I learned that it was just a symptom showing me that I needed to dig deeper, I was struck by this question. If I am not the depression, then who am I? Who is Julia beneath her pain and suffering? Who am I when I am dissociated from this repeated story? I realized that I am me, not the version that is filled with mental incapability and stuck in the dark, but that I am an ultimate being of light, filled with love and bliss. I am a small fractal in life, living this existence to experience and challenge myself through depression so that I can heal and help others. You see, most people who are faced with a problem continue to suffer because they neglect to search for the meaning behind the problem, behind the pain. Any illnesses, whether mental or physical, is there to teach you something. It's a calling from the universe to look closer, to analyze what in your life could be causing this "symptom" to show up, and why now? When I was depressed, I just felt depressed, I did not know why and I certainly did not bother searching for answers. I just wanted someone to tell me what was wrong with me.

Suppose you are struggling with depression as I was. There are a few things that tend to happen: Usually some stressor or negative event in your life occurs and you do not know how to cope with the stressor, so instead, you push it down. Most people tend to suppress it and write it off. Often, you let this build up over time and it becomes a prolonged suppression, you start to burn out. As it continues to build, BAM! One day you are absolutely depressed and you don't know why. The fact is that there is always a preceding event or events that lead to depression. It begins with small moments where you may not speak up, where you let others bully you, or where a negative situation keeps repeating itself and you don't know how to deal with it, so you just internalize it. Eventually, it creates a snowball effect, and thus you are hit with depression. Depression develops over time based on past events and then eventually, it hits a peak, an accumulation of emotional pain or suppression. Once you are at this peak, that's when everything becomes too overwhelming. You are unable to cope and you find yourself too depressed to handle simple daily tasks because they are too unbearable.

Having depression forced me to connect with myself. The pain that kept me still caused me to look inward. This helped me reconnect with the essence of who I am. Whether you have depression or not, it is essential for you to connect with your truth, and that means daring to peel back the layers of your "self." I started peeling back my layers out of desperation to find out who I really am. And, despite all the mistruths I had been telling myself for years, that I wasn't good enough, I discovered that I was so much more than I had thought!

2. Disconnection from Social Connections

Besides connecting with yourself, it's also important for you to have social connections. As animals, we can only survive and thrive when we are connected with a pack. Think about prisons and how the worst punishment is solitary confinement: isolating one of the prisoners and keeping him or her locked away from other people. This psychological torture is sometimes enough to cause the prisoner to have a complete mental break down and go crazy. In today's technological era, we are living in a world where instant connections are easily accessible through online communities. People mistakenly believe that this means they are connected. The truth is, this "online connection" is misleading because we are actually disconnected from not only each other but also from ourselves. Although we can connect with people across the globe within seconds, we are missing key connections to humanity and ourselves. With the touch of a finger, we can send messages through this online network, reaching millions across the world, yet this connection is all a pretense covering up what we all really need, which is face-to-face human connection. Although the online community might seem like it's helping us move forward, in reality this connection is causing most of us to feel even more lonely each day. It's a mask that society wears, overriding the emotions that lay underneath.

Why have the rates of depression and anxiety risen so much over the last few decades across the world? There are two possible contributing factors: The first one is because we are all becoming more connected through the online community but lacking this connection in real life. Most people tend to isolate themselves more and more every day. Social scientists have been studying a question for Americans, "How many confidants do you have?" What they found is that most people have no one that they can truly rely on.[19] Being that we are social creatures, we thrive when we are surrounded by others. However, it's not as simple as just being surrounded by other people. It goes much deeper than this. We have to feel a sense of mutual connection that bypasses superficial levels. We have to feel that the other person sees and understands how we really are. This is how we feel connected.

The second reason may be because we are living in a "super-connected" world influenced by technology more so than previous generations. We are integrated into one

216

another's lives via television, internet, and social media. Whereas previous generations were limited to their local communities, today we can compare our imperfect selves to the air-brushed, filter-photography versions of the best and brightest worldwide. There is no way we can ever live up to the numerous ideal role models that parade across our computers and cell phones. Of course, there are additional factors which lead to anxiety and depression and this theory of media's impact on our self-perception is only speculation, but the fact remains that personal social connections are extremely vital to our wellbeing and inherent in our nature. That is why being super-connected can actually lead to an intense feeling of disconnection or in other words, feelings of isolation, loneliness, anxiety, and depression.

When I attended *Unleash the Power Within* event in Los Angeles earlier this year, I was reminded of how important it is for us to be connected with other people. The event was a magical one and I took home with me many lessons that will last a lifetime. I attended the event with my dear friends, Tamara and Ryan. I remember the first day we got there, everyone was a bit tense and socially awkward. We were all there for the same reasons, hoping to gain some sort of revelation and change our lives for the better, but there was an apparent barrier between most people. Everyone had their guards up and you could feel the disconnections. As the weekend progressed, we could feel the barriers slowly fading and melting away. By the third day, everyone was completely open, smiling, and free. We could sense the invisible walls that were once present dissipate as we all connected to love and appreciated each other's presence. We were all filled with gratitude and love for each other's company.

Tony Robbin's event taught me that we may all appear different, but we are all connected as one, all magnificently part of the interconnected web of the universe. Unfortunately, our egos make us want to see each other as belonging to different groups. By design, the human brain creates an illusion of separation which makes us feel isolated from one another. The truth is that we all thrive off connections. The event showed me how truly connected we all are. One of the exercises we did at the event was connecting with three other people and sharing with them our biggest fears and challenges in our current life as well as our biggest hopes and dreams. As we shared our stories with each other, we all realized that we were afraid of the same things. We also discovered that we all craved the same things: love, connection, and recognition. I looked around at the sea of people in the stadium, and almost everyone raised their hands as Tony Robbins asked about our fears and wants. Being surrounded by 10,000 people, I saw people break through their barriers, let their walls down, as we all hugged each other feeling united, and danced the night away. Oftentimes as we go through our journey, we may feel very alone. We forget that we are all interconnected in this fabric of life and that we rely on each other for our basic human needs and survival. This is why connection is so critical for our wellbeing; and for those who lack it, they must cultivate it in their life in one way or another. I often isolated myself from other people because I was afraid of the depth of sharing that would come with building these relationships. However, being isolated made me feel even worse. Connection will bring you closer to home, closer to the oneness we all share.

At the *Unleash the Power Within* event, we were pushed beyond our limits and it was incredible! It made us realize that we could do anything that we set our mind to. As mentioned earlier, I even walked on hot coals without getting burned! It was not the task that was a miracle, the miracle was that I overcame my fear. Standing in line, waiting to walk on hot coals gave me a rush of anticipation like no other. Once I crossed it, those who had crossed ahead of me congratulated me. This was such an incredible feeling of connection to the universe that I've never felt before or since.

3. DISCONNECTION FROM A LIFE PURPOSE

During college, I took an English class that focused on monsters in society, what they mean, and why they are significant in our culture. To my surprise, it was a fascinating topic that opened up my perspective to our fears and needs as a culture. During one portion of the class we had to analyze zombies to determine what they represent. I discovered that we all have a fear that we will be unable to reach our potential and will be destined to do "zombie work" for the rest of our lives. When you think about it, daily life for most individuals consists of constantly doing minuscule tasks that are often boring, deadening, and suck the life right out of them. This work continues day after day, a routine that never stops. Endless e-mails are deleted only for another 20 to appear in your inbox. You complete one task at work and then there's another . . . and another . . . and another. The pile of work never ends. This cycle goes on and on—just like a zombie, once killed, only to return to haunt you again. We are attracted to zombies and monsters because they give us a psychological break from our reality, but if you look at it closely, maybe we are so obsessed with these monsters because they signify something much greater—a fear we have that life will always be this way: boring and deadening. A zombie life does not equal true fulfillment. What we really want is a life in which we feel ALIVE!

Working at a job that you hate or one that adds no value to your life will always create a disconnection from your truth, from the reason why you are here on this planet. When you're chasing someone else's dreams instead of your own, it's easy to become unhappy and unfulfilled. This leads to the need to know your purpose in life. When you do not know your life's purpose, you will often feel lost in life. We all want to create meaning in life, and without this foundation, we will wander through life with constant uncertainty and unhappiness. Most people are stuck in dead-end jobs while they wonder why they are so unhappy. This really comes down to doing your life's mission, something we will create in a coming chapter. When you are performing meaningless work or hate your job, you will see life from the perspective of tackling a zombie every day only for more to come. That is why it is important to understand what your life's purpose is. This disconnection urges you to find a deeper meaning as to why you are here. Now I completely understand that most people are not blessed with the ability to work at whatever job they want to because they have bills to pay and a family to feed. I am not disregarding that this might be your current reality, however, I want to encourage you to not be stuck in this trap. Oprah Winfrey once said, "Do what you have to do until you can do what you want to do."[25] So, if you're working at a job you hate, let it motivate you until you can chase after your dreams. While you're working at this job, though, don't let it prevent you from chasing after your dreams and living your life with purpose.

To know our life's purpose, we have to know our values and whether or not we are living according to them. Disconnection can also result from us not upholding our values and doing the things that we truly love. Many of us live lives to please others, do what society tells us to do, focus on making money, and chase material things that are supposed to lead to happiness. It's no wonder that so many of us are so unhappy. We value one thing but we do the complete opposite because the rational mind tells us that in order to have X, Y, and Z, we need to suffer and do the things that we do not like doing because that is how we will survive in this world. We remain at this basic survival-instinct level, unable to bypass the comforts of the material world and stretch toward our goals. In a future chapter you will have a chance to explore your values and see if you are living according to them.

On Maslow's Hierarchy of Needs, the second most basic thing we need after physiological needs is safety and security. When we feel that we are not safe and secure, we may suffer from anxiety whether we are aware of it or not. The feeling of safety and security comes in many forms: It can be having an environment where you feel comfortable and unthreatened. It can mean feeling safe with those around you. But it can also mean having a clear vision for the future. When you can envision what the future will look like, you are calmer. Those who are unclear about what the future holds will constantly live in a state of anxiety. This is why setting goals for the future and having a mission is important. It gives you a sense of direction, even if the path to get there doesn't unfold exactly as you plan.

4. DISCONNECTION FROM CHILDHOOD TRAUMA

As I mentioned in the previous chapters, healing childhood trauma is an essential part to connecting with your true self. Childhood is one of the most vulnerable times in our lives. When we are young, we often take the blame for bad things that happen. We tend to internalize the events and if we never process them, these events remain ingrained in our nervous system waiting to be triggered. During one of my therapy sessions, a client that came in to see me for depression and anxiety realized that he had blamed himself for his parents' divorce. They divorced when he was 14, and since he was still an adolescent, he could not quite understand what was happening. Instead of recognizing that his parents' problems had nothing to do with him, he developed this belief that it was his fault. He carried this belief into adulthood along with feelings of blame and guilt. This created problems with relationships in his life.

Reconnecting with your childhood trauma helps you let go of experiences of the past so that you can move forward in your life without holding onto beliefs that are not true. When you first begin to heal from your childhood trauma, it's like shaking a snow globe. Everything in the snow globe might appear beautiful and serene from the outside, but once you shake it up, you stir up snowflakes that weren't visible before. In the same way, when you explore your childhood trauma, you stir up many parts within you that you didn't know were there. It can bring up uncomfortable emotions and feelings, such as things that you did not want to face. But just like the snow globe, after it's been shaken, the snow slowly settles back into place, clearing the view and providing you with a new sense of clarity and perception. But if you look carefully at the snow globe, you will notice that the flakes have not settled back into the exact places as before. In the same way, once you shake up your childhood trauma, something will change inside you. The parts of you that needed healing will have healed.

5. Disconnection from Nature

In an earlier story, I told you about my disconnection from nature. At the epitome of the depression, I stopped leaving the house. Every single day I would stay in bed for hours, cooped up in the house. The longer I stayed in the house, the harder it was to get out. That went on for about two years until that moment of grace came when I felt the need to go outside for a walk. Going on that walk immediately made me feel better and, for a moment, I forgot about the depression I was in. In today's world, most of us are too often leading a life where we are always busy. Being busy is good if you are being productive. Being busy can function as a distraction, which may or may not be beneficial, but it can also be detrimental if you do not take time for yourself to reconnect with nature, which is an essential part of our essence.

Nature is our biology, so it makes sense that if we are neglecting this side of our primitive nature, we end up becoming unhappy and disconnected. Biologist E.O. Wilson founded the idea of biophilia which is "humanity's innate need to connect with nature and the natural environment."[26] In this fast-paced world where we live, most people are spending plenty of time in a car or in an office but not spending much time outside in nature. It's easy for us to get stuck in our routines and only wait until we have a holiday to actually go outside and breathe in the fresh air. Think about when you are outside at a park or at the beach, what does that feel like? Did you ever notice the sense of calmness that floods over you when you are connected with nature? Being able to connect with nature is a key factor to reconnecting with your essence.

RECONNECTING WITH THE SELF

Practicing Self-Love

"I think the greatest wound we've all experienced is somehow being rejected for being our authentic self. And as a result of that, we then try to be what we're not to get approval, love, protection, safety, money, whatever."[27]

—Jack Canfield

All of the meditation in the world will lead you to realizing that you just need to love yourself and be you, all of you. I did not know what love really meant because my first experience with love from a man was ripped away from me. My dad left our family when I was really young and this wounded me deeply. My parents had gotten a divorce and his leaving impacted me for many years. I remember being daddy's little girl, but one day he just disappeared. I was too young to understand it all, but what I did know from that point on was that I did not deserve love, because if I did, how could he leave? There were periods in my life when I observed other people who had a beautiful relationship with their dad and witnessing that triggered a sense of abandonment in me.

You see, experiences from our childhood leave imprints on us and can influence us for a lifetime. Although I take full responsibility of my life now, there were many years where I blamed him for who I was. He was my scapegoat. I repeatedly entered unhealthy relationships because I did not feel like I was worthy of love. I was scared but craved the attention and love so much that it didn't matter who I was with, as long as I was not alone to face myself. And when I met a really amazing guy, his love was too overwhelming for me. The truth was that I didn't know how to be loved because I felt so damaged.

Love begins and ends with YOU. You are the person you have to spend the rest of your life with so learn to accept yourself. Learn to love yourself unconditionally. Cultivate a relationship with yourself beyond any other because if you do this, when things get tough, you can ground yourself, no matter what happens. At the end of the day, you have to grow old with *you* and if you don't enjoy your own company, how do you expect others to? Yes, other people may be with you along the journey, but in the end you are it! Learning to love yourself outside of society's ideals for physical beauty as well as what society deems as worthy is extremely valuable. Do not let the opinions of other people get you down or define who you are. You are so much more than your physical appearance. You are beautiful on the inside and outside. Your worthiness transcends all forms of external validation. I know what it feels like to succumb to the thoughts, voices, and opinions of society. It can be painful, those thoughts and voices can become embedded in your mind, but you can refuse to let it define your self-worth and your view of yourself.

Growing up in an Asian family, where most women are petite and under 105 lbs., it was tough on me as I went through my adolescent years and it affected me even when I became an adult. To the Asian culture, women should be incredibly thin and anything beyond 105 lbs. was a spectacle and anomaly to them. Because of my cultural upbringing, I was constantly criticized for being overweight because I had curves and was bigger than the rest of my family. Even when I was only 108 pounds, my family would tell me that I needed to watch what I was eating.

This constant criticism caused me to have extremely low self-esteem which I've had to work on as I got older. A few years ago I was back home in New Mexico visiting when I had found my journal entries from when I was thirteen years old. At thirteen years old, I was counting calories and bulimic. I went as far as getting an Adderall prescription because I heard it would make you lose weight. The extremes that I went to in order to make myself feel better were incredible and it didn't stop there. If I was not being bulimic, I would attempt to starve myself, or take diet pills that made me feel absolutely insane. I went to great lengths to try to lose weight in hopes that it would help my self-esteem. It continued into my early twenties, where I decided to have multiple plastic surgeries because I didn't feel like I was pretty enough.

I hoped that if I changed the way I looked on the outside, it would change the way I felt on the inside. But it did not. All it did was leave me with ugly scars and I still did not feel like I was good enough. So, learn to love yourself from within, because that is the key to your transformation! Losing weight and becoming thinner might increase your short-term confidence but it's all temporary. You must do internal healing work in order to really boost your self-esteem and that is why it's crucial to develop self-love.

Believe it or not, an important lesson I learned was that I needed to *thank* my dad for leaving me. You might be confused to why I thanked him. Honestly, if it were not for him leaving, I would not have become the woman that I am today. I wouldn't have learned how to be independent and to help others through their pain.

So, remember: Anyone who has hurt you in the past, be it your parents, friends, ex-partners, whoever it was, *thank them* because they, in some way or another, helped you get to where you are today. You might not understand it yet, but you will as you continue on this journey.

EXERCISE E8-6: SHIFT YOUR PERCEPTION
OF REALITY

1. Take a few minutes and write down the major people or experiences that have left a negative impact in your life.

2. Describe them from your perspective back then and then ask yourself, "How has this experience or person actually helped me to be better?"

You see, all it takes sometimes is a small shift to alter our perception of reality. For years, I made my dad the antagonist to my story, but when I was able to see things differently, I saw how he influenced me to become the protagonist in my own story, and everything changed.

"Self-love" is the strange concept of truly loving and accepting oneself fully and unconditionally. If you are like me, this idea is foreign, so you can grasp it but you don't really understand what it means. When I first began my own self-development journey, I felt the exact same way. I read tons of articles and books on self-love and how to practice it, but I was never fully able to implement it. Now, self-love is not an easy concept. It does take initiative and effort to achieve it, and for most it might be a lifetime journey.

It all sounds cheesy and, yes, maybe so. But the truth is that the process of falling in love with yourself is the key to ultimate happiness.

Now, I'm not saying fall in love with yourself in an egotistical way, because sometimes that can happen. In reality, the people who are narcissistic actually have no sense of self-love. They do not even understand it. They use their ego as a way to cover up the fact that they hate themselves. The self-love I am talking about is a love where you accept yourself fully and unconditionally, and you embody the essence of who you are—all of you, every single nook and cranny of your body and mind. It is accepting yourself as you are, right now, in this very moment. It's not waiting until you are skinny or have the perfect body. It's not once you change something about your appearance that will make you feel better (in reality it does not and, even if it does, it is only temporary). More than that, it is accepting that you are a human being with a mind, body, and spirit that is designed perfectly. Self-love is when you can embrace that you are you—unique and perfect, even with your imperfections, just as you are, and you can still love yourself. It's accepting all of the idiosyncrasies that make you, YOU! It's when you can wake up every morning, look at yourself in the mirror and be truly grateful for yourself and tell yourself, "I love you." "You're absolutely fricking amazing!" This is when you will have a sense of affinity with the core of who you are, as a brilliant human being.

Now, self-love does not mean completely ignoring things that you need to change for the better. It is accepting yourself as you are now, and at the same time allowing yourself room to grow into the best version of yourself without beating yourself down for your current shortcomings. Everyone has things that they need to work on and you are no exception. Part of self-love is working on your transformation and refusing to settle for mediocrity because you know that you can achieve better.

Once you fall in love with yourself, life will feel much easier and you will feel a sense of peace within yourself. You will be able to handle anything that comes your way and not let it define who you are or break you down, because you know that you are good enough and that you deserve everything in the world.

At first, the thought of doing this might sound silly. It might even make you cringe or panic—because, who are you without your wounds and the victim story you keep telling yourself? Who are you underneath all of those pretense layers? I know you're afraid of the pain, afraid of the hurt, and afraid of the truth. You think you are broken because you've been wounded, but the truth is that your wounds are what make you beautiful and you are far away from being broken. Have you ever met another person who has not been damaged in one way or another? I bet you haven't, even if you thought you did. People only portray a superficial version of themselves to the world so that they can blend in. But if you ask most people, deep down, they all have the same set of problems, fears, and worries. That is what makes us human.

Let's use me as an example. When most people meet me, they think I'm beautiful and that my life is perfect. There have been times when I have told people about my depression and all they could say was, "How can you be depressed? You're so beautiful!" as if being *beautiful* means my life is perfect. People will often have a misconstrued perception of who you are based on what they see or think they know about you. To other people, it might have appeared that I had it all together and that my life was perfect because, honestly, I worked really hard at putting on a show for other people to see. I worked so hard to cover up my pain, to be strong, and to be the person who had it all together. But every time someone complimented me and told me that, "I was beautiful," I would cringe. All I could think of was how I felt so ugly on the inside.

I thank this pain because it sparked an eternal search for self-love and acceptance within me. Make a conscious effort to thank your pain because it is what helps move you and pushes you to grow.

So how can you fall in love with yourself? With all that you are, the pain, the wounds, the suffering—all of it?

Below are a few steps you can follow to get started on this self-love journey:

STEPS TO ACHIEVING SELF-LOVE:

1. GET TO KNOW YOURSELF

Are you always doing things to please others and make them happy? What about you? What makes you happy? Part of the self-love process is getting to know who you are, your likes and dislikes. So, pay attention! What makes you happy and what makes you feel scared? What motivates you? What keeps you stagnant? Most importantly, why do those things make you feel the way that you do. Grab a paper and pen and create a list of the things you like and do not like. Write a definition for yourself of who you are.

2. PRACTICE SELF-CARE

Self-care can come in many forms. What's important is that you do what makes you happy and feel good. Whether it's taking a nice bath to relax or treating yourself to some ice-cream. Spoil yourself a little and do small acts that make you feel good about yourself.

3. MAKE YOURSELF A PRIORITY

Most people hide behind others by giving all the love they have to everyone except themselves. When you are giving away all your love and not making yourself a priority, you are depleting yourself of the love you need to help you flourish and grow. This also creates an imbalance in your life because you are giving, giving, giving and not receiving anything in return. Maybe you get affection or attention and love from other people sometimes, but the most important love you need is the love you have for yourself. So, this means making yourself a priority and being okay with it.

4. REFUSE TO COMPARE

You may know this, but comparing yourself to others is the thief of all joy. It will rob you of your happiness and make you feel small. You can never win if you compare yourself to other people. Everyone is unique in his or her own way, and so are you! You have your own journey to take, so do not waste time comparing it with others.

5. BE KIND TO YOURSELF

This means refusing to sabotage yourself. It means refusing to tell yourself negative things or beating yourself up over the small things. Instead, show yourself some kindness and compassion when you mess up or when things do not go your way. For example, if you made a mistake, don't punish yourself by telling yourself things such as, "I'm a failure" or "I always mess up." Instead, honor yourself for what happened and tell yourself something like, "It's okay that I made a mistake. Everyone makes mistakes. What can I learn from this mistake?"

6. Know your Worth

The core of most of our problems stems from the fact that we do not believe that we are worthy or deserving. It's easy to continue to feel sorry for yourself and let your story dictate your life, but I challenge you to do the opposite. I truly believe that everyone on this planet is worthy of love, success, and happiness. But no one is going to go and get these things for you, so you have to do it yourself. This can be hard because most of us have ingrained beliefs that we are not good enough and not worthy. Know that reversing those beliefs will be a process but knowing your worth can be something as simple as saying, "No," to something you do not want to do, or not accepting a job that does not pay well. As you come to know your worth, you can start making decisions in your life that reflect your true—and newly discovered—value!

7. Invest in Yourself

Most people avoid investing in themselves—investing in the things that really matter. Let me tell you that investing in myself and my self-development journey has been the most rewarding thing I could have done! You can invest time and money into material things and experiences, but at the end of the day, you will still not feel complete. Investing in yourself means signing up for the class you've always wanted to take, learning new things, going to a self-development event. Investing in yourself is finding ways to make you look deep within yourself and figuring out how you can become your best self.

Exercise E8-7: "Self-Love" Exercises

A. Journaling

Review the 7 steps from above and answer the following questions:

◇ What makes me feel happy, excited, or scared?

◇ What motivates me?

◇ What are some self-care acts I can do to help me feel better?

◇ How can I prioritize myself in my life? What are some things I can do?

◇ When the voice of comparison pops up, what can I remind myself of?

◇ How can I be kinder to myself? What are some things I can do?

◇ What am I worth? (It might be easy to fall into the trap of thinking you're not worthy, but try the opposite and write down the reasons why you ARE worthy!)

◇ What are some things I can do to invest in myself?

B. Mirroring

1. Look at yourself in the eyes in a mirror and say, "I love YOU," and really feel it. Let it penetrate your body. This technique is called "mirroring." It's a tool that I learned from Lisa Nichols, a transformational leader. The first time you do it, you might feel silly and awkward. It might also be an extremely emotional experience.

Whatever you feel, just be with your emotions. Honor them and be present.

2. Say it to yourself every single day and repeat it as much as you can throughout the day. There will be days where you will not believe it but say it anyway. Say it until it resonates throughout your entire body. Say it until you believe it. The day that you truly fall in love with who you are will be the most important and revolutionizing day in your life.

Imagine... being completely and unconditionally in love with yourself, free from self-judgment and self-condemnation. What would that look like? How would you feel?

Loving yourself goes beyond traditional acts of self-love. Taking care of yourself and your needs is not enough. You have to really learn to love every single part of you, everything that is unique about yourself and that makes you YOU!

C. 50 THINGS

Take some time and write down 50 things you love about yourself. It could be something small or something big. Any quirks or idiosyncrasies you have, write them down, too! When you first start this exercise, it might take you some time to complete it. However, just continue to add to it every single day. Over time, you will have the list completed and you can refer back to this list when you are feeling down about yourself.

D. Accomplishments

Another way you can start to build self-love is through identifying your accomplishments. Oftentimes in life, we pay a tremendous amount of attention to our mistakes, yet we forget to recognize our own accomplishments. When you can direct your attention to the things that you have achieved, you will develop higher self-esteem and self-love.

1. Grab a pen and paper or journal.

2. Give yourself 15 minutes of quiet time so you can focus on this exercise.

3. Begin by writing down 50 things that you have accomplished throughout your life. Any accomplishment counts—even if it may seem insignificant. Just write down everything you can think of. Maybe it's learning to drive a car, maybe it's graduating school, maybe it's winning an award or breaking a bad habit. It doesn't matter. Just write it down.

4. Use this list of accomplishments to remind you of what an incredible human being you are and add to it as needed. Over time, you will visually see how much you've already accomplished in your life, and that is something to be proud of!

E. Healing Yourself—Words of Affirmation

What are some words you've always wanted to hear from the people closest to you, whether it's your family, friends, or from yourself? What are you waiting for someone to tell you? Create a list of affirmations you can repeat to yourself on a daily basis.

Post these affirmations everywhere you frequent whether it's in your kitchen, bathroom, or car. The more you see these affirmations, the more reinforced they will be. You can even set up reminders on your telephone with these affirmations as another way to reinforce them.

Examples:

- I am enough.

- I am safe.

- I will always be there for you.

- I'm proud of you.

- I love you.

- I appreciate you.

Reconnecting with You

The key to happiness is
doing things that make you happy!

To reconnect with who you are, remember to start doing things that light you up and make you happy! This was one of the best lessons I learned along my journey—*do what makes you happy*. Wow! You must think this is such a simple concept. Yes, it might sound simple, but I find that some of the simplest things are often the hardest to do. Doing things that made me happy was a hard transition for me. Actually, it had never dawned on me that I had the right to do things that lifted me up. One day, I discovered I could break free from my depression by *breaking free from my depression!* Let me explain.

During an extremely difficult time in my life, two years of deep and dark depression, I had lost myself. Every single morning when I woke up, I could not pull myself out of bed. I laid in my bed in deep despair wondering how things had gotten so bad. I could not seem to get out of my own head. Negative thoughts were swirling through my mind and tormenting me. It was like being in a prison. But that one day, while I felt chained to my bed, in a moment of grace, I had a sudden realization: *I needed to do something that made me happy*!

When you are extremely depressed, it's much harder to get out of bed than you might think. But in that moment, I was blessed with a sudden motivation to get up! So, I got up, got out of bed, and went to a hiking trail near UCSD in San Diego. As I got to the trail, I felt an immediate sense of relief. Hiking was one of my favorite things to do, but I had given it up when I became depressed. When I came to the end of the trail, I stood on top of a cliff that looked down to the great Pacific Ocean. I was enamored by the magnificent view, as the sun glistened on my skin and I felt a warmth that made me feel incredibly happy again.

As I stood there and took in the beauty of the moment, being fully present, I was reminded that I had forgotten to do things that I enjoyed—something as small as taking a walk in nature. I had been so stuck in my head that I forgot that there was an incredible world out there just waiting to be embraced. From that day on, I began to slowly do more things that I enjoyed each day. It did not matter if they were small, seemingly insignificant things. They all contributed to me breaking out of my head.

That moment of happiness gave me a push, but what happened afterwards was even crazier— in fact it was a magical, synchronistic moment. It was a few weeks after my boyfriend and I had broken up. I was staying at one of my friend's house in downtown San Diego. One morning as I was heading to work, I went out to my car and found some papers flapping on my windshield. I usually toss advertisements like this, but for some reason, I was drawn to this little booklet. I took it with me inside the car and decided to have a look at it. I read through it and it seemed interesting. It was filled with little affirmations and quotes. As I flipped to one of the pages, the first line read, "Do what makes you happy." As I read this, I got chills all over my body. I looked around me to see if anyone was there. I thought to myself, *Is this a joke? Am I dreaming? What were the chances of something like this happening? It was just last week that I kept thinking to myself, "Do what makes you happy."*

Whatever forces out there that worked together to make this happen, are beyond something I can comprehend. What I did know was that it was an affirmation and reminder for me to never forget that when you do the things that make you happy, life will be much more enjoyable and you will discover how to be fully present in each moment.

When we are constantly in our minds, busy living our lives, and doing what we think is necessary, we forget to do the things that we really enjoy. So, make this a priority in your life. Put it on your "To Do" list: Try to do one thing every day that really makes you happy!

EXERCISE E8-8: WHAT MAKES YOU HAPPY

1. Create a list of things that make you happy, really happy.

2. Brainstorm some ideas of how you can do at least one of these things daily, even if it's just for a few minutes.

3. Take action.

CHASING AFTER "ENOUGH"

For years, I chased after things. Whether it was money, prestige, a respected job title, or success, I was on an endless wild goose chase, unable to catch my breath. I was in the proverbial rat race, like so many others in America. I felt like a lab rat, part of some sort of experiment in which the faster I ran, the more it led to nowhere. I believed this chase would give me some kind of happiness, but as I reached the top of my emotional ladder, there were few moments when I felt accomplished, then the accomplishment faded and I was left with a familiar feeling of emptiness. My chase to be "enough" had led me astray, left me bewildered, and beyond confused. I was a chaotic mess, desperately searching for something more, something to fulfill my needs of being seen, heard, and understood.

I kept seeking answers beyond my own means. Every single person I met, every single experience, all the external things I sought after, never filled this empty void I felt within. Instead, it made that void grow deeper as I kept chasing after this bliss that I believed existed outside of me. This search has taught me many valuable lessons, given me so much wisdom, and I have finally understood the meaning of it all. The truth is that I had always been enough; I had just forgotten. Although this has been the most challenging voyage of my life, reconnecting to this truth has altered my life forever.

You can travel through space and time, always seeking a new thrill or a new destination, but one of the most important lessons I have learned is that the *destination* is not the answer. *Life is not about waiting to arrive. It's about recognizing the eternal truth, that our arrival is here and now, in the present moment.* It's crazy to think that most of our life we are constantly on a search to be "enough"—good enough, pretty enough, smart enough, rich enough, popular enough, loved enough.

The list is almost endless. We embark on this search hoping that we will come home when we've found what makes us feel whole and complete. Most of us believe that once we obtain our dreams, once we have that perfect career, once we have that perfect partner, once we have all the money that we need, we will finally feel like we are "enough." We believe that this external world quantifies our inner value. This is so far from the truth. If you are constantly on this search, there is no happy ending. You will come to realize that once you are there and have "obtained it all," you will still feel like something is missing. The puzzle piece that you are desperately pursuing has already been found, it has always been a part of you. All the answers and fulfillment you have been seeking is an intrinsic part of your nature, waiting for you to discover it. You do not have to go far to find it. It's here. It always has been.

The eternal search to come home, create meaning, and be happy will always be out of your grasp if you are seeking it in the exterior world. The only thing this search really shows is that you do not believe that you are "enough," and that is why you keep on searching for things that will fill this gap. When you notice that your life is all about this search, shine some light on it and realize that the more things you chase, the further away you will drift from this reality. The only way for you to feel like you are enough is to begin appreciating yourself for all that you are, regardless of your material possessions, status, and recognition. When you can feel enough even when you have nothing, you will be at peace. This is because the gap you were trying to fill will disappear. Your search to be enough will no longer be necessary.

Part of self-love is self-acceptance. Of everything, this is probably the most difficult thing to accomplish. I know as you read this, your inner critic is probably coming out. That little voice is probably saying, "How can I accept myself when there are so many things wrong with me?" Look! Let me tell you:

YOU ARE ABSOLUTELY PERFECT
JUST THE WAY YOU ARE.

YOU ARE ENOUGH.

YOU ALWAYS HAVE BEEN
AND YOU ALWAYS WILL BE.

The universe created you for a reason, and if you believe in the power of the universe, you have to realize that everything it created is perfect just as it is. Think about the trillion of cells that make up your body, each being able to function on its own with an infinite intelligence. Do you think this is all by accident? Human design goes beyond our imagination and is something beyond our comprehension, so how can you doubt the magical creation that is your life? So, start learning to accept yourself and accept all of you.

This is a process, so start small. Start by giving yourself small compliments every single day. Let these compliments slowly permeate to your mind and help you transform your story of not being enough to being perfect just the way you are. You can repeat the mantras and affirmations in this book to get these new *thoughts* to develop into new *beliefs* about yourself.

Loving yourself means you should stop seeking external validation. Chasing after being enough, seeking external validation is a game that has no ending.

This pursuit of external validation is a chase that will lead you nowhere. Why do so many people look to the external world for validation? Because it satisfies the ego. But this satisfaction of the ego is only temporary. You might feel good for a few brief moments and then the ego will begin to search for something else to satisfy its needs. Think about how much you need other people's approval to feel good about yourself? Are you constantly waiting for other people to approve of you? Maybe it's your family, friends, coworkers, or boss. Do you rely on their approval to feel good about yourself? If you can relate to this, and most people will, I invite you to look inward and ask yourself why you need this external validation. How does it make you feel? Why is it important to you? Does it really fill the gap and satisfy your needs of feeling whole? The truth is that when you love yourself truly and unconditionally, you won't need this validation from other people. You will just know the truth, that your essence in itself is enough. You do not need to be anything other than who you are, right now.

When things get tough, channel your higher-self. Don't let your lower-self win.

EXERCISE E8-9: SELF-ACCEPTANCE MANTRAS

You can do this exercise by reading it silently or out loud to yourself. However, for more effect, it's best to repeat these mantras while you are meditating and already in a blissful state. This will ensure that it will permeate into your subconscious mind.

SELF-ACCEPTANCE MANTRAS:

"I love and accept myself just the way that I am. I release any feelings of self-hate that I once held of myself. I accept all the mistakes that I have made in my life and I forgive myself for them. I no longer feel the need to criticize myself. I replace all negative words that I use to describe myself with positive words. I am patient with myself.

"I love my body and I treat it with respect. I let go of any insecurities that I have ever felt about myself. I am strong and empowered. I am beautiful and strong. I am in perfect health. I have a burning energy source inside of me and I am worthy of all things wonderful. I release any self-sabotage that holds me back from living my life to its greatest potential.

"I no longer judge myself. I am not a victim. I take great care of myself. I take this journey of healing one day at a time. I love the person that I am as well as the person who I am becoming."[28]

—Carly Marie

Self-acceptance means accepting *all* of you, the good as well as the bad. This means that you have to accept your *shadow self* as well as your *light self*. Like the yin and yang in Chinese philosophy, we all have two sides that make up who we are, and this gives us balance. The *light self* contains all the amazing and beautiful qualities about your "self." The *shadow self* is the side of you that you may perceive as ugly or negative. It is usually tucked away, hidden because you don't want others to see it.

You need to reconnect with the essence of who you really are and own all the disowned parts of yourself.

"Beneath the social mask we wear every day, we have a hidden shadow side: an impulsive, wounded, sad, or isolated part that we generally try to ignore. The Shadow can be a source of emotional richness and vitality, and acknowledging it can be a pathway to healing and an authentic life."

—Zweig and Wolf, *Romancing the Shadow*

The "shadow" is a concept in psychology that was first developed by psychiatrist Carl Jung. The shadow is actually another archetype within our psyche. It is the side of ourselves that we try to hide, deny and repress. The shadow part of you is often tucked away and hidden, a side of you that you conceal.

Just as *archetypes* help to shape our *heroic side*, they also shape our *shadow side*. After we have been bruised by negative events in our past, the negative characteristics of our archetypes exert their influence over our perspective, attitude and behavior. Consequently, we can react in ways that are foreign to our true self, but aligned with these archetypes. This creates a major conflict within us, making us miserable and angry at ourselves and the world. We end up fighting with ourselves, but we have no idea why. This is why it is critical that you discover your "shadow self" and determine which archetypes are influencing it. Once you explore your shadow and understand it, you will be able to start reintegrating your "shadow self" into your whole identity and achieve that Yin-Yang balance.

The *shadow* is comprised of the parts of ourselves that we view as ugly: jealousy, rage, greed, selfishness, lust, etc. These negative traits can be seen as the weaknesses in the archetypes mentioned earlier. Sometimes we are in denial of our shadow selves; we notice these shadow traits and qualities in others but refuse to acknowledge that they are a part of us as well. Working with the shadow will help you admit to these negative traits and allow you to reflect on the dark sides of you—because the negative parts that you hide from yourself will eventually destroy you.

Sometimes we view the shadow parts as something we need to suppress, and this may cause us to repress certain traits within our personality. We bury this darker side of ourselves because we are afraid that someone might see that part of us and they will reject us if they know that part of us exists. This leads to internal chaos because we end up rejecting parts of who we are. In reality, everyone has both a light and shadow side to their personality. If you look at the story of Dr. Jekyll and Mr. Hyde, you can see that it represents the light and dark sides that everyone has, although in that case, it was in the extreme. We all have a light side and, equally, we have a dark side. Together they complete us and make us whole. Many people may feel that the shadow self is negative and that we have to punish ourselves for having it. Don't torment yourself with this false belief. Instead, just accept the fact that, like everyone else, you have a light side and a shadow side. Both are simply aspects of our personality that we can work with.

Shadow work is necessary for our healing. If we refuse to deal with our shadow side, according to Dr. Joe Vitale, we are creating a ticking time bomb:

> **"Suppression is building bombs.**
> **When you bury an emotion, you bury it alive."[30]**

A few of the shadow parts that you must work with:

- Shame
- Guilt
- Jealousy
- Greed
- Being Judgmental

In order to work with this shadow side, we must confront the negative emotions and beliefs that lurk beneath the surface.—Soon you will begin to create a more balanced relationship with yourself. Here's how to get started:

Working With Your Shadow

1. **Get to know your shadow.** Bring the dark side of you out into the open and take an honest look at it. Reflect on the damaging impact your shadow side has on your life, because it's better to look your enemy in the eye than to be ambushed unexpectedly. Evaluate and explore your shadow side. Otherwise you can be destroyed from within by negative emotions that you are not even aware of. The shadow is typically the negative personality traits which we may deny within ourselves. These traits are anger, jealousy, a judgmental attitude, greed and shame. The shadow is also present when you feel triggered by other people. These are times when something they do causes an intense reaction in you and makes you upset. Sometimes the shadow can be your limiting beliefs and reality statements. Shadows include ideas like, "I'm not good enough," "I'm not loveable," or "I'm flawed." Take some time to identify the parts of your shadow, or the negative things that you constantly tell yourself, which can be qualities of your personality that you view as bad.

2. **Own your projections.** Realize that what is triggered in you by others, is also a reflection of yourself. What you see in another person that you view as bad or horrible is also within you. You also hold this component in your personality. This is why when your shadow appears, evaluate it and own your projections. Think this way: When you are triggered by others, what emotions come up? How do these personality traits appear in your personality?

3. **Honor your emotions.** We all have moments in our lives when we're not feeling at our best, but that does not mean that you have to run away and hide or push down those feelings, because eventually they will resurface. When working with the shadow, I encourage you to be brave. Sit with your emotions when times are tough and let those uncomfortable feelings surface. Write about the way you're feeling and give yourself time to really feel them. Then ask yourself, "Why do I feel this way?" "Where do I feel it in my body?" "Where do these emotions lead to?" It's okay to feel sad, hurt, frustrated, or angry. You see, there's always an underlying reason why we feel the way we do, even though we might not see it at first. If you keep looking inward, you will get a better understanding of yourself. So, do not be afraid to let yourself feel these emotions. You are not the only one struggling with this. No one, and I mean NO ONE, can avoid experiencing these feelings. There is a plus side to the discomfort you are going through in this process. It will help you grow. These are your *growing pains*.

4. **Re-own the disowned parts of yourself through compassion.** Understanding your shadow might come easily, but being compassionate to yourself when it shows up is another story. When faced with our shadow self, we tend to push it away. We deny it, reject it, and do not give ourselves permission to let it be. When these negative emotions show up, it's extremely important to be kind to your shadow, because it is part of who you are. So, when dealing with it, be explorative and compassionate at the same

time. Pretend that you are talking to your best friend. Let your emotions run their course, then tell yourself the things that you might tell a best friend who is going through tough times.

5. **Working with the Shadow.** The best way to work with your shadow is through journaling or meditating. When you journal or meditate, you can talk to this part of yourself. Richard Schwartz, the creator of Internal Family Systems, advocates for a therapy approach that incorporates talking to different "parts" of ourselves.[31] We will use this technique to help you connect with your shadow side.

EXERCISE E8-10: DIALOGUING WITH YOUR SHADOW AND/OR PARTS

1. Identify the shadow or part of you that you want to work with*.

2. Write or meditate and ask the part of you to present itself. You can just write or think about the part that you feel like talking to and exploring.

3. Ask the part what its role is in your life. Ask it what it needs to tell you.

4. Thank the part for trying to help you and release it.

5. Let the part know that you will always connect with it when it needs you.

If there is a part of me that is feeling angry and frustrated, I would first identify this part through journaling or meditation. (I will explain both ways separately below so you can understand how to complete the exercise.)

A. JOURNALING

◇ Identify the shadow. The shadow could be an emotion or a belief.

◇ Answer the questions below. Let the answers flow to you as you are journaling.

◇ Thank the shadow and release the emotion by writing down your intention or saying out loud, "I release this anger that I am holding onto."

The goal here is to help you connect with the part and speak to it. The *part* is generally an automatic response or the subconscious speaking to us, usually the first response that comes to mind. For example, consider these *asks* (bold) and *answers* that follow when journaling. This *shadow* is *anger*:

1. **"What is your role in my life?"**

   "To alert you when your boundaries are being invaded."

2. **"What do you need to tell me?"**

   "You need to have firm boundaries."

3. **"What are you trying to teach me?"**

   "You need to express your voice when your boundaries are being crossed."

Now, thank the shadow and release the emotion. For example, say out loud:

> "Thank you for trying to help me. I release you (the anger or the emotion) that I am holding onto. I allow myself to move through this emotion and forgive myself for the attachment to the anger."

Additional journaling questions to work with your shadow:

- Judgment: How are you judging others? What does this reflect about yourself? Usually, when we judge other people, it reflects back to something or some disowned parts of ourselves. These judgments might originate within you and are displaced onto others as a mirror reflection.

- What are some qualities in other people that you dislike and cannot deal with? What can these qualities show you about yourself?

- What are your triggers? What makes you upset, angry, and defensive with others?

- What negative things do others say about you that you refuse to accept? How does it make you feel?

- What emotions do you rarely express around others? When did you begin to hide these emotions? Emotional suppression and repression show some areas of shame buried within yourself.

- What was one of your darkest moments? A time when you were self-destructive. How were you acting and behaving? Write a heartfelt letter to that version of you showing her/him compassion, understanding, forgiveness, and acceptance. You can review this later when you have moments of similar feelings.

- What is your biggest fear? How does this fear influence your decisions, habits, outlooks, and relationships?

- What are some shameful moments in your life?

- What anger do you still hold onto?

- What resentment do you still hold onto?

- How can you release these feelings?

- Describe your most self-destructive behaviors. How do you feel when you are doing them? Explore the motives behind these self-destructive behaviors. Can you think of why you do them?

- When was the last time you were mean or aggressive towards another person? What was your motive behind it? What feelings and thoughts were you having?

- What are you jealous or envious about in another person? What emotions come up?

- What does insecurity teach you about yourself?

- Do you feel like you are good enough? Why not? When you finish answering this question, write down the reasons why you are good enough.

- What are the most troublesome emotions that you deal with on a daily basis? What are some ways you can deal with these troublesome emotions?

B. MEDITATION

1. Close your eyes and take a few deep breaths. Let yourself begin to relax as any thoughts, feelings, or worries fade away.

2. Once you have a few minutes of relaxation, think in your mind about the part you want to work with. Identify the shadow. The part could be an emotion or belief. Where do you feel the part in your body? Or does an image or sensation come up? Be aware of the part.

3. Ask the part:

   • What is your role in my life?

   • What do you need to tell me?

   • What are you trying to teach me?

4. Let the answers flow to you as you are sitting in meditation.

5. Thank the part and release the emotion by imagining a black cloud (the emotion or belief) floating away from your body.

6. Take a few deep, cleansing breaths, and begin to come back to your full awareness.

Example:

I take a few deep breaths and then I close my eyes and try to feel the part in my body. I notice a sensation at the top of my head; it feels like steam. I ask the part, "What is your role in my life?"

The part answers (usually you will hear a thought come up naturally), "I am protecting you because your boundaries have been crossed."

I say to the part, "Thank you. I understand why you're here and I honor you for it, however, I am ready to release this emotion so that it does not ruin my day." I take a deep inhale and imagine a black cloud of anger floating away from my body.

Rewriting Your Story

Our stories are a combination of past experiences, history, values, and core beliefs that we operate from. They are the driving forces behind our actions and everything that we do. Our story can anchor us to a reality and limit us from doing anything that does not match that story. Most of us are unconsciously addicted to our story. We secretly like the drama that takes place in our lives. We sabotage our lives when things are going great because there is some part of us that believes we're not worthy of happiness. The mind is extremely resistant to change, and that is why sticking to our story based on our past is easier than rewriting a new one. I am sure there's a narrative you've been telling yourself up until today. I bet that narrative is full of sad stories, limiting beliefs, and untouched hopes and dreams. I get it. We all have a story, but we don't have to let that story dictate the rest of our lives. We can re-write our story to have a different, a happy and fulfilling, ending.

Can you imagine how wonderful life would be if our personal story focused on our biggest hopes and dreams—our desires, happiness, and greatest outcomes—rather than just our pains? For me, my story was that I was not good enough and that love and happiness were not available to me. So, I lived my life according to this story for a huge part of my life. Everything I did was based on this story. Any decisions I made aligned me with this story I kept telling myself. In a way, I actually prevented myself from seeing what was available to me by believing this mental block. I did not know it, but I was creating my own self-fulfilling prophecy, that love and happiness could never be available to me.

When you operate from a story of darkness, you can't see anything other than that darkness. I was so stuck to this story that I did not see anything else besides it. Before I had my spiritual awakening, my life was like this: Every day, I felt a heavy cloud above my head. Everything I saw around me was bleak and dark. This was all that I could focus on and all that I could see. My spiritual awakening was the first time I saw the world in a different light. I got glimpses of what true happiness and bliss could be. Sometimes we see the world through tunnel vision, based on "our story" or the "reality" we've created for ourselves. When we view the world with tunnel vision, we blind ourselves to opportunities because we are blocking out those opportunities. As your life continues to unfold, realize that your story is absolutely malleable. This means that you have the ability to change your story. You do not need to wait for a spiritual awakening to decide you want to focus on the positive things in life. You just have to decide that you are going to rewrite your story.

Unhealthy storylines will keep us stuck, so rewriting your story is a way to self-liberation. You can write your own script to this screenplay that is your life. With everything that you've learned so far, it's time to put it down on paper. Whatever story you've been telling yourself this far, it's time to let go of that one and write yourself a NEW story. This is the time to get creative and use your imagination. Imagine, if you had no

255

limitations in the world, who would you be? What would you do? What would you create? Who would you love? Take this chance to write down everything you want your life to be and post this somewhere where you can read every single day. Let this be a reminder that you are not a victim anymore; that you have the power to create the life you deserve to live. Let this story motivate you as we work on closing the gap between who you've been and who you are going to become through this process of self-realization.

EXERCISE E8-11: REWRITING YOUR STORY

1. Write down the story you are currently telling yourself about your life.

2. Look for any cognitive distortions, negative beliefs, and exaggerations you have that are affecting your current reality. Challenge any current assumptions you have. How can you change those thoughts and beliefs?

3. Rewrite your story. This time, make it a positive one. Include everything you want your life to be. THINK BIG. There are no limitations here.

4. Remind yourself that this new story is absolutely possible! As we continue to create a path for you on your self-development journey, you will inch closer to this exciting, new reality.

"Now that we are progressively unhooking you from the past, it's time to find your passion and mission in this lifetime."

~ *Julia*

CHAPTER 9:

REWARD

A Shift in Perception

"What you choose to focus on becomes your reality."[1]

"If you're serious about changing your life, you'll find a way. If you're not, you'll find an excuse."[2]

—Practical Thoughts from Jen Sincero

A S A VICTIM of depression, it was not until I realized that I had a choice concerning my depression that I was able to overcome it. I want you to know, whatever it is that you are going through or suffering from, you have a choice. And when you make this decision, your life will change forever because mine certainly did! Reclaiming my power and taking accountability for my life helped me overcome "this thing" that was weighing me down for so many years.

Learning to take responsibility for my life and not blaming circumstances that happened to me in the past forced me to take back control. When you realize that you are the one who is in charge of your life, you know with certainty that you can create the life that you want. So, take responsibility for your life. Know that you are the creator of it and you can change it. For change to happen, all you have to do is have a shift in your perceptions.

It's easy to focus and ruminate on past negative events. Focusing on past negatives events and how much they have damaged your life doesn't change anything. It doesn't move you forward. Instead, you have to look past these events and change your perceptions. A perception is an understanding or interpretation of an event that is happening and is at least in part based on your experience of what happened previously. We all form our perceptions from a combination of things: genetic predispositions, past experiences, prior knowledge, and emotions and traumas we went through that shaped our current reality. This creates the lens through which we view the world, and sometimes this lens can be clouded and full of preconceived notions. Most of our perceptions are based on a combination of past experiences, what we think we know to be true and what we identify with. Our perception can also be the meaning that we attach to a specific event, which can sometimes be warped based on our previous experiences.

When you do the internal work of self-discovery, you have to open yourself up to expanding your awareness and insight about the events in your life. Reality consists of both an objective reality and a subjective reality. In order to separate yourself from the truth (objective reality) and your false interpretation (subjective reality), you have to evaluate what you attribute the truth to. An *objective reality* cannot be proved; but in terms of self-development, we want to look at it as the "truth" versus our subjective reality, which is the reality we create in our minds based on our thoughts.

Subjective reality is a personally-constructed reality, usually consisting of an elaborate reality we create about ourselves and our environment based on filters. These filters combine our perception, thinking, emotions, memories, imaginations, and interpretations of events. It's similar to a Snapchat filter, where everything is morphed into something unreal.

Think back to an event in your past that changed your life forever. What meaning did you associate with that event? For me it was an "aha!" moment when I realized that I am the creator of my life, and this shift in perception was when I began to realize that I am an infinite being with limitless possibilities. I also realized that I was the only one standing in my way. As a child, because I didn't have the necessary coping skills, I did not realize that I had the power to live an uncompromised life full of magic. But as I revisited my past and discerned that I am no longer a small child, incapable of achieving the things that I want to do, I was blessed with relief. I finally understood that when you alter your perception of an event and change its meaning, you can modify your reality.

During the "Unleash the Power Within" event, I learned an extremely valuable tool. I knew that shifting my perception was important, but Tony Robbins introduced to me an even more crucial component to shifting your perception, making it so much easier: When you are aiming for change, "start small." Tony Robbins said that all you have to do is create a "2 millimeter" change every single day, and eventually that will add up to exponential growth.[3] When most of us try to change, we start by looking at the big picture and we become overwhelmed. We are crushed beneath this huge mass of goals, dreams and to-do lists—everything that we have to change. This stress and feeling of being overwhelmed are absolutely unnecessary. The fact of the matter is that change takes time, there's no easy fix when it comes to personal development. You have to do the work. But instead of looking at the big picture, you only have to focus on breaking it down into small, actionable steps. Of course you still need to have the big picture in mind so that you have a roadmap to guide you to where you want to go, but you only have to focus on the small steps to get there. Take an action every single day—one step at a time. It's the same process that you would use to attain any personal goal, like losing 30 pounds. You do it slowly, over time.

When I began writing this book, I experienced this intense feeling of being overwhelmed. At first, writing an entire book about my self-discovery journey and overcoming depression seemed like a daunting task. I had thoughts like, *Do I really have enough information to share with the world about my journey? I've never done anything like this before.* If I had continued to focus on the information I had or did *not* have, I would have become overwhelmed and maybe even stopped writing altogether. Instead, I just kept writing every single day, until one day, I finished this entire book.

A *shift in perception* frees you from attachment to your thoughts and perceptions, but it also creates the space for you to open up to new perspectives that can be positive and transformative. I made myself consciously switch from thinking about how massive an undertaking this was to "I'm going to write a few paragraphs every day." In an earlier chapter, we identified cognitive distortions in our life. One major cognitive distortion that can hold you back is the catastrophizing distortion. Many of us always imagine the worst-case scenario, so we act and respond out of fear. When you have a shift in perception, you can rewrite the worst-case scenario to a best-case scenario! Instead of thinking, "What if the worst-case scenario happens?" transform this question into, "What's the best thing that could happen?"

I'm familiar with this situation because it is something that I've struggled with. With any situation that came my way, my first instinct was to start imagining the worst-case scenario. This thought process threw me down a rabbit hole where I got lost imagining more endless negative outcomes.

But . . .

What if things actually worked out?

What if you can do it?

What if you are good at it?

What if you can learn this new skill?

What if there are no limits to what you can achieve?

Have you ever thought about it this way? This is a valuable lesson that I had to learn. I had to learn to master my negative "what if" questions and channel them to positive "what if" questions.

Most of our lives we spend doubting, criticizing, and avoiding our potential selves because we are so caught up in the worst-case scenarios.

Below, you can transform these thoughts so that you start questioning things in a more positive light and reevaluate where your thoughts stem from. Learn how you can change these thoughts so that you can do the things that you are most afraid of.

EXERCISE E9-1: WORST AND BEST CASES

◇ Think of a situation that could be a worst-case scenario. Write this situation down. How does it make you feel when you think about it? What are the thoughts associated with it? What are your current beliefs about it?

◇ Now think about the opposite, the best-case scenario. What does that look like? How do you feel? Just thinking about the best possible outcome should give you some immediate relief. The key is to practice this exercise until it becomes second nature and your default setting is to think of positive outcomes.

FOCUS ON THE SOLUTION- NOT THE PROBLEM

All too often, not only do we tend to focus on negative outcomes but we also tend to focus on the problems. This problem-oriented mentality prevents us from being able to overcome our challenges and only increases stress in our minds, which is counterproductive. We may believe that focusing on the problem has some benefits, but it only does in an extremely narrow sense. Focusing on the problem will maybe prevent you from creating the same problem in the future, but it will not help you resolve it. So, that time wasted spent on thinking about your problem will have no value. When you're stuck in this mindset of focusing on the bad things, there will never be an end to your worries. If you keep doing what you are familiar with, then you will keep getting the same results you've already had. That's why it's absolutely necessary to shift this bad habit so you can learn to resolve your issues instead of magnifying them. I know that for many of us it's a default to focus on the negative. I too can at times succumb to this bad behavior and oftentimes can fall into this trap. However, I've established how important it is to make choices in your life. You can start doing things that will help and support you on your journey, but you also have to let go of the habits that are blocking your successes.

Regardless of how challenging the problem may be, if you think long and hard enough, a solution will appear. So instead of letting yourself focus on the problems, learn to focus on the solutions. Where your attention goes, energy flows. This means that whatever you focus on will generate a higher frequency that will cause you to attach to the problem. This drama in your head will never end if you don't smash it as soon as it begins. The more you practice shifting your focus from the problem to the solution, the easier it will be come. When you are faced with a challenging situation, ask yourself, "What are the possible solutions I can create for this problem?" "What are the steps necessary for me to overcome this situation?" A problem or challenge will be the end-all only if you let it be, so challenge it instead!

When adversity comes at you, find a space for solitude and reflection. Let yourself focus on the solution and see what surfaces. Oftentimes, just the perspective of a third party can help you. Sometimes we can get so focused on the problem that we forget to use the resources we have: friends, family, research, reading—any resource that can help you think outside the box. This is usually when the solution will magically appear.

EXERCISE E9-2: FINDING SOLUTIONS

1. Define the problem.

2. Shift your focus. What are three (3) possible solutions for your problem?

3. Reach out. Connect with your resources. Who can you ask for help? Ask three people to suggest a solution to your problem.

4. Create a list of things you CAN do instead of what you can't do.

5. Write it all down. Believe it or not, just the act of writing things down on paper stimulates your brain and boosts brain activity so that you can come up with even more solutions!

REALISTIC OPTIMISM

At the core of most self-help books is the idea that we need to develop a positive outlook on life and focus on the positive things in life. Of course, in this book, like the others, I have focused on this concept as well, but I speak from my personal experience of overcoming depression. Every little thing you do and every little shift you make in your life will lead you closer to the life that you want to live. However, I want to remind you to also be realistic about what you want to achieve. Whether it's overcoming depression, or just developing a mindset that will help you conquer your life and have it be at your mercy instead of letting it dictate your every move, make your goals and expectations realistic. Since self-development is a life-long journey and it takes time for things to unfold, don't be discouraged if you aren't making fast progress. This book is designed to help you on your journey, but it is not a magic formula where change will happen overnight and all of your problems will disappear.

That is why it is important for you to have "realistic optimism" so that you do not get disappointed when things do not work out exactly as you anticipated they would. "Realistic optimism is the ability to maintain a positive outlook without denying reality, and actively appreciating the positive aspects of a situation without ignoring the negative aspects. It means aspiring and hoping for a positive outcome, and working toward those outcomes, without assuming that those outcomes are a foregone conclusion."[4] *Realistic optimism* restores balance to your life. You are not a Pollyanna, only seeing lollypops and balloons in your future, but neither are you a pessimist, expecting doom and gloom around every corner. You are willing to deal with the negatives while capitalizing on the positives.

MEDITATING AND STRESS MANAGEMENT

Combating your negative programming can be done through many different avenues. One of the most useful tools I've discovered is learning to meditate. Meditating is the best way to quiet your restless thoughts and gives you a break from your overactive mind. Meditating also helps to reduce the chatter and mental fog caused by information overload from everyday experiences. Moreover, it is a way to avoid wreaking havoc on your physical and mental health.

Meditation? Bo-o-or-ing! I'm sure you've heard a million times that meditating is good for you, but you just cannot seem to get yourself to do it. I will be completely honest; meditation has completely changed my life and I will attribute my freedom from depression to it. Surprised? There's a reason why it's becoming so mainstream—because it works! So how does meditating really help you? Well first, it shuts up that annoying voice in your head that you hear all the time! Imagine going on a vacation to the Greek Islands for the very first time. You just got off the plane and are headed straight to the ocean. You're cruising through Santorini's cobblestone streets, mesmerized by the blue and white hues of the beautiful Greek homes.

You find a quaint restaurant with spectacular views of the ocean. You walk up to the edge of the restaurant, taking in the magnificent views. You take a deep breath, inhaling in the fresh air. You feel at peace, fully enveloped in the moment. Oh wait, there's no chatter in your head! Just a sense of stillness and appreciation. That's weird! There you go. You just experienced a quick meditation. Now, how peaceful was that? Was it nice not to think about the past or worry about the future? The mind is constantly overactive and, thus meditation is a necessity! Meditation helps you dissociate from your thoughts and gives you a break from the mental chatter. In addition, there are so many health benefits to meditating:

- Reducing stress and anxiety

- Promoting emotional health

- Enhancing self-awareness

- Improving memory and focus, among others.

Meditating helps with your perception because it provides an accessible part of you where you can safely review past traumatic events and the meanings you attach to them. You can even change how you look at them (shifting your perspective). A few moments of stillness also breaks the cycle of repetitive and limiting thought patterns that you associate with a particular event.

Richard Davidson, a pioneering psychologist discovered that meditating altered the brain's wiring and increased gray matter in the brain, which is responsible for improvements in self-awareness, empathy, increased memory, and reduced stress. Meditation not only alters your brain chemistry but has been proven to improve people's overall health. Even just a few minutes of stillness each day is enough to create subtle changes in the brain. These subtle changes lead to massive growth over time.[5]

In addition to meditation being able to change the gray matter in our brains, it also can help regulate our brain waves. When we are constantly stressed, we will have more incoherent brain braves. However, if we learn to meditate daily, this can change our brain waves, and in turn reduce our stress levels. During the 1970s, Les Fehmi, a pioneer in biofeedback studies, discovered that there was a method for teaching people to change their brain waves from beta to alpha levels. This was accomplished through narrow-focus meditation.[6] In other words, meditating while you are focused on a specific thing. Meditating while narrowing your focus changes your brain wave patterns. When you are able to change these brain waves, your life becomes more balanced overall. If you look at the different brain waves below[7], you can see that prolonged practice of meditation causes a person to have more coherent brain waves which results in better stress management and overall mental health. That is why meditation is essential to creating a more cohesive life.

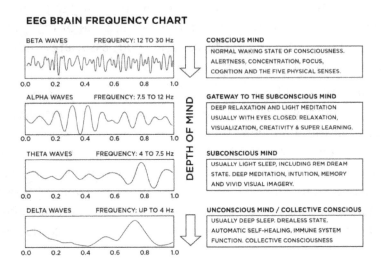

https://www.mind-your-reality.com/brain_waves.html

You may have misconceptions about meditating. I know I did when I first started. You probably assume that it's annoyingly time-consuming and boring. How could it be possible for me to just not think—and for how long? You probably think meditating is sitting with your eyes closed and trying to fight yourself to block out the thoughts that flow in. This isn't necessarily true. There are many different kinds of meditation that can be relaxing or fun. Anytime you are learning a new skill there is always a learning curve, but think back to the Four Stages of Learning. There will be a point where, like riding a bike, when meditating will become just as easy and effortless.

For example, you can do a walking meditation where you are fully present. This is best done outdoors, where you can breathe and feel nature in all its glory. Go to your favorite spot. When you are there, really focus on being present and in the moment. Feel the sensations of the external world as they collide with your internal world. For example, if you are walking in a park, begin to notice the small nuances that are happening. Try to connect with that moment. If you see a beautiful flower, look at it deeply. Appreciate the vibrant colors. Feel the softness of the petal against your skin. If you feel a breeze, close your eyes and really take in that fresh air. Feel how it refreshes your face and ruffles your hair. With each step you take, feel the earth beneath you and feel how connected you are to the Earth. Most of us have had moments of meditation at one time or other, we just didn't realize it. Have you ever been completely wrapped up in your favorite song, singing at the top of your lungs, or dancing and laughing under the moonlit sky with someone you love? If so, you have experienced a form of "walking meditation."

Meditating is essentially any small moment when we are fully present and not listening to the chatter of our conscious mind.

Many of us continue to live in the past or worry about the future—both of which are completely out of the grasp of our control. Of course, this is normal because not knowing what will happen in the future is a common fear, so we often hold onto the pain of the past for dear life. Consequently, we forget to live in the present and enjoy the "here and now," which is all that we really have. Eckhart Tolle explains it this way:

"All you have is this moment. The past is gone and the future isn't here yet. Thoughts of the past happen in this moment. Visions of the future happen in this moment. Your point of power is now."[8]

Meditating has numerous health benefits and it also helps give you the ability to manage stressful situations. Most people are so busy with their lives every day that they forget to do something as simple as breathing. When you're "too busy" chasing whatever it is that you are chasing, in the end it will have unhealthy repercussions. That is why it is necessary to learn how to relax and take care of your mind and body. In addition to meditating, take time every day to help you relieve some stress. This will help you remain in a calm mood and give you clarity as you go through your day.

Side note: As you begin your meditation practice, understand that it might take some time before you feel its full effects. You may need to practice a few times before you begin to feel lighter, less stressed, and in the flow. Try to be consistent and persevere at it. You will reap surprising rewards if you are committed to the process.

EXERCISE E9-3: MEDITATION

MINDFULNESS

For beginners, I recommend mindfulness. Mindfulness is simply the act of being aware of your thoughts and not attaching emotions to them. To practice, do the following:

- Find a comfortable place to sit or lie down, a place free from distractions.
- Close your eyes and take three deep, long breaths.
- Begin to be aware of the thoughts that you are currently having.
- Let them float in and out of your mind like a cloud floating in the sky.

- Then imagine that you are taking a step back and simply watching these thoughts.
- Here, you are viewing them as if watching them on a big screen TV, but yet, you are not emotionally attached to them.

There you have it! You have just done a one-minute meditation. You can start with just a minute or two and slowly, gradually, build up to more time.

WALKING MEDITATION

A *walking meditation* is best done outside, where you can breathe, be fully present, and feel nature in all its glory.

- Go to your favorite outdoor place.
- While you are there, focus on being present and in the moment.
- Feel the sensations of the external world as it collides with your internal world. For example, if you are walking in a park, begin to notice the small nuances that are going on.
- Try to connect with that moment. If you see a beautiful flower, look at it deeply. See the vibrant colors that it exudes. Feel the softness of the petal against your skin. If you feel a breeze, close your eyes and really take in that fresh air. Feel how it refreshes your face and ruffles your hair. With each step you take, feel the ground beneath you and feel how connected you are to the Earth.

Most of us already meditate, we just don't realize it.

BREATHING

Breathing is a process that is unconscious and automatic. However, if we consciously regulate our breath, we can help to manage our moods, feelings, energy levels, and reduce stress. Think about a time when you were tense, upset, and angry. How do you start breathing? Did you notice how rapidly you were breathing while you were feeling these negative emotions? You discovered earlier that stress can induce a response from your sympathetic nervous system when you are tense and stressed. That is why we must learn to regulate our breathing in these types of situations. Spending some time each day focusing on your breathing is not only calming and centering, but will allow you to better regulate your body and mind.

EXERCISE E9-4: BREATHING TECHNIQUES:

Practice these breathing techniques starting twice a day and see how much it will begin to improve your calmness and decrease your stress levels

A. NADHI SODHANA (PURIFYING BREATH)

This breathing technique involves alternate nostril breathing. It helps quiet the mind and is known as one of the best exercises for reducing stress and anxiety. This technique also helps settle the nervous system.

How to do Nadhi Sodhana:

1. Sit up tall, in a relaxed and comfortable position.

2. With your right hand, cover the right side of your nostril with your thumb.

3. Inhale through your left nostril and close it with another finger.

4. Exhale through your right nostril and release your thumb. Inhale through the same nostril and breathe out through your left nostril as you close the right nostril with the thumb again.

5. Alternate between both nostrils. When you feel like you are comfortable with the exercise, inhale for 4 seconds then exhale for eight (8) seconds.

6. Repeat up to ten (10) minutes.

B. BREATH OF FIRE

This technique of breathing originates from Kundalini yoga and meditation. The Breath of Fire is a rhythmic breathing that focuses on a short inhale and exhale. It is great because it helps rejuvenate your body in a fast and efficient way. The Breath of Fire will purify your blood and re-oxygenate your whole body, leaving you feeling refreshed, centered, and calm. It can help you regain control when dealing with stressful situations. Most importantly, it helps strengthen and balance your nervous system.

How to do The Breath of Fire:

It will take time to build up to the optimum level for the Breath of Fire, so don't be in a hurry. As a beginner, start with 30 seconds at a slow rate. Here is how Amber Scriven of *Do You Yoga*[9] says to do this exercise:

1. "Sit up tall, lengthening the space between your navel and your heart.

2. "Breathe in and out through your nose and start to pull your abdomen in during the exhale, while you press it out during the inhale. Imagine your belly filling up with air during the inhale and use your abdominal muscles to push the air out during the exhale.

3. "Start to shorten each breath and pick up the pace. The breathing should be loud and quick.

4. "Try to equalize the inhale and the exhale in both strength and length."

Imagine yourself panting like a dog, but through your nose with your mouth closed. Push your belly out with each pant. I know this is a funny image but it is the easiest way to visualize it.

Amber adds, "Tingling is completely normal (and quite wonderful!). After a while, you may do 2-3 sets of 30 seconds with a few smooth, long breaths in between. One day in the future, you will reach four minutes at a rate of four breaths per second."

C. UJJAYI BREATHING:

Ujjayi Breathing is a *pranayama* (breathing exercise) in Yoga[10] that can help you calm yourself and invigorate your mind and body while relaxing you deeply. This breathing technique is especially beneficial for our purposes because it helps you block out distractions while creating a space for awareness and relaxation within yourself.

How to do Ujjayi Breathing

1. Sit up tall, in a relaxed and comfortable position.

2. Inhale and exhale deeply through your mouth. Feel the air as it passes through your body.

3. As you exhale, contract the back of our throat, and softly whisper the sound "ahh" as you exhale.

4. Once you feel accustomed to breathing like this through your mouth, close your mouth and begin to breathe through your nose.

5. Let your inhalations and exhalations fill your lungs up to full expansion. Focus on the breath as you breathe in and out. Concentrate on the sound of your breath and let this sound bring you into a deeper sense of relaxation.

CREATING A VISION—THE HERO!

Have you ever thought about what your dream life looks like? Every person needs to have a purpose, something that they are trying to accomplish in life. A vital part of the Hero's Journey is finding this sense of purpose. At the depths of my despair as I went through my depression, I felt so lost and lacked a purpose in life. This lack of purpose made me question the meaning of being alive and made me wonder, *What's the point of it all*? As I worked through my traumas, healed old wounds, and learned how to change my behavior, I was left with not knowing what to do next. At this point, it was crucial for me to uncover my purpose in life. It was not until I defined my vision and understood what I really wanted out of life that I became motivated to chase after my dream life and tap into my superhero potential. My life purpose and mission became the driving forces that pushed me to reach the greatest depths of who I am.

Now that we are progressively unhooking you from the past, it's time to find your passion and mission in this lifetime.

Beyond the limitations you have set for yourself, who are you deep down to the core? It doesn't matter what you believed in the past. It doesn't matter if you've failed a few times, if you bombed a test, if you didn't have a successful or healthy relationship, or if you were unable to make money to support yourself. The future is bright and you can create anything that you want for yourself. You just have to start! It is time to reclaim your power and acknowledge the limitless potential you have. But first, you need to discover your calling!

TAPPING INTO YOUR POTENTIAL: FINDING YOUR TREASURE

"The whole idea is that you've got to bring out again that which you went to recover, the unrealized, unutilized potential in yourself. The whole point of this journey is the reintroduction of this potential into the world . . . It goes without saying, this is very difficult. Bringing the boon back can be even more difficult than going down into your own depths in the first place."[11]

—Joseph Campbell

Remember in high school or college when you took chemistry and learned about *kinetic* and *potential energy*? *Kinetic energy* is energy that is in an object because it is in motion. *Potential energy* is energy that an object has due to its relative position to another object. You can basically view yourself as a being who contains both kinetic and potential energy. All of us have potential within us, waiting to be accessed. Your potential energy is your higher-self or inner-mentor, silently waiting until potential energy transfers into kinetic energy. Once you tap into this potential, you will build momentum and become the kinetic energy, or the person you've always wanted to be. All you have to do is start learning the new behaviors and beliefs that can free you from negative behavioral patterns. Start by letting go of any preconceived notions of who you think you are and what you've learned. Make a conscious effort to break the bonds that connect you to the past, which is an archaic version of yourself. By doing this, you will begin to open up the potential for awakening the hero within you and tap into a greater gravitational force of happiness and freedom.

First, you must figure out what it is that you really want, and you have to clarify your values. Something that you find valuable has a huge significance in your life. It's something you strive for or something you live your life according to. Values are important because they are the motivating factors in helping us create fulfilling lives. They are "the driving force behind you," according to Tony Robbins,[12] as they are the reasons behind our thoughts and actions.

Growing up in America, a nation of extreme consumerism and materialism, taught me that the most important things you should value are *money* and *material gain*. The more you buy or have, the more valuable you are to society. This corrupt perspective has caused a huge epidemic of unhappiness. In the end, this plethora of material things equates to nothing of true value. Children are taught that if they don't have the latest cell phone or brand-name shoe, that they themselves have no value—that they are not enough. As this thought permeates into their belief system, it teaches them that the only way they will ever be happy and fulfilled is if they buy more things. Since the values of most people are so distorted, it's no wonder that depression rates continue to rise.

So, how do we reverse the effect of society that has led us to believe that we are not enough unless we have all the things, statuses, and power in the world? We have to look deep within ourselves and evaluate what it is that we truly value.

Values represent our individual essence and what matters to us. They are the compass and guide to living a life according to what's really important to us. Values are either intrinsic or extrinsic. When something has intrinsic value, it has value in itself and not because you can get something out of it. When something has extrinsic value, there is usually an outcome you gain from it. When most people are posed the question, "What do you value in life and what are the most important things to you?" many people answer this question at a surface level. They believe that money, status, and possessions demonstrate their true value. However, if you dive deeper, you will come to understand that these values actually give you things much deeper—such as *love, freedom*, and *happiness*.

The brain will attribute value to many things on a logical level. You can look at money and a beautiful car and know that they have value, but what is it about the money and the beautiful car that give them value? If you analyze this, you will realize that you give value to these things because they can produce some desired outcome—for example, helping you gain status, freedom or recognition. These items would not be valuable if they did not give you something that you wanted, so they only have extrinsic value. On the other hand, you might look at a worn-out, used book and see no value in it. You see no value in it because it does not produce the results you want it to produce. In other words, it doesn't add to your status, freedom, or recognition.

You can also assign value to something intrinsically. This means that you value this object or action regardless of any desired outcomes. There are no expectations that you will get anything from this; you just value it because it is important to you. These intrinsic values for most people are often love, happiness, and freedom. Overall, extrinsic values are really a cover-up for intrinsic values. Intrinsic values are what is really important to you at the core. The superficial stuff is just a way for you to reach for the intrinsic value you desperately seek. When we are unaware of our true values, we risk becoming stuck in a "value trap."[13] A value trap is something that you believe is giving you real or intrinsic value when, in fact, it does not.

For a long time, I always valued having material possessions because I felt that they would give me the status and recognition I desperately craved. I thought these "things" would make me feel as if I were enough and that it would solve my problems. However, after some time, I realized that these material possessions never truly fulfilled me. They did not complete my intrinsic value of "being enough." Every time I bought a new item, I was ecstatic and high for a few hours or days until the high wore off. Then I still felt the same way as I did before— insufficient. This put me in the "value trap," tricking me into believing that the more things I obtained, the more whole I would feel. This need for more drove me absolutely insane.

It drove me into depression as I kept trying to fill my void. Because I put so much value on external things, I never truly felt fulfilled. Tony Robbins said, "Success without fulfillment is the ultimate failure."[14] This quote has remained embedded in my mind. I had thought that material possessions equaled "success" and that this "success" would make me whole. If you focus on external values, you will never be truly satisfied. Fulfillment is necessary for you to be truly happy and thus it is absolutely necessary for you to define your values.

Defining your values will help you focus on the things that are most important to you and help you evaluate if you are living according to them. When you live according to your values, you will feel aligned with your true purpose in life! We're not only going to look at your surface level values, but we are going to dive deeper to explore what you truly value in life.

EXERCISE E9-5: DEFINING YOUR VALUES

Take a look at this *Chart of Values*. This is a list of values recognized by experts in the field as the most critical for our wellbeing. (For the complete list, see James Clear's self-improvement website[15].)

Pick out your top five values. If you have a value that is not listed below, feel free to add it to your list. This exercise is about you and what's important to YOU! Think about what these values mean to you. Grab some paper and write about their meaning and how they contribute to your happiness:

AUTHENTICITY	FREEDOM	MASTERY
ACHIEVEMENT	FUN	MEANINGFUL WORK
ADVENTURE	GROWTH	MONEY
AUTONOMY	HAPPINESS	OPTIMISM
BALANCE	HEALTH	PEACE
BEAUTY	HELPING OTHERS/SOCIETY	PLEASURE
COMPASSION	HONESTY	RECOGNITION
COMMUNITY	HUMOR	RESPECT
CONNECTEDNESS	INDEPENDENCE	RESPONSIBILITY
CONTRIBUTION	INSPIRATION	SECURITY
CREATIVITY	INTEGRITY	SERVICE
FAITH	KNOWLEDGE	SPIRITUALITY
FAME	LEADERSHIP	STABILITY
FRIENDSHIP	LEARNING	SUCCESS
FREEDOM	LOVE	TEACHING
FUN	LOYALTY	TRUST
GROWTH	MAKING A DIFFERENCE	WEALTH
FRIENDSHIP		WISDOM

Look at your list of values. Can you break them down even further? For example, perhaps you wrote down that wealth is one of your values, think about it deeper. What does wealth bring you? Does it bring you freedom? Does it buy you time to spend with those who are important to you? Does it provide you the opportunity to do all the things you've always wanted to do?

After defining your values, take a look at your life and think about it. Are you living up to your value system? Or, is your life not really connected with the values you hold dear? Sometimes when you live life in a way that does not satisfy your values, you tend to be disconnected from your true or higher self. You are like a plant whose roots have been cut off. Being disconnected from one's true self can lead to unhappiness and dissatisfaction in your life. This disconnection from your values is like the "value trap" I mentioned earlier. You chase one thing because you think it will bring you happiness, but in reality, it might take you further away from what you want to attain.

Once you are able to define your values and decide if you are living up to them, the next step is to identify your life purpose. Identifying your life purpose will allow you to integrate the essence of who you are—your values, gifts, and talents, and ways you can serve others—with your dreams for the future.

Figuring out your life purpose can be challenging; but, with this book, the tools that can make this process seamless for you are right at your fingertips:

Let's first take a look at your strengths. Instead of focusing on what you're not good at, let's focus on what you have already excelled at. What you are good at is another clue to what you're meant to be doing with your life! To help you figure out what you have to offer to the world, we are going to do a strengths-finder exercise. What is a strength? A strength is a natural way of thinking, feeling, or behaving that is absolutely innate in you.

This **strength formula** lets you see
what ingredients go into a strength:

Talent

(a natural way of thinking, feeling, or behaving)

+

Time Investment (time spent developing your skills and
building your knowledge base)

=

Strength

Or, re-stated: *Talent + Time Investment = Strength*

EXERCISE E9-6: STRENGTH-FINDER[16]

Your Strength-Finder

Below are a series of questions that will help you discover your
true strengths. On a sheet of paper or your journal, answer
them and see whether your answers agree with what you think
your strengths are:

Clues to Your Strengths:

◇ What activities are you naturally drawn to?

◇ What type of activities do you seem to pick up quickly?

◇ In what activities do you automatically know the steps that need to be taken?

◇ During what activities have you had moments of subconscious excellence when you thought, "Wow! How did I do that?"

◇ What activities give you a euphoric feeling or "kick" either while doing them or immediately afterwards, and you think, "When can I do that again!?"

Identifying your strengths gives you clues into your true purpose in life! As you start to define your life purpose, your strengths play a critical part. They point you in the direction of your true purpose in life.

Ask Yourself:

◇ What do I have the most fun doing?

◇ What is something that I can get lost in? (like reading, my hobby, jogging, playing sports, etc.)

◇ If I had all the money in the world, what would I do?

◇ What am I passionate about?

◇ What makes me really happy?

◇ What does success mean to me? What does it look like?

◇ What are the most important things in life to me?

◇ How do I want to contribute to the world?

◇ What do I want to be remembered for when I'm gone? What do I want my legacy to be?

The Ikigai:

The Ikigai is a Japanese concept that gives you the *formula to happiness and meaning in life*. The word, "Ikigai," basically means the reason you get up every morning. The Ikigai is the common ground between:

◇ What you love

◇ What you care about

◇ What the world needs

◇ What you can get paid for[17]

EXERCISE E9-7: IKIGAI

Write down your Ikigai using the list above. This will provide clues as to what your purpose in life will be. The Ikigai can serve as a compass to navigate a fulfilling life and career and is one method you can use to define your life's purpose. I like using the Ikigai because it gives you a visual representation and you can see the connections.

Look over this diagram and explore how your Ikigai can help you find your life purpose:

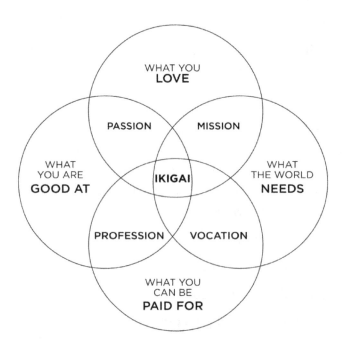

LIFE PURPOSE STATEMENT

There is so much power in the clarity of knowing why you are here. That is why it is extremely important to determine your life purpose. Having a life purpose will guide you to living a happy, fulfilling life. It will also be a reminder that you are living for something much bigger than yourself. Give yourself some time to contemplate this. What is the legacy you want to leave behind? What is your purpose in this life? How do you intend to accomplish it? And what is the reason behind this life purpose? When you know your "why," this will be your driving force and you will never give up. Tony Robbins said, "Fear will drive you until you find something so powerful that it pulls you towards the direction of your dreams."[18] If you want to leave something behind for future generations, you have to lay down the foundation so that others can model after you.

When you live your life on purpose, you will be doing things that make you happy and excited! You will live passionately and wholeheartedly while pursuing something you love. Singer, actor and songwriter, Marc Anthony, once said it this way: "Do what you love, and you'll never work a day in your life."[19] Having a life purpose provides a blueprint for you, and you will work even harder because you know you're doing something that you love!

So start thinking! What is the one thing you want more than anything else? Be specific and clear when describing it to yourself. Know what you want, when you want it, why you want it, and how you intend to get it. THINK BIG! What makes you get excited? What are you passionate about? What do you want to have? If you could do anything in the world and you had enough money to do it, what would you do? There's no possibility of rejection or failure as you brainstorm about this. Stretch your mind to take in the possibilities! What would you do? Who would you be? What would your everyday life look like? How would you spend your time?

Write your thoughts down on paper or type them into your phone so you have your thoughts and dreams handy. This is meant to be interactive, and I have something I want you to do. I want you to be clear on your life purpose; so, do the exercise below:

EXERCISE E9-8: LIFE PURPOSE

1. List two unique personal qualities that you know you possess. You may select from the qualities below or write others that describe your tendencies, approach to life, and personality:

◇ Creative

◇ Intelligent

◇ Enthusiasm

◇ Humorous

◇ Knowledgeable

◇ Courageousness

◇ Compassionate

◇ Artistic

2. List one or two ways you enjoy expressing those qualities when interacting with others. For example:

◇ Inspire

◇ Empower

◇ Uplift

◇ Support

◇ Cultivate

◇ Educate

◇ Create

3. List your top two (2) passions:

4. List your top two (2) strengths:

5. 5. List two worldly causes that are extremely important to you (mental health, homelessness, environment, etc.) or ways that you want to impact the world:

6. Look at your answers to 1-5 and create a statement that shows your life purpose:

Here is an example of a purpose statement. (This one is actually mine!):

My life purpose is to use my creativity and knowledge to inspire, uplift, and empower others to reach their fullest potential and create their dream life.

Another example of a life purpose statement:

To use my gifts of intelligence, charisma, and serial optimism to cultivate the self-worth and net-worth of women around the world.[20] —Amanda Steinberg

The following two quotes from Napoleon Hill really changed my life:

The secret to getting everything you want and doing big things is having a definite purpose.[21]

From the very moment that you make this choice, this purpose becomes the dominating thought in your consciousness, and you are constantly on the alert for facts information and knowledge with which to achieve that purpose. From the time that you plant a definite purpose in your mind, your mind begins both consciously and unconsciously to gather and store away the material with which you are to accomplish that purpose.[22]

When you have a definite purpose, you can forge a path for yourself in this world. Moreover, following that path makes it easier to live aligned with that purpose! You will no longer feel lost or confused, but have a sense of clarity about what it means to be alive. Having this purpose will connect you to your higher self and it will be the foundation of your life.

Once you've decided on your life purpose, it's time to pick one thing that you can specialize in. Specialized knowledge is extremely powerful, so dedicate your energy to that one thing. Before I gained clarity in my purpose, I made the mistake of trying to learn as much as I could about everything and became, in a sense, a "jack of all trades." I thought this was the answer. As admirable as that is, it is self-defeating. My energy was spread out across so many different subjects that I became even more confused as to my purpose. Spreading your energy thin like this just leads to more indecision! This is because we get "information overload." We are living in a technological era and constantly being fed SO MUCH information that at some point, we cannot process it all. The truth is that our conscious minds are only able to process 120 bits per second[23]. It's easy to get distracted and be pulled in many directions because we are bombarded with much information each day.

What's the solution? *In order to gain mastery in any subject, you have to spend time, dedication, and focus into that ONE subject*. So, pick something that you can focus on and give it your all. This is where you will gain power. Spend the necessary time to develop your skills in that one area and one day this skill will become your talent. Staying focused on mastering your art will align you with your purpose, and the end-goal will eventually manifest itself as your new reality. So now is the time to "Put all your eggs in one basket and watch that basket grow"[24] (Andrew Carnegie).

You see, your potential is infinite. You just have to focus and tap into that power! Once you are clear on your purpose in life, it's easier to navigate through life without feeling lost and confused. Defining your life purpose is an essential part to the Hero's Journey because it is the roadmap for the rest of your life! Create a timeless vision for yourself and dare to live a life beyond boundaries. Let yourself take risks and embark on a journey that will help you transcend your consciousness.

Having a vision is the *first step*. When you have a clear sense of purpose, you can use the powers of the archetypes to help you achieve and accomplish your goals! For example, engage the Thinker, the intellectual side of you, to create a concrete plan to help you accomplish your vision. Your plan of action is your *second step*. What are the steps necessary to get from where you are now to where you want to be? Knowledge without action is useless. The more you plan and prepare, the more you will achieve. (I do want to warn you, though, not to let endless planning prevent you from taking action. Some people try so hard to get all the steps perfect that they never quite get around to actually taking them.) To move forward, you must take action. The *third step* is to break down your goal into small, actionable steps. How can you break the steps down even more so they are workable? What do you need to do now for the best possible outcome?

These three steps will help you have an overview of exactly what you need to do to get from where you are now to where you want to be. Sometimes it is easier to lay it out visually as a diagram. Personally, I like using a mind map when I am setting and planning to reach a goal.

This is fun! Create your own Mind-Map!

EXERCISE E9-9: CREATING A MIND MAP

Grab a blank sheet of paper and a pen.

1. Write down your main goal in the center of a page.

2. On another sheet of paper, write down ten steps you need in order to help you reach your goal.

3. Go back to the page with your main goal. Draw connecting lines to the center and write down each of the ten steps you need to take. This completes your Mind Map!

4. Further break down those ten steps you need to take into small actions that you need to take.

5. After creating a mind-map, it is critical to track your progress. Keep this mind map nearby and check off the items on the list as you complete them. You can review this when you feel like you are not inching closer to reaching your goal.

6. If additional steps pop up along the way don't be afraid to add them to the mind-map. This map will continue to grow as you proceed along the way to attaining your life's purpose.

Here are two examples of my personal mind maps so you can see what a mind map looks like:

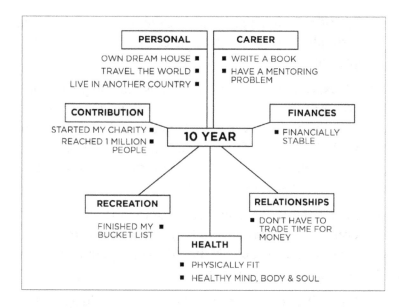

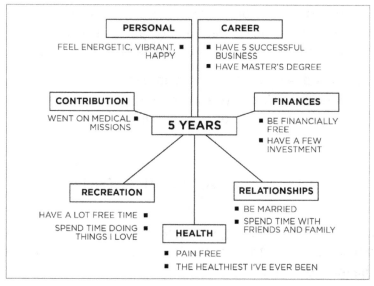

When setting a goal, always remember the word S.M.A.R.T.[25]:

◇ **Specific**: Create a goal that is exact and targeted. Keep it simple. Your goal should be clear and specific so that you can focus all your efforts on it.

◇ **Measurable**: Choose a goal that is meaningful to you (You can measure it in terms of: net worth, how you feel, happiness level, etc.). What would it mean if you achieved this goal? It is important to have a measurable goal so that you can track your progress and stay motivated.

◇ **Achievable**: (Has it worked for someone else?) Consider all areas of your life, starting now. Your goal should be attainable; it should stretch your abilities but still be possible to reach.

◇ **Realistic and Responsible**: Your goal should also be realistic based on any constraints you might have. It should also be relevant and responsible. It should be a goal that moves you toward what you really want.

◇ **Timed**: Always set a target date for your goal. Having a deadline will give you something to focus on and make sure that you complete it in a timely manner.

OPTIMIZING YOUR GOALS

Once you are done setting your goals, it's time to factor them down and optimize them to see how you can reach your goals in the most efficient way.

CFAR has a "goal factoring" technique in which you can reduce your goals down so that you can reach them more easily and effectively. You can use this technique to help you factor down any goals. It's similar to factoring in algebra class, when you have an equation that is factored down to a solution. Many people tend to focus on the in-between steps, but typically there is one thing that you can do which will trigger massive growth toward your goals.

To factor down your goals, do the following exercise:

1. Pick a goal that you want to accomplish. You can pick one from your mind-map to focus on and practice.

2. Decide why it is important for you to reach this goal.

3. Once you know your "why," think of the action steps you need to take to accomplish this goal.

4. Create a list of action steps you need to take to reach this goal.

5. Brainstorm possible ways you can tackle the goal; focus on the ones that are more efficient and will help you reach the goal faster.

6. Think of your goal and what it will cost you. Will it cost you money, time, effort?

Example:

Before I became a life coach and hypnotherapist, I considered going back to school to become a psychologist. That would mean that I would need to go back to school, obtain my Bachelor's, Master's, and Ph.D. degrees to get there. To get all three degrees it could take me up to an additional six plus years. I had a limiting belief that people would not trust me if I didn't have X, Y, Z credentials that to prove that I was reliable and good at what I do. Even with my background as a psychiatric nurse, I did not feel qualified enough to help people. However, as I looked at my main goal of "being able to help people through helping them shift their mindset," I realized there were many alternatives I could take to reach that same goal. That's when I brainstormed different things that I could do to help me get from where I was to where I wanted to be. Instead of going the traditional route, I decided to take workshops to learn about Neurolinguistic Programming, enrolled in Marisa Peer's Rapid Transformational Therapy program, and continued reading books to help broaden my knowledge of different methods I could use to help people transform their mindsets.

Notice how I used the S.M.A.R.T technique: I named specific traditional steps to reach my goal, and then named specific non-traditional steps that could get me to the same goal. The goal was measurable because it let me achieve my life purpose. The steps were realistic for me. The steps were timed and had a target date because they let me reach my goal within the time-frame I was considering.

I also laid out my steps in a Goals Schematic so that I could quickly glance at my options and keep track of my progress. You can make one, too. Mine shows how I found two equally viable paths to take toward my goal. List your short-term and long-term goals and follow the exercises below to create a schematic that maps out realistic and practical ways to achieve your goals.

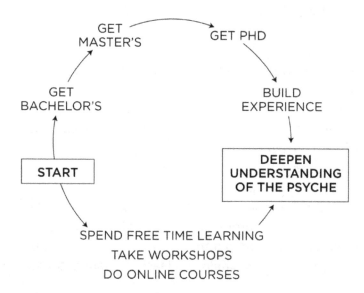

Once you have completed the above exercises, you will have a roadmap laid out to guide you on your journey. This roadmap will help you stay focused on your end goal, whether it's overcoming fears of the past or creating the life of your dreams.

HARNESSING ARCHETYPES TO SUPPORT YOUR LIFE PURPOSE

You have seen how several of the *archetypes* can be used to help you determine your Life's Purpose and explore ways to achieve it. Look over the four archetypes below and see how they can help to enhance the steps you are taking toward your Life Purpose. These archetypes are redefined as a way to support you on your journey. You can harness the power of these archetypes to help you on your journey.

CHANNELING THE LIGHT ARCHETYPE - BIOLOGICAL CONSTELLATIONS

Once you have a clear sense of purpose, you can use the powers of the archetypes to help you achieve and accomplish your goals! The following Jungian archetypes are often grouped together as *biological constellations*. They tend to energize each other and provide you with additional strength. Consequently, as biological constellations, they will help you tap into your true potential. They can also enable you to add new dimensions for potential to your life purpose. The following exercises will help you learn to channel them:

THE HERO- DREAMER-MAGICIAN

The Hero's role is to keep you aligned with your higher self. It's the part of you that contains all of the answers. He embodies everything that is honorable and true to all 12 virtues. You can combine the Hero's strength with the daring nature of the Dreamer and Magician to make your dreams a reality. The combination of all three archetypes gives you the power to create new possibilities and realize your dreams. The Hero also has a "vision" or a life purpose that guides him along his journey.

The Hero will help you with your creative vision. Engage in the Law of Attraction to help you create the reality that you desire. Spend at least ten minutes a day doing this visualization exercise where you imagine that your dream has come true. What does that look like? How do you feel? After you do the visualization, write it down. The more you visualize this image and read about it, the more likely it will become true. Your mind cannot discern imagination from reality, so the more you visualize your vision, the closer you are bringing that image into reality. When I became a hypnotherapist, I learned from Marisa Peer that the mind is constantly working for you, to help you create the reality you want, however, in order for it to do this, it is necessary for you to tell it and feed it the things that you want it to help you achieve.

THE SAGE (THINKER)

The Sage (Thinker) archetype is also known as the wise old man. This archetype is blessed with wisdom, knowledge and power. The Sage will help you utilize your brain to come up with steps that will help you reach your goals. Because he is the seeker of truth, he will constantly challenge himself (and you) with self-reflection questions which help you both grow and master critical skills. His meaningful introspection helps him brilliantly come up with solutions and much better ways to accomplish things.

The Sage will act as your inner guidance system, never letting you get far off course—if you listen to him. He will keep you from making impulsive or thoughtless mistakes. You can use meditation to connect with the sage part of your higher self. Ask him: What do I need to know right now as I travel this leg of my journey? What is the wisest step that I can take next? How can I prioritize my life so that it aligns with my purpose?

THE LOVER

The Lover is the part of you that is emotional and seeks connection. It's also the part of you that will give your work all the effort you need from the bottom of your heart. This fills everything you do with passion, and this passion creates a magnetizing radiance that touches the people around you.

Life is lackadaisical without passion. So, whatever it is that you want to accomplish, do it with tenacity and draw from the burning passion you have within. Use 100% effort in whatever you do, because this energy will take you to greater potentials.

To reconnect with your Lover, do things that ignite the fire within you. What is something that you love to do? That brings you endless joy? What brings you a sense of motivation and hope? Connect with this side of yourself whenever you notice that your spark is fading and you need a boost of encouragement.

The Lover is also about connecting with other people through love. This can be through intimate relationships or just friendships. If you are lacking connection in your life, brainstorm some ideas about where you can connect with other people, either people you are close to or even those in need. Spend some time volunteering at a charity or feeding the homeless to help you reconnect with other communities.

The Lover embodies living from the heart and not just the mind. It's great to be practical and analytical when the situation calls for it, but remember that if you live motivated only by logic and reason, life will not be as rewarding. When you live life from your heart, your life will overflow with abundance and passion. It will lift your quality of life and allow you to feel fulfilled while you follow your dreams.

THE WARRIOR

The Warrior is the part of you that will take action and persist through it all, even when faced with the most adversity. It will help you fight with purpose. The Warrior is the one with confidence, strength, discipline, and bravery.

The Warrior will help you move toward your vision, breaking down your plan into small steps, and help you do this every day. It has the drive and willingness to overcome any challenges. It is the go-getter. It will build up your internal strength so that you can rely on it when facing any ordeals. The Warrior also embodies patience, resilience, and perseverance, which will all be discussed in the next chapter.

"The process of failing helps us learn and grow through reflection. It opens up our perspective and shows us a new path we need to take in order to succeed. Through failure, there is a trajectory to extraordinary greatness."

~ *Julia*

CHAPTER 10:
THE ROAD BACK

Failing Forward

OKAY, SO NOW that you have defined your life's purpose, you are inching closer to the special world of the hero. The journey continues and does not stop here. The hero's journey is a treacherous one and it's only for the brave! When I defined my life purpose, I was so excited and filled with creative energy! It gave me the boost I needed and it helped encourage me to start living and doing what was necessary to achieve my end goals. However, no one told me how hard it would be! I had built up all of this momentum when I learned my true purpose. I designed a plan, became creative, and started living aligned with "my purpose." I was doing everything I thought I needed to do, but somehow, I felt like I had gotten nowhere. The momentum built up and lasted for several months. I was on fire, sparked by creativity and imagination and everything felt so right! I felt vibrant and alive until one day, the momentum stopped, fear kicked in, and I became discouraged. I was in the middle of creating inspirational videos and workbooks, and then the feeling of being overwhelmed took over my entire life. It felt like the depression was kicking in again and I felt like a failure. "I can't do this!" I thought frustrated with myself. "I'm a failure and I can never finish what I start. Stupid me for being so optimistic. Maybe this 'live your life on purpose' is all bullshit."

The voice of my ego had kicked in again and it was there with a vengeance. It's true—the biggest battle you will ever have in your life is the battle you have with your own mind. I let the vicious thoughts take over my newfound self and they made me feel weak and small again. For six months, I was frozen in time, suspended once again by this heavy cloud hanging above my head. The thoughts continued, verifying that I was not good enough and that I was not capable. During this time, I was really unhappy and disappointed in myself. I woke up every day dreading the alarm. I went to work every day feeling more lost and confused. At this time, I was slaving away working for someone else's dream, feeling further and further away from my own. I continued to lean on meditation and reading self-development books to increase my motivation. It faltered. Nothing seemed to work.

Then one day, one of my girlfriends asked me if I wanted to go to a Tony Robbins event. Desperate for help and a way to pull myself out of the rut, I agreed. Attending "Unleash the Power Within"[1] reminded me that all I had to do was reconnect with my higher purpose. I had been so caught up in my mind and ego that I had forgotten my purpose. At the event, I remembered how much I wanted to help people and that was all that mattered. I reconnected with my purpose and reminded myself that the journey will not always be smooth-sailing, but as long as I am persistent and patient, I will inch closer and closer to my goals. So, what I had viewed as a six-month failure, was actually just a detour that was taking me to something better. It's funny how life works, when you're in a rut, sometimes someone shows up along the way to help you on your path. In this case, my friend Tamara was my guide and Tony Robbins was my mentor, reminding me of what I'm capable of.

DISCOVERING HOW TO "FAIL FORWARD"

This six-month ordeal was a crucial learning period for me. It served to remind me that the road to success is not a straight one and that slow progress is better than no progress. There will be ups and downs, just as life ebbs and flows. However, despite my failures, I had to remember that I will always "fail forward." More importantly, hidden within each failure is an important lesson to be learned. Think of it as falling *up* instead of *down* the stairs. Most of us have tripped while running up the stairs. Notice that if you are already moving upward, you tend to fall *up*, not down—*forwards*, not *backwards*. Yes, you pause for a moment to get your footing, but then you continue climbing upward. It's the same with life: *As long as you have momentum and are traveling forward in your journey, so what if you mess up and fail?* Like falling forward, you will fail forward! You haven't lost any ground. Just get up and keep on going!

It would be amazing if we could reach success without all the hardships that come along with it, but this ideal is unrealistic. Unfortunately, life just does not work this way. Part of the Hero's Journey is encountering challenges along the way and learning to bounce back from defeats. The truth is that the only way we can really learn something and grow is if we experience things firsthand—by dealing with failure, feeling the pain, and getting back up and deciding to try once again. *The process of failing helps us learn and grow through reflection. It opens up our perspective and shows us a new path we need to take in order to succeed. Through failure, there is a trajectory to extraordinary greatness.*

RESILIENCE

As I faced this painful growth period, I had to build my resilience and patience. Because I had already committed to this journey, there was no point in turning back. I just had to push forward and master the art of challenging my negative thoughts and beliefs. Being resilient meant that I had to continue to bounce back even though I felt scared and unsure of what the future held. Being patient meant that I had to let life unfold on its own without trying to control situations and outcomes.

Throughout your journey, there will be many trials and tribulations. They are all there to help you build resilience and patience. In the past, I might have let a roadblock stop me in my tracks and prevent me from moving forward. For a while, I had this belief that "I always give up when things get hard," and that was my reality. As time passed and I continued through my journey of self-discovery, I learned that the key to succeeding is resilience. Let's be real, it's easy to give up when things get hard, but when you can surpass the adversity, still survive and make it to the other side, this is where you will obtain the gold. Resilience will massively help you as you go through the trajectory of life. It is a skill that you need to master in order to thrive. Instead of running away, giving up, and feeling helpless, gain the courage to face the adversity bravely and confidently— like a Hero.

Resilience is often needed in aspects of our everyday lives: when facing unexpected situations and challenges, handling daily stress, dealing with difficult people and confrontations, or managing extreme tasks, etc. It is even more important when it comes to facing life-altering situations. When you learn to build resilience, you will be able to overcome any trials and tribulations that come your way. Resilience, along with perseverance, are the keys to moving past the hurdles in life so that you can do what you're meant to do—and that is to flourish! Life will continue to inflict setbacks, but you do not have to succumb to these setbacks every time they accost you. The key is learning to weather the tough times. How? By remembering that you have a purpose, and that you now have resources that you can draw from.

Being resilient means that you will not give up no matter what happens. Being "resilient" means you will continue to nurture and value yourself through the tough times and adversity that come your way. Your resilience will build naturally as you go through The Hero's Journey, but there are always times when you might come to a halt. Your way may be blocked. It's important to show up with a massive amount of courage and flexibility. Learn to adapt to extreme setbacks and difficulties, and remember that in time, these will pass. You will not be in the heart of your deep despair forever, your life will continue to fluctuate with good and bad times. This is the natural rhythm of life. However, how you deal with the situation you are facing is what matters. This is when it's extremely important for you to push through and continue building your resiliency. This resiliency comes through strengthening your sense of self, creating positive self-images, and managing your emotions and impulses in healthy ways.

If you take a look at the most successful people in the world, they can fail one thousand times and still not give up. This is the faith that you have to build within yourself. Know that things will eventually work out as long as you keep trying. You never know what lies ahead. Sometimes a curveball can send you to your next biggest breakthrough! However, if you stop before reaching the finish line, you risk missing the huge opportunities that are to come. If you continue to persevere, I promise you will not regret it.

RESILIENCY IN THE FACE OF PAIN

It's easy to remember past traumatic moments and stress over how they negatively affected your life, but you have to look beyond these events if you want to heal and fulfill your purpose. One of my friends was sexually abused by her father when she was a child. She had to go through many years of therapy to heal this part of her. Rather than choosing to be a victim of this abuse, she decided to become a social worker and help abused children. You can see how resilient she is. She did not let her past dictate her future. Instead, she used it as a way to help others.

I remember the first time I met Melanie, there was something calming about her. My best friend had told me about her before we met. He told me he thought we would get along very well, and I was surprised to find this comfort in her I felt when we first met. I knew we were similar in many ways and we got along just fine as my best friend had predicted. I remember having a conversation with her while we were at dinner one night when she decided to open up and tell me her story. We talked about how we both wanted to help other people, Melanie being a social worker and I, a nurse. At that time, I told Melanie I admired what she did because I didn't feel like I could handle it. I liked helping other people but the mental aspect of it seemed challenging.

When I was younger, before I decided to pursue nursing, I thought I wanted to become a psychologist. However, I decided on nursing because I was worried about the mental strain associated with becoming a psychologist. This was further reinforced when I did a psychiatric rotation in nursing school reading all of the horror stories from patient charts. I felt sad reading about the experiences these people had gone through, and could see how they had become mentally ill and stuck in a psychiatric ward. The empathetic pain I felt as I read the stories made me want to push away this calling. So, when I talked to Melanie and she told me she worked with sexually abused children, I was in awe. Hearing about the children who were abused broke my heart.

Thinking of how overwhelming it must be to deal with their experiences, I asked her, "How are you able to work with these children? Doesn't it really impact you in a negative way? It would make me really depressed."

Melanie gracefully answered, "The reward of being able to help these children is very fulfilling. Knowing that I can help them through their experience makes me feel happy. I can relate with these children because I was also abused as a child."

When Melanie told me this, I felt a deep pain for her, not being able to imagine what it was like for her to go through what she did, but also amazed by her kind heart despite it all. She gave me permission to share her story in the hopes that it will help someone else.

Melanie's story is one of gut-wrenching pain, but a story of true resiliency and amazement, a true transcendence from pain to love. Melanie was sexually abused by her father from 3-4 years old up until she was a teenager. She remembers being "daddy's girl" although ironically, he was the one that caused her so much torment. How is it possible for someone that gave her life was able to do this to her, an innocent and young child? His abuse began a long journey full of pain and suffering for Melanie, however, this eventually led to her healing and resilience. After the abuse by her father began, Melanie lost most of her memories, only recalling fragments. The only memories she recalled was when she felt terrified it was her "turn" to sleep with her father while her brother slept with her mom.

This abuse stopped when she became a teenager, when her dad developed dementia, only to be followed by abuse from her older cousin who moved in with their family. He had recently experienced a psychotic break. Her cousin began the abuse by gaining her trust as he played with her and her brother—until one day he decided to "groom" her. This incident opened a can of worms for Melanie and the memories of her father's abuse "flooded "back in. She was stuck in confusion, feeling scared and helpless. The abuse continued until an emotional conversation Melanie had with her dad as they were moving to a new home during her sophomore year of high school. She begged her dad to not let her cousin move in with them again. She was crying profusely and finally blurted out through her tears, yelling, "Because he abused me!" at which time her dad responded, "No, he didn't, and if he did, then it was your fault." Her dad's shocking response struck her. She could not believe that the only person she thought she could rely on, not only disregarded what she said, but also blamed her for the situation.

After she moved to her new home, she kept herself locked in her room so the incidents with her cousin decreased and finally came to an end. Even though that was the end of her trauma, it was the beginning for a whole other set of problems that began as she came to terms with the abuse she experienced as a child and teenager.

The abuse had changed Melanie forever, robbing her of the innocence of being a little girl. Her entire personality and demeanor changed from being a "loving and carefree" girl to a girl who shut down entirely and became "soul-less." During this time, Melanie was, as she described herself, "numb, cold, and was there as a body, but [my] soul was completely destroyed and not present." She was "withdrawn and absent." She became a high-achiever in school, which was the only thing she felt she had control over. In despair from all the abuse, Melanie attempted to commit suicide. She was lucky to have a few friends at the time who helped her. Nevertheless, she still felt "emotionless" and "did not trust others."

When Melanie turned 18, she became the sole decision-maker for her dad's medical care since her parents were not legally married. Her dad's dementia had progressed to the point that he needed around-the-clock care. She eventually decided to withhold care, which was in contrast to her mother's wishes, further complicating the many emotions she had about her dad. By that time, she was also in therapy to process the abuse from her dad, but her anxiety in high school peaked and she was completely unstable emotionally. Shortly after her dad died and a relationship she was in had failed, she moved to another state, in an effort to "start over."

As an adult, she was in a co-dependent marriage and still numb to emotions. She presented herself as if she had everything together. She was putting on a "mask" every single day and did not even know she had it on. She still had trust issues, difficulty opening up, and intimacy issues. When it came to relationships, Melanie told me, "My heart was cold." Plagued by anxiety and panic attacks, she even had out-of-body experiences (moments of disassociation) which were misdiagnosed as seizures after she collapsed several times. She had been through three cycles of serious depression, admitting, "I have high anxiety." She had been in therapy for many years with a diagnosis of PTSD and depression with high anxiety. Three years ago, Melanie had a "mid-life crisis," a complete mental health break, about three years ago that led her to leave her job and her marriage. Finally, she took eight months to focus on nothing else besides healing and rebuilding herself.

Currently, Melanie is in a much healthier state and feels more whole, but she still has to consciously work to overcome her negative thoughts, feelings of worthlessness and anxiety. Despite of her previous traumatic experiences, Melanie has been able to overcome it all and transcend her pain. She has overcome the trauma and abuse by doing yoga and practicing regularly. Yoga played a very significant role in her healing. It allowed her body to release years of harm (as we know the "body remembers"). She was also in therapy on and off until she began working with her current therapist about five years ago. They connected immediately and she truly believes her therapist has been an instrumental part in her healing process. She has been the compassionate, strong, supportive, consistent, honest and raw person she needed to thrive. For the first time in her life, religion and spirituality became important to her. She began studying and practicing Buddhism and sought asylum with a very loving and supportive church. Naturally, this led to a lot of outdoor time, which was important to her. She also participated in Native drumming circles regularly and experienced sweat lodges and journeying, common healing practices in the Native culture. In her deepest, darkest moments, she found love in God. The relationship she built with Him has been paramount in her healing.

Last but not least, she leaned on her loved ones for support. Being raised as an oldest child to a mother who survived genocide, she was not taught how to accept help from others. She got to the point where she was so weak, she had no choice but to allow others to help and love her. She finally began sharing her feelings with her mom. She called on friends for support when she needed them. She opened her heart and, for the first time, allowed someone to see the deepest parts of her broken self. This required her to share a vulnerability she did not know she had. That someone is now her husband. He was the mirror she needed to hold herself accountable for her healing and the motivation for her to continue doing so.

Melanie was able to overcome all of this due to her resiliency. Throughout her life, she wanted to give up many times, but even in the darkest of moments, there was something in her heart that told her "better days are ahead." She would tell herself, "just one day at a time." When things were really tough, it became "one moment at a time," and she still lives by that. Her mantra became "my blessings will match the size of my struggle." She can truly say that today. She has made it out of the darkness. The light within her keeps that darkness away and keeps her going.

The life she lives now is nothing she could have even dreamed of! She feels beyond blessed in so many ways, and she knows that she is deserving of this incredible life. The encouragement she would like to share with others is that, through all the pain and suffering, it is so worth it to keep moving forward. All the hard work, all the darkness and the ugliness are what allows us to know the beauty in life. Without darkness, there's no light. She truly believes nothing is ever wasted. Everything that occurs plays a role in growth and healing. You just have to find the lesson within it.

Now that Melanie has passed the hardest struggles of her life, she is able to pay it forward by helping adolescents who have been abused. She graduated with her Master's in social work and is a Licensed Clinical Social Worker. She has worked with many diverse communities in her career, and her purpose for going into social work was to help others along their healing journeys. She feels that so many people played a role in her healing as an adult, but she fell through the cracks as a young girl; so, her passion is working with young children and adolescents. Her goal for the future is to set up yoga therapy with adolescents who have been sexually abused.

Through it all, Melanie's biggest lesson is that she has learned that life can be hard and dark and scary, but you can choose to move forward with your experiences and lessons by using them to help you grow. There are many things in her life that she did not get to choose or control, but she can choose her own perspective. She can truthfully say she is blessed with the life she's lived and that she can understand now why everything happened the way it did. Every single thing that has transpired has gotten her to be the person she is today. And she finally loves herself, the person she has become through her trials and tribulations. That has been the hardest lesson of all: learning to love herself and be compassionate through it all, because she is deserving of love. There is no one in the past, present or future who can tell her story as their own. She is the only person who can tell her story and she is damn proud of it.

As you read Melanie's story, I'm sure you saw glimpses of the Hero's Journey and the role Melanie took in creating the life she has always deserved despite going through the horrible events in her life. She is a role model for true resiliency, of being able to overcome hardships and not letting them trample you.

I am honored to be able to share her story in the effort to inspire you, regardless of what your story is, because there is always a way for you to surpass your suffering.

LESSONS FOR US ON RESILIENCE

1. Failure is a gift; within it is a lesson.

2. Everyone has fear and doubt. The key is to learn how to tackle it without letting it overwhelm you.

3. Being resilient means realizing that you have control over your life. You are not a victim and you have a choice to create change in your life.

4. When you are resilient, you are committed to the process and the journey. You make it your priority to do what you need to do to get to where you want to be.

5. Challenges are part of building resilience. With each challenge you are building a stronger backbone.

EXERCISE E10-1: BECOMING MORE RESILIENT

1. Set aside some time to journal and reflect on your life.

2. Think about your own personal story.

    *   How often did you consider giving up or punishing yourself for your past?

317

- And most importantly, how did you transcend your pain in the past?

- What steps did you take to overcome it and how far have you gotten?

Remember: We all have a story we tell and they are all equally important. Most of us will punish ourselves and let the road of disappointment bring us shame and guilt, which pushes us further away from our goals and building the life that we deserve. However, when you look back, can you tell how resilient you were? Furthermore, continuing to build your capacity for resilience will help you learn to deal with difficult situations and give you a backbone to survive anything that comes your way.

A key to building resilience is not giving up even when you are facing the worst situations. When you feel like giving up, do this simple exercise to help you put things into perspective: Create a list of all the successes you've had along your journey. Remind yourself of all the progress you've made. Remember that transformation is a journey of a lifetime. Channel the hero within and know that every hero has to go through the same phases of their journey that you are experiencing. And finally, you, like them, will come back home, healed, fully-aligned, and on purpose.

PATIENCE

"In the depth of winter, I finally learned that within me there lay an invincible summer."[2]

Everything in nature comes in cycles, like the seasons: Spring, Summer, Fall and Winter. Plants grow in cycles that function like clockwork. Each season is appreciated for its own purpose and provides its own benefits and challenges. Spring marks the end of a cold winter, sprouting out new beginnings, a fresh start and a renewal of life. It is a time of cleansing and restoration, a time of transitioning from the harsh winter. It's the time to plant new seeds, physically and metaphorically. It's about getting clear on what you want and setting your intentions for the rest of the year. Summer is a time for fun and achievement, when everything comes into full bloom and you're at the peak of the growth. It's the time to take action, to move toward your goals. Fall is a time to slow down and reflect on the journey by harvesting your lessons. Winter is a long dark period, marked with deep stillness and silence. It is the time of inner-exploration and celebration, waiting to start a new year or cycle again.

When you observe plants, you see this beautiful cycle that signifies the important stages that life goes through. The act of gardening is a wonderful process that offers valuable life lessons. When you tend a garden, you work with it. You prepare the dirt, get your hands all dirty. You plant the seeds, water, and fertilize the garden, and you pull the weeds to help the garden grow and maximize its potential. Through the process of gardening, you learn what is necessary to give it life and turn it into a brilliant work of art. The process of gardening is the same as the process of becoming the hero, a self-discovery journey to nourish your soul. You are the garden, the whole of who you are. When you are planting the garden, you are planting seeds of your own growth. When you are watering the plant and showering it with love, you are helping yourself to grow and flourish. When you are pulling the weeds, you are removing bad habits and perhaps negative thoughts so that you can maintain this beautiful garden. Once the garden is beautiful and complete, it's the start of a new cycle, a new beginning, a new lesson to learn.

As you embark on this self-discovery journey, remember that just like the seasons, there is an appointed time for everything. There will be times when you will have massive growth, and there will be times when things will slow down. There will be periods of great pain, but also periods of deep happiness.

There will be moments of transition and moments when the transitioning turns you into the person that you were always meant to be. Most people tend to resist when things slow down, but this is a necessary part of your development, so do not fight it when it happens. Resistance is like paddling upstream on a fast-flowing river, trying to fight the current to no avail. You will only cause yourself needless stress and frustration because you will be unable to make progress. Fighting the current will not help you move along any faster and it definitely will not help you travel up the stream. Instead, learn to love the "down time." Use it as a time to reflect on your journey so far and let life flow as it naturally does. In reality, progress and growth happen when we are not forcing things. Instead of engaging in frustrating and self-defeating behaviors, this is the best time to foster patience. Patience is an amazing coping skill that will provide you emotional freedom. It is easy to become frustrated when things do not go your way, but patience will help you reframe your frustrations and give you perspective. If you can be patient, it will be far more satisfying when you finally experience the fruits of your labor.

I'll be honest; being patient was not one of my greatest qualities. Growing up in a culture and society where everything is readily available did not give me patience. With the rapidly growing technological era, everything you want and need is conveniently available at the click of a finger. This time period is marked by a focus on quick fixes and the next magic pill solution. However, it is important to realize that these short cuts do not work when it comes to change and transformation. Like the old saying, "Rome wasn't built in a day," you have to take time and effort to build something, and this empire you are building is a happy and well-lived life. Nothing worthwhile comes easily, and perhaps there is a reason for this: We need the struggles of the journey to teach us important lessons, such as resilience and patience. Being patient was a quality I had to develop along my transformative journey. When I was younger, I had this very demanding attitude where I felt that if I wanted something, I needed to have it immediately! If I didn't get what I wanted, I would throw a fit. But, like I mentioned, throwing a fit is basically being resistant to the true reality, and it definitely didn't help me get what I wanted. Learning patience became normalized as I graced through the beginning of adulthood and learned the value of patience. I had to learn that being patient is absolutely necessary, especially when it comes to something as challenging as change. Life cannot only be defined by outcomes. We need to let go of the belief that if we don't get what we want immediately, it means we have failed. Life, like our journey, is a process.

I remember Tony Robbins' wise words: "...[Most] people overestimate what they can accomplish in a year, and underestimate what they can achieve in a decade!"[3] The short term seems to be what most people tend to fixate on. When you are rebuilding yourself and learning to tap into your potential, be reminded that great change will happen gradually, and that there are many layers that you have to unveil before you can get to the core of who you really are, which is a brilliant human being with so much potential!

SURRENDER

A lot of times in life, we try to control everything around us. The truth is, we've never had control in the first place. If you think about it, the universe has been around for approximately 13.8 billion years and the earth has been here for about 4.5 billion years. The human lifetime is only a blip in this infinite timeline. Do you really think that you can control every single outcome in your life? You might think "yes," but the reality is that the intelligence of the universe has been around and working on its own without your help for eons.

Of course, as humans, having fear of the unknown causes us to want to control as much as we can. We have to develop a faith and trust in the universe that everything will work out according to plan. The fact that you are alive and breathing is a miracle in and of itself! The fact that you are here reading this is a miracle. The fact that you are able to experience life is a miracle. Think about it; A power beyond your knowledge and understanding created you because it knew that you had a purpose and that you were meant to be here. The fact that you are here means that the force of the universe wanted you to be here for a reason. If the force of the universe can create you, be reassured that the universe would not have given you this chance at life, or purpose, without giving you the resources necessary to achieve your biggest goals and desires.

One of my biggest tests of faith came when I first started my business. I struggled with attracting clients into my life. I had put so much effort into creating the business, that when I was not getting clients, I was extremely disappointed. I automatically assumed that I was a failure because my plans did not manifest as I intended. I was what Gabrielle Berstein called the "manic manifestor,"[4] because I kept trying to force my way to get what I wanted because I was afraid of losing control. I went down the spiraling hole into a dark area of fear, comparison, guilt, and failure. It was not until I finally released the outcome, took the pressure off myself, and surrendered, that I finally attracted the clients that I really wanted. What surprised me was that this process was suddenly effortless.

The art of surrender is of course an art to master, and it is not an easy one. However, the more you do it, the easier it becomes. Surrendering does not mean that you are giving up. It only means that you are letting the forces that are greater than you take care of the things that are out of your hands. Remember, the universe is always guiding you in the right direction even when it might not feel like it.

There are many times in life when we will face difficulties. It is in these trying times that we must learn to surrender and shift our perspectives. Surrendering helps us let go of the need to control and frees us from expectations of the outcome. When we realize that we are not in control, and that is okay, this small shift in perception helps us release our attachment to suffering. Whatever situation you may be in, remember that the universe is here to support you. Surrender, let go and shift your perspective. Once you do this, you will gain a sense of relief and clarity from the situation you are facing.

When you are facing these difficulties, I want you to observe the conversation you are having with yourself. What are you telling yourself? What is the quality of this conversation? Are you being kind to yourself or are you speaking to yourself with a critical and negative voice? What is the narrative that you are telling yourself as you deal with this difficulty? Imagine if this were your best friend. Would you have the same conversation? Would you beat a friend down who was in a tough spot? I'm sure you wouldn't.

When faced with a difficulty, it is extremely important that you become aware of how you are talking to yourself. Remember to be kind and compassionate as if you were talking to your best friend. Ask yourself, what needs to be healed? How can I upgrade my beliefs and self-image? Then surrender and ask the universe to meet you and provide guidance. You will be surprised at what the universe has in store for you.

My friend Kelly once told me that the biggest surrender you have to make is to "surrender to the journey." This is the truth. Sometimes we are so focused on the outcome that we end up forgetting to enjoy the journey as we go through it.

When you think you've surrendered enough, surrender even more. Ask yourself, "Who was I when I started this journey? Who am I now? How far have I come?" Let these questions remind you of how far you've already come. It's important to surrender to the journey but it's necessary to surrender to the outcome. Many of us are so focused on our goals that when we don't reach them the way that we thought we would, we become extremely disappointed in ourselves. When we become disappointed with ourselves, we then begin to criticize ourselves and talk down to ourselves. This creates more pain, anger, and frustration. When you are in a state of frustration, you put on a mental filter and you discard all the opportunities that may be around you. This blocks the things that may come your way. The universe doesn't always give you what you want, but it always gives you what you need. So, the moment that you are attached to an outcome, it will create a negative vibration and you will not attract what you want. Sometimes we think that we know what's best for ourselves, but we really do not. When you're struggling with an outcome, let go and release it. Only this will lead you to true freedom.

A story to inspire you to surrender and trust the universe is the story about the life of Michael Singer. In his book, *The*

Surrender Experiment: My Journey into Life's Perfection, Singer details the story of his life and how surrendering led him to live a life beyond his wildest imaginations. Singer was a man who just wanted to be a yogi and meditate. He set out on an adventure to go live in solitude and meditate alone in the wild. He decided that this was the only thing he wanted to do. He also decided that he would surrender to the universe and just let things happen as they are supposed to, even when it was not what he wanted. He said, "What would happen if we respected the flow of life and used our free will to participate in what's unfolding, instead of fighting it?"[5] Thirty years later, he had built a thriving yoga community in a beautiful forest of Florida and became a billionaire, among other achievements. His life is proof that we must trust the process and let life unfold on its own instead of imposing our will on it.

Exercise E10-2: Surrendering to the Journey

A Prayer to Help You Shift and Surrender[6]

From A Course in Miracles

(Please note that the author has substituted words "the Universe" for the word "God" in this atonement prayer to accommodate the broadest range of beliefs.)

◇ I perceive (the form of the problem, issue, sickness or person) as causing me to suffer. I recognize that this suffering is not the Universe's Will and that I have been mistaken in choosing to believe it. I don't want to believe this suffering any longer. I ask You, Spirit, to heal my perception in this instant.

◇ As much as I want this form of suffering to cease, I accept that I must desire to have my perception healed MORE than I want the seeming form of the problem healed.

◇ The singular cause of the problem regardless of the level of suffering, or where I see it, is my perception of the problem (guilt/fear).

◇ I deny anything that is not of the Universe's Loving Will the power to hurt me or others. There is only one Power, which is the Universe's Will. The ego has no power unless I choose to believe it.

◇ I accept the divine undoing of the singular cause of my issue, which is always fear and guilt.

◇ I accept and I RECEIVE the Loving and healing Will of the Universe to replace the ego's wish for suffering.

◇ I claim and RECEIVE my eternal guiltlessness which is the Will of the Universe. Fear and attack fall away as I claim my divine innocence.

◇ I accept abundant miracles as my Inheritance.

◇ I accept that my "will" is now joined as one with the Universe's Loving Will.

◇ I surrender my personal responsibility for the seeming problem, as I give it over to the Spirit.

◇ I accept that my Holiness reverses all the laws of the world.

◇ I accept that the Universe's Laws always overrule the ego's laws of this world, i.e., sickness, pain, scarcity, conflict, death, etc.

◇ I accept that healing in the Universe is always certain and has already taken place, because healing is always the Universe's Will for me.

◇ I accept that my perception is healed, so the effects/symptoms MUST heal as well (the timing depends on my degree of trust in the miracle).

◇ I accept that my only responsibility now is to trust implicitly that the Universe's Loving Will has ALREADY healed the cause of the problem, regardless of any continuing appearances to the contrary. Appearances are just that--appearances only and not real. I choose to trust implicitly in the Universe's Loving Will.

Forgiveness

Forgiveness is the path to all healing and the key to freeing oneself. Forgiveness helps free us from the pain others have inflicted upon us and also the pain that we have inflicted upon ourselves. When I was younger, I held a lot of resentment against my father for abandoning our family and starting a new family. How could he have done that to us? I held onto this pain for many years and I let it eat up my life, burning like a hot coal within me.

As I continued on my self-discovery journey, I realized that the only way I could free myself was if I forgave him. A very important lesson I learned was that people do the best that they can with what they know at the time. This gave me a shift in perception and I was finally able to forgive him. I did not only forgive him but I also forgave so many other people in my life, including anyone that had hurt me in the past.

Is there someone who has wronged you in the past and you've been carrying this baggage around with you? Have you made a mistake in the past and continue to hold onto guilt, shame, and fear, punishing yourself for it? Are you ready to let go of the pain, anger, and resentment so you can heal and move on with your life? Like the old saying tells us, "Holding onto anger and resentment and refusing to forgive is like drinking poison and waiting for the other person to die." You might ask, "Why should I forgive someone who has done me wrong?" Let me ask you, how has holding onto this pain affected your life? Is it improving the quality of your life? Most often, holding onto unnecessary pain will prevent you from living happily and creating a fulfilling life for yourself. To clarify, forgiving someone does not mean that what they did was right. Forgiveness is simply a way to let go of emotional baggage that you might have held onto. When you forgive someone, you are freeing yourself and giving yourself the gift of freedom!

Forgiveness enables you to release the hurt, pain, and resentment that you've held onto. It allows you to heal, discover fresh air and sunshine, and to learn to trust again. People are not perfect. Don't expect them to be. There will always be someone who says or does something to hurt you. It may be intentional or a just a well-meaning comment, but unless you forgive, you cannot move forward toward your dream life. Unforgiveness is a ball-and-chain attached to your ankle. Do not expect to climb any incredible mountains in your life journey with that extra weight dragging you down.

Most people struggle to forgive because they believe that forgiveness justifies the pain that has been caused to them. This is not true. Pain is a part of life and it is something we cannot avoid.

Exercise E10-3: The Ho'oponopono Prayer[7]

When the hurt is ingrained so deeply in your psyche that you do not know how to start forgiving, you might want to try the Ho'oponopono Prayer. "Ho'oponopono is an ancient Hawaiian practice for forgiveness and reconciliation. It's more than the prayer alone; it's a process of making things right in your relationships..." It is a "family ritual [that] focuses on working through problems together, openly expressing feelings, and releasing each other."[5]

What makes this prayer so effective is that it zeroes in on repentance, forgiveness, gratitude, and love. By praying the four phrases of the prayer (below), it opens up the pathway for you to fix and restore a relationship that has been damaged.

Imagine that the person who hurt you is sitting across from you. Say the following phrases, in any order, silently or out loud:

1. I am sorry.
2. (Please) Forgive me.
3. Thank you.
4. I love you.

This prayer[8] is effective when said privately, thinking about the person who hurt you and you honestly forgive him or her. Or, if the situation allows, the two of you can go through this ritual together. That's how it is really designed to work. If this is not possible yet, maybe after you have privately forgiven the person who hurt you, at a later time the two of you can reconcile.

If you would like to know more about this Hawaiian prayer and the ritual that goes with it, you can find it online at: https://healingbrave.com/blogs/all/hooponopono-prayer-for-forgiveness.

EXERCISE E10-4: SELF-FORGIVENESS

It's important to forgive other people, but it's also important to forgive yourself and acknowledge yourself for how far you've gotten. Write a letter to yourself and forgive yourself for all the mistakes you've ever made. Forgive yourself for the pain you inflicted upon yourself. Forgive yourself for rejecting the love that you truly deserve.

To help you start the process of self-forgiveness, fill out the list below with your own name in the blank. Read this to yourself often so that you can honestly forgive yourself and be free from self-condemnation.

_____ (name) I honor you for _____.

_____ (name) I am proud of you for _____.

_____ (name) I forgive you for _____.

_____ (name) I thank you for _____.

_____ (name) I appreciate you for _____.

_____ (name) I acknowledge you for _____.

SHIFTING TO A PLACE OF GRATITUDE

Most of us are conditioned to focus so intently on the negative things in life that we often neglect the positive things. When we're not busy focusing on the negative things, we tend to focus on money and the ways we think it will solve all of our problems and make us happy. We live in a world that prioritizes material things over things with true value, love, and happiness. Consequently, we tend to neglect the abundance that we are actually surrounded by. We constantly look to the external world to provide us with enrichment, we become stuck under this psychological ignorance of the truth, aiming to be rich financially in hopes that it will fill us up and make us feel like we are good enough. We are so sure that money and things will fulfill our every need. This reality is much further from the truth than you can imagine.

I noticed that many of my patients and I both shared the following experience: At one time or another, we all believed that more money would bring us happiness. Yes, money can provide comfort and security, but it is not the solution to all our problems. Many celebrities "have it all" but still suffer. This suffering can manifest itself as addictions or even depression. Take Robin Williams, for example. A successful comedian and actor, he delighted his audiences with his personality and humor. Despite being able to lift the spirits of others, he suffered for years with deep depression and ended up committing suicide. His case is a prime example that even if you have fame and material goods, you might still be unhappy. We have so much to be grateful for, and money should be on the bottom of that list.

If you look below at Napoleon Hill's *The Twelve Riches of Life*[9], you will realize that financial gains are at the bottom of this list for good reason.

1.   A "Positive Mental Attitude" (PMA)

2.   Sound physical health

3.   Harmony in human relationships

4.   Freedom from fear

5.   The hope of achievement

6.   The capacity for faith

7.   A willingness to share one's blessings

8.   A labor of love

9.   An open mind on all subjects

10. Self-discipline

11. The capacity to understand people

12. Economic security

This is where gratitude comes in. Gratitude is the act of appreciating and attributing value to something you may have, whether it's a thing, event, place, memory, or just the fact that you are alive and healthy. When you shift to a state of gratitude, your view of the world will start to change. You will gain a new sense of overall well-being. Creation in and of itself is a miracle. So, when you feel envious of what other people have, think about all the amazing things you do have in your life. Be grateful that you are alive! Many of us take this gift for granted, but being alive is a miracle. Think about the fact that your heart keeps beating and you keep breathing even when you are asleep. Think about the trillions of tiny cells that make up your body. They are all operating individually to keep you alive. I mean, how incredible is that? Think about getting a small cut on your finger and how your skin immediately begins to heal the wound all by itself. Thank the universe for giving you this body, this mind, and the chance to experience life and enjoy it—even with its ups and downs.

For me, overcoming depression meant that I had to begin to notice the wonders of the world. It began with small moments that sparkled, moments of deep gratitude, and appreciation. In any moment in life, especially when things are rough, you have the option of switching from a state of fear and lack to one of gratitude and love. This small shift will help you realign with who you are: a magnificent being who is capable of so much more than what you have allowed yourself to do.

So, give thanks for this human experience! Give thanks for the fresh air you get to breathe. Give thanks for the magic of your beating heart, pumping blood out to nourish your body. Be grateful for the sun, the earth, the breeze, and the ocean. Be grateful for how nature constantly provides for us. Have you ever looked around you and soaked it all in? Have you ever seen a newborn baby take its first breath (if not in real life, at least on TV)? There is a moment filled with love, excitement and wonder when the father and mother catch their first glimpse of this beautiful baby. Imagine the newborn baby as you when you were first born. You came into this world with everything you needed. Unfortunately for many of us, in the course of life, painful experiences have made us forget that we are already filled with everything we need to create the amazing and abundant life we deserve. This journey is meant to help remind you that you are already equipped with everything that you need. All it takes is a moment of gratitude to remind you.

It is crucial for you to practice gratitude every single day. The easiest way to do this is to keep a gratitude journal handy. Every morning or evening, write down at least 10 things you are grateful for. This will encourage you to focus on the positive things right at the start and end of your day. In my experience, the morning is the best time to do this because being grateful in the morning will make it much easier to remember what is important to you as you go throughout your day.

EXERCISE E10-5 THE "HEART OF GRATITUDE" MEDITATION

◇ Find a quiet place, free from distractions. Sit down in a comfortable position.

◇ Take a few deep breaths as you let the day fade away. Connect to this moment and feel fully present. Once you feel deeply relaxed, close your eyes.

◇ As you begin to relax, turn your focus to your heart. Place your hands over your heart and feel the rhythm of your beating heart. Feel the pulse as the blood from your heart fills up your body and revitalizes it with life. Feel the force, the power, and the strength of your heart. As you feel the power of your heart, take a moment and give thanks to this incredible beating heart that is giving you life. Really feel gratitude for the chance you have at living. Take another deep breath and think about something that you are truly grateful for, whether it's a memory, someone in your life, or even this opportunity to reconnect with your essence. Breathe in that gratitude that you have for whatever it is that comes to mind. Then magnify this feeling of gratitude you are experiencing 100 times, 500 times, then 1,000 times. Really feel the feelings and sensations that you are experiencing as you envelop this feeling of gratitude. Stay in this sensation for a few minutes until you feel ready to come back to reality.

◇ When you are ready, slowly come back to your full awareness. Begin by feeling your fingers and toes. Then let in the sounds around you. Feel your body begin to awaken as you wake up to your surroundings feeling refreshed and filled with gratitude.

◇ Repeat this process daily every morning for at least 30 consecutive days and you will begin to notice some shifts and changes in your levels of appreciation.

"Remember that wherever you are, whatever you are doing, life does not have to be perfect. You do not have to be perfect. You just have to get started and you will figure out the rest along the way."

~ *Julia*

CHAPTER 11:

RESURRECTION - THE

WORLD NEEDS YOUR

LIGHT

⁓

A FTER THE HERO travels through the first two stages of the journey, Separation and Initiation, it's time for the Hero's Return and Rebirth. This parallels the stages of our lives—we transition from birth to adulthood, and from adulthood to death. This journey through time marks the cycle of our lives. We experience the beginning of life, then grow and learn. As we develop through adolescence and adulthood, we live, learn, and become wise. As we approach the end of life, we are blessed with the opportunity to share our stories, to leave behind something of value for the ones who come after us.

The Hero's rebirthing process is incredible, but with it comes growing pains. Nobody tells you about the growing pains during your rebirthing process, as you transform into the Hero you've always been deep inside of you. Growing pains is one of the most crucial parts of your journey and it's not always pleasant. You will still be attached to your past as you develop new aspects of your personality that embody the hero. This attachment to the past version of yourself will create an epic internal battle within you. It will feel like a tug-o-war. Sometimes you will inch closer to your full potential and other times you'll be pulled back in the direction of comfort from the past.

This in-between phase will cause extreme discomfort as you disconnect from the past and try to become who you really are. This period is a time when you are eradicating the ego and experiencing the death of the outdated version of yourself. This is the death of who you once were so you can be reborn again into the new you. You might be confused with who you are as you separate from the "identity" that you believe was once you and develop into the new version of you. Think of it like the transformation of a butterfly. The butterfly starts as a caterpillar (the old you). It goes through a transition stage, where it wraps itself and forms its chrysalis (transition phase). During this stage it may look like nothing is going on, but big changes are happening inside. In the same way, as you transition to your hero, you may not be actively doing things, but all the activity is going on inside you.

As the internal changes are being firmly fixed, you are re-emerging and creating space for yourself to metamorphosize (be reborn) into the butterfly. As you go through this rebirthing process, you will break out of your comfort zone, shedding off old layers of previous conceptual frameworks that you lived by, and stretch yourself until you reach your best self. Although the process doesn't come easily, it will enable you to eventually spread your wings and fly.

Let these words from Jenny Markas encourage you:

When you find yourself lost in the darkness and despair, remember it's only in the black of the night you see the stars.[1]

If it were not for the depression, the devastating setbacks, and tragedies in my life, I probably would have never been able to see the light. The truth is that the drive to create an extraordinary life is usually based on harsh experiences. The darkness of hitting rock bottom drove me to reach extraordinary heights. Although at times the darkness kept me small, it also helped me realize that there is a world full of possibilities outside of that mesmerizing darkness. You have to realize that the darkness is not the entire universe. If you look up at the sky, most of it might seem dark, but the stars are always there sparkling through the night and lighting up the sky. There is a light that is separate from the darkness that has been surrounding and invading you all these years.

This light has always been a part of your essence, the flame that burns inside of you. It is the torch of the hero. So, when you catch a glimpse of that light, go after it. When you reach it, do not forget to let it in. Let it slowly seep into your soul and fill your body with the magnificence of life. Let it penetrate through your essence and fill you up with infinite amounts of love and happiness. Just as the night sky has stars that are there whether we see them or not, your life contains light, whether you see it or not. When you are able to face the darkness and still find the light shining at you from within, jump at the opportunity to explore the light and begin to master yourself. As you discard the old habits and limiting beliefs that have kept you in darkness, you will emerge as a new, stronger and deeply joyous person.

Sometimes in the midst of it all, you might feel a sense of frustration and confusion because you cannot understand why things are unfolding the way they are. But have faith in yourself and in the universe, that the universe will guide you to where you're meant to be. When I was depressed, I was constantly filled with doubt and fear and that was all I could focus on. I didn't have faith in anything, and certainly not in myself. Once I began to realize that nothing in my life would change unless I changed it, I began to believe in myself and my ability to become the best version of myself—someone who is free from depression, living in awe and happiness every single day.

Begin to develop this sense of faith within yourself and let it help you on your journey. This faith is not necessarily faith in religious terms, but more so relying on your own abilities to be the master creator of your life. Believing that everything and anything is possible is half the battle. Once you recognize your own internal power, you will experience a massive shift in perspective and motivation. From then on, whenever you are faced with challenges and difficulties, you will know you have something you can always rely on: your internal and infinite wisdom.

Many of us tend to disconnect from this part of ourselves, and so it's easy to be misguided and pulled in life's different directions. We continue to be busy, and to push this part away because we have forgotten what it's like to let our deepest Self guide our decision-making. Only when we are faced with major difficulties do we scramble and try to connect with our true selves, because at that point, we have nothing else we can rely on. Yet, every single one of us has this internal guidance system that will help us when we are in dire need of it. Actually, this internal wisdom is available to us all of the time, even when we're not in dire need. It can help spark the creativity within us. It can inspire us to chase after our dreams, create a new magical future that is marked with endless possibilities.

If you look at the world around you, there is so much beauty to be seen, but many of us forget to look or do not take the time to appreciate it. We negate the magic around us because we are so enveloped in our minds, stressing over the past or worrying about the future. Eckhart Tolle's book, *The Power of Now*, has completely changed my life. He opened up my eyes to a new world, one that I never noticed before. You might be at the beginning of your self-discovery journey. I hope that as you read my book, I am able to spark something in you that moves you to look deep within yourself while connecting to each precious moment in your life. We cannot live in the past or the future—only the present. Allow yourself to be inspired by each present moment.

Think about one of your most treasured memories. Maybe it was at your graduation. You were surrounded by family and friends, feeling deeply connected to each and every one of them. Were you filled with joy and happiness and a sense of completeness? Or maybe it was falling in love for the very first time and being overcome with a joyful oblivion that you had never experienced before? These enchanted moments are moments of true bliss, when you were fully "present" and enjoying the "now." Unfortunately, as life gets busier and bogged down with anxiety, many of us get caught up in our minds and totally forget that we can actually experience this same bliss in everyday life. We possess the power to create those magical moments, and it begins with *being present*. Being present means being relaxed in your body while experiencing what is currently going on around you. This helps you connect with a part of you that is not stuck in the past or anxious about the future. When you are fully present, you free yourself from the chatter of stressful thoughts swirling around in your mind. Being present breaks the chains that are mentally and emotionally holding you prisoner.

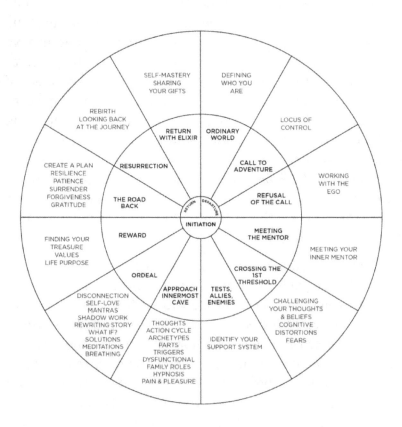

STAGES OF THE HERO'S JOURNEY[2]

Look how far you have come in your journey! You have faced down your demons, fears and your stubborn ego, and yet, you have persevered and learned how to detach yourself from what's been holding you back for years. I am so proud of you! You no longer allow the past to tyrannize your present. The old version of you has died, and a NEW YOU is being reborn. This birth is the beginning of a new chapter in your life. You are embodying everything that is the hero within.

Remember that, in life, you will constantly be faced with challenges and obstacles. You know now that how you deal with these obstacles and challenges is your path to growing and self-realization. With each obstacle is a chance for you to learn and grow. Not only that, but when you and I learn these lessons, we are able to share them with others. Hardships are part of the journey and, in all honesty, make life a bit more exciting. Can you imagine a utopian world where you had everything exactly the way you wanted it? You would probably go out of your mind with boredom. Our minds and hearts are designed to thrive on challenges. Challenges make us stronger.

When you are struggling, remember to look within yourself. Deep inside, you have a toolbox packed with everything you need to handle what you are facing. You just have to make a choice. So, choose happiness, choose abundance, choose love. Maybe in the past you chose fear or depression or resentment. You pulled them from sources outside yourself, not realizing that the universe had already equipped you with the right tools in your mind and heart to push those obstacles out of your way.

Life is meant to be magical and when you realize that you can co-create it, you will come into your superhero role and begin to live the life that you deserve. The world needs you and your light to shine through and help raise the vibration of the planet.

So step into your power—because YOU are your SUPERHERO!

Let your spirit soar as you embrace this truth.

COURAGEOUS IMPERFECTION

Be proud of yourself for embarking on this journey, for being brave and bold, and willing to overcome the darkest parts of who you are. Give yourself credit for picking yourself up, for standing tall, and realizing that your imperfections are what make you perfect. Most people are unwilling to try because they are afraid, but here you are, transcending conventional beliefs and fighting bravely for your personal psychological freedom.

Remember that wherever you are, whatever you are doing, life does not have to be perfect. You do not have to be perfect. You just have to get started and you will figure out the rest along the way. I know, I had no idea what I was getting into when I first began my own journey. But after all this time, I prevailed. And when I look back at who I was and who I've become, I can say that I am 100% proud of the growth I've made. And you can feel that way too!

ENLIGHTENED HUMILITY

This journey is challenging and sometimes your biggest challenges and failures will humble you. That's okay. They help you realize what's really important in life, and that is *human connection*. For years, money and material wealth were what I believed would make me happy. As I grew during my journey, I discovered that sharing moments of happiness with the people I love is the most important thing in life. So, do not isolate yourself. Let other people in and let them help you. Sometimes the journey will feel lonely, but all that means is that during that period, you are meant to rely on your internal strength because the person you can always depend on is you. So be kind to yourself. You will achieve enlightened humility when you find the balance between success and failure, being with people and being alone.

SACRED EMBODIMENT/ UNAPOLOGETIC DEVOTION

There will never be a time in your life where there will not be many more things to learn. So, keep learning. Keep challenging yourself. Keep pushing yourself to be the best that you can be. And at the end of the day, know that you did the best you could in whatever situation you faced. Never accuse yourself of not being enough or not doing enough because you put yourself out there and that is all that is required of you. Even if things do not work out, it's okay because you still did everything you could in your power. Oftentimes, when we fail or things do not go our way, we punish ourselves for it and we beat ourselves down for it. But sometimes things do not work out for a reason—and you might not know that reason now, but in retrospect, you will look back and see the meaning of it all.

One of my Rapid Transformational Therapy (RTT)–clients once dealt with uncertainty about his future. We did a regression and went back to a few scenes from his past. When he was in his twenties, he was beginning his residency as a medical doctor. He had just moved away from home for the first time, and he felt like he was a "real adult." He was excited but nervous about what was ahead. Despite that, he was eager to embark on this new adventure. Over 30 years later, he was beginning another new chapter in his life. He was dismayed that he was experiencing some of the same feelings of uncertainty that he had when he was younger, and it threw him for a loop. He felt like he was in his twenties again and just as unprepared.

As we talked about it, he came to the realization that, although he was nervous about the future, seeing how far he had come and what he had accomplished, helped him feel a sense of pride and relief. You see, it does not matter what stage we are in life or how old we are, at one point or another, we will feel fear of the unknown and of what the future holds. The way to deal with this is to just give ourselves some time to grow and heal. Then, one day we will look back and see how far we've come. So, if you're worried of what the future holds, it's okay. I'm here to tell you that everything will be okay, and it will unfold as it should, beautifully, with maybe just a few hiccups along the way!

"I decided to leave my secure and stable job as a nurse to move abroad and live in Barcelona, Spain. I was ready to leave the norms of society and to venture across the world to build a new life and chase after my dreams."

~ *Julia*

CHAPTER 12:
RETURN WITH THE
ELIXIR—YOU ARE YOUR
SUPERHERO

AS I SOJOURNED through my journey of transformation, I learned so much along the way. I've learned the meaning of self-love, of compassion for all the parts of me, of acceptance, of surrendering and much more. I've obtained the "elixir of life," the highest expression of who I am. I'm continuing to learn as I grow through this transformative journey to reach higher stages of human development.

*Such humble gratitude for 'what is' becomes the foundation
for receptivity to 'what is possible.'[3]*

And thus, my gift to you, is this "elixir" or memoir of how I started as a depressed little girl and metamorphosed into the woman I am today—a brave soul, full of love and appreciation for the world.

The depth of my despair had led me to embark on my Hero's Journey, starting as a girl who was extremely insecure and unhappy with herself and her life. Along this journey, I've learned how to truly love myself and to believe in my power. I've met amazing people along the journey who continue to nourish me and aid me on this journey. I've learned to surpass the voice of my ego, allowing me to focus on the abundance that life has to offer, such as amazing friendships, a business I created, making a powerful impact on others, and traveling the world. I've been able to eradicate limiting beliefs that I had placed on myself for so many years and have begun to develop a healthier belief system that supports my dreams. I've released my ties to depression. I've started my own business in which I live fully aligned to my mission in life: to help people overcome the limitations of their mind so they can create a fulfilling life for themselves. The journey has led me to writing this book, to inspire people, and to continue my own personal development so that I can show up in the world in my superhero suit. I've managed to complete one full circle of the Hero's Journey and now I'm ready to embark on my next adventure.

At this stage of your journey you have faced your fears, gone through countless battles, learned your lessons, and now you are ready to integrate all of this knowledge and wisdom into your new identity and self, the superhero within. Joseph

Campbell said, "We're not on our journey to save the world but to save ourselves. But in doing that you save the world. The influence of a vital person vitalizes."[4] As you continue this journey and spread your elixir, remember that if you make an impact on even one person's life, that is enough. This impact will create a ripple effect in which that person will make an impact on someone else, and so on.

So, remember, that deep within each of us is a "Hero" waiting to be unleashed. This hero within can be your guiding compass. Comprised of the Archetypes you have chosen to work for you, your hero will express the person you want to be. All the answers that you need are tucked inside your deepest self. You just have to be open and willing to connect with them.

The journey I went through is also possible for you, so I dare you to embark on your own journey of transformation— because life is too short for you to stand still. You don't have to be stuck in inertia, or dragged down by the darkness of depression or limiting beliefs—because YOU are the SUPERHERO of your story! All that you have endured up to this point has not been in vain. The growth that you have experienced along your journey leads to an expanse of knowledge, an expansion of your horizons. And when you have gone far enough in your self-discovery journey to discover your true happiness, then you, too, can return and pass your "ELIXIR" on to someone else.

The end of the Hero's Journey takes you back to the ordinary world where you started. This time, however, you are much wiser than the original version of yourself. You have been transformed by going through a series of ordeals and coming out victorious. You are different on the inside and it shows on the outside. You are stronger, wiser and well-equipped to face any challenges that life throws at you in the future.

Moreover, now there is new adventure awaiting for you to embark on. The end of each chapter means the beginning of another one. The future holds many amazing expeditions, waiting for you to take the next step along the "the pathway to bliss."[5]

Follow your bliss.

If you do follow your bliss,

you put yourself on a kind of track

that has been there all the while waiting for you,

and the life you ought to be living

is the one you are living.

When you can see that,

you begin to meet people

who are in the field of your bliss,

and they open the doors to you.

I say, follow your bliss and don't be afraid,

and doors will open

where you didn't know they were going to be.

If you follow your bliss,

doors will open for you

that wouldn't have opened

for anyone else.[5]

—Joseph Campbell

I hope this book has helped you on your quest, and that this quest is one of many to come. Each new Hero's Journey will demand that you stretch yourself beyond what you thought you could do or be. Don't let yourself get discouraged or thrown off course just because the path is cluttered or uncertain. Dig deep within yourself for the inspiration and grit to take on the challenge of each new Hero's Journey.

Remember who you are.

You are the light in this world.

Remember who you are.

Pure love and light.

Remember who you are.

You are divine power.

Remember, remember. remember.

So, there you have it—traveling through a world full of limitations and opening yourself up to a world full of possibilities.

Exercise E12-1: Circle Back Home

When you complete your journey, and have returned home a victorious hero, strong, impassioned and free, ask yourself these questions:

◇ What changes have I made since I embarked on my Hero's Journey?

◇ What did I learn?

◇ What can I share with the world about my story?

◇ What is my elixir? What was my greatest revelation?

◇ What are my next steps? Where will my next journey take me?

EXERCISE E12-2: SHARING THE LOVE

◇ Find a quiet place, free from distractions. Sit down in a comfortable position.

◇ Take a few deep breaths as you let the day fade away. Connect to this moment and feel fully present. Once you feel deeply relaxed, close your eyes.

◇ As you begin to relax, concentrate at the Heart Center and bring your hands into prayer position. Focus on the rhythm of your beating heart. Feel the pulse as the blood from your heart fills up your body and revitalizes it with life. Feel the force, the power, and the strength of your heart. Begin to feel the love that embraces your mind, body, and spirit. Let this love penetrate through your entire body. Then magnify this feeling of love you are experiencing 100 times, 500 times, then 1000 times. Really feel the feelings and sensations that you are experiencing as you envelop this magnitude of love.

◇ When you are in this absolutely blissful state of love, imagine you are sending love energy from your heart to all life forms. Imagine your love energy in a bright white light, extending from your heart and connecting with the hearts of all life forms and sending them healing thoughts. Feel as you send this love to uplift the spirits of all existence. Say out loud, "I pray to uplift all lifeforms with my love. I pray to help those who are suffering and in need. I pray to raise the vibration of the planet. As you are sending out this energy, imagine this light, lighting up the planet Earth. Let it surpass Earth into the atmosphere outside of Earth. Then let it continue to grow beyond the atmosphere and into the galaxy. As it reaches the galaxy, it continues to expand into the other galaxies and throughout the entire universe until you are connected with eternal bliss and love.

◇ Stay in this feeling of connectedness with yourself and the universe for a few minutes. Really enjoy it.

◇ When you are ready, slowly come back to your full awareness. Begin by feeling your fingers and toes. Then let in the sounds around you. Feel your body begin to awaken as you wake up to your surroundings feeling refreshed and filled with gratitude.

THERE'S MORE TO THE JOURNEY...

Update

Last year, on October 24, 2018, during a meditation with my inner mentor, or my Hero Within, I was impressed with the urgency to go to Spain. I couldn't quite understand this, but I felt it was a calling that would lead me to the life that I've always wanted.

JOURNAL ENTRY

Today I met my inner mentor. Her name is Iris. She told me she was my guide and that she was here to help me realize my dreams. I saw her waiting at the door in a small town, where there were a lot of people around me shopping. It was like a scene from Beauty and the Beast. *When I met her, I felt her warmth, and she was happy and excited. She told me to continue to work on my workbook and meditation videos, that my words will reach many people and help raise the vibrations of the planet. She told me to be patient, to take my time. Everything that I want is on its way and will come to fruition, she said. She told me to go to Spain, which had been a dream of mine for the past three years. I told her that I was scared. She told me that I have answers waiting for me there and that I will discover so much about myself. She told me to meditate, read, and work on my book every single day. She told me to forgive, to let go. She told me she is here to guide me along the way, and that I will know when the time is right to leave my job. She gave me gifts—gifts of faith and trust, in her and in the universe.*

Flash forward to today, a year later, I decided to leave my secure and stable job as a nurse to move abroad and live in Barcelona, Spain. I was ready to leave the norms of society and to venture across the world to build a new life and chase after my dreams.

This meant that I had to disconnect and cut cords with the person I've been all along in my life and grow into the person I am meant to be—a badass therapist and coach. The journey was not easy and it continues to have its challenges, but I will say this: taking this risk was the best decision I've ever made. It was time for me to live authentically and fully, to express all of who I am and change the world at the same time.

Have you ever had a moment where everything in your life just made sense? I had that magical moment here in Barcelona, as I was swimming in the Mediterranean Sea at sunset. I was immersed in warm water as I stared at the majestic sky and fluffy clouds full of beautiful colors. "I am exactly where I am meant to be," I thought to myself. There was a hint of familiarity, almost like déjà vu, but how could that be? I've never been here before. I knew it was a validation from the universe that I was exactly where I needed to be.

"For what it's worth: it's never too late or, in my case, too early to be whoever you want to be. There's no time limit, stop whenever you want. You can change or stay the same, there are no rules to this thing. We can make the best or the worst of it. I hope you make the best of it. And I hope you see things that startle you. I hope you feel things you never felt before. I hope you meet people with a different point of view. I hope you live a life you're proud of. If you find that you're not, I hope you have the courage to start all over again."

—*Francis Scott Fitzgerald*

A MESSAGE FROM JULIA

I HAVE ALWAYS BEEN filled with curiosity and a love for adventure. I shared much of my life story so that those who are struggling can see that I have written his book from personal experience and that what I discovered really works! Now I'm on a mission to change the world. I am hoping that everyone who reads this book can take what I have written and transform their own lives.

If reading *Awaken the Hero Within* has prompted you to honestly explore your thinking, your beliefs, and your dreams for a happy future, then I have done my job. You can climb out of the dark pit that you have been in. You can move ahead in your life toward an awesome future. The time to start has always been and always will be, NOW!

About the Author

*Every great dream begins with a dreamer.
Always remember, you have within you the
strength, the patience, and the passion to reach
for the stars to change the world.*

—Harriet Tubman

EVERY SUCCESS STORY begins with a dream, a dream that someone never gave up on. As Julia explains, as she discovered herself and realized what her true purpose is, she decided to chase after her dreams. She took a chance and gained the courage to live a life that she could only ever imagine. Now that dream has become a reality. She now wants to share her dream with the world. She wants to provide a toolbox that is accessible to everyone, to inspire, uplift, and empower each person to pursue their dreams.

The meaning of life is to find your gift. The purpose of life is to give it away.

—Pablo Picasso

Julia's mission is to raise the vibration of the planet one person at a time, aiming to spread happiness and help humanity overcome the obstacles of the mind. Julia strives to empower people through providing tools for them to explore and discover their true authentic selves. She is truly on a mission to guide people to discovering who they are beneath the layers of society, in hopes that we can all become happier in life, and ultimately, raise the vibration of the planet.

Create the highest grandest vision possible for your life, because you become what you believe.

—Oprah Winfrey

As she says, "Our dream and vision creates our reality. My vision is to create a community that promotes self-love, self-healing, and self-empowerment. When we become the best version of ourselves, then everyone that we meet, we influence in a positive way. This will then raise their vibration and will cause a ripple effect to where the world is a much happier place."

Julia is a Licensed Vocational Nurse (LVN) with a background in psychiatry. She is certified as an NLP (Neuro Linguistic Programming) practitioner and life coach, and is also a Rapid Transformational Therapist (RTT) and hypnotherapist.

Free Strategy Call

For a limited time, Julia is offering a
Free Strategy Call
for readers of *Awaken the Hero Within*

Book Your Appointment Here

www.thedreamlifefoundation.as.me

PLEASE LEAVE A REVIEW

What Did You Think of *Awaken the Hero Within*?

First, thank you for purchasing *Awaken the Hero Within*. You could have picked any book, but you picked mine, and for that I'm grateful. I hope it added value and quality to your life. If so, it would be really nice if you could share this book with your friends and family:

- You can post your thoughts to Facebook, Twitter, and Instagram.
- You can leave a review on Amazon. Your feedback and support will help me to greatly improve my writing on future projects and make this book even better.
- You can also use the hashtag: #awakentheherowithin

— Julia

ACKNOWLEDGEMENTS

~⚬~

THE WORLD IS a better place thanks to people who are willing to love unconditionally and support those they love. My life couldn't have turned out the way it did without the support of the ones who always believed in me, supported me, and saw me for who I am.

Having an idea and turning it into a book is as hard as it sounds. The experience is not only internally challenging but also incredibly rewarding. It has been a healing journey to create and write this book and I'm so grateful for the experience that has pushed me to grow beyond known heights. None of this would have been possible without my family, friends, and editors.

First I would like to thank my mom Jean Luu for teaching me how to be a strong and independent woman. I couldn't have become who I am without you. You not only gave me life but you have always supported me and loved me unconditionally. I love you with all of my heart.

Secondly, I would like to thank my sister Linh Nguyen for always being there for me no matter what happens. You've helped me to grow into the woman I am today with your tough love, sister. I wouldn't have it any other way. I am so grateful for our amazing bond together. Thank you for always having my back.

Thank you to my two brothers Son Nguyen and Lucas Low-Luu. I am grateful you are both in my life and have always cared for me.

Thanks to Mike Sygula, founder of Truth Theory. You were there for me through my process of writing and creating the book. Thank you for your support and belief in me. I truly value your kindness and generosity with the creation of my book.

I would also like to thank my friend Tamara Shnarr, my soul sister. You've always been a sun who brightens up my world. Thanks for believing in me and encouraging me. I appreciate you so much, and our aligned journey together.

I would also like to thank my friend Kelly Graver for being my rock. Kelly, you are an incredible woman who stood by my side through every struggle and encouraged me. You helped me truly believe in myself and who I am and for that, I am forever grateful.

Thanks to all of my best friends and those who have been with me since day one and have watched me grow into the woman I am today. My journey getting here would not have been possible without you guys supporting me through my growth: Mimi Kingsada, Jenny Chu, Suzann Ho, Jessica Duong. You guys are literally everything to me. I'm so glad I have you all in my life and that we can grow old together.

Mimi Kingsada you are my sister and best friend! Our bond together is incredible and I'm grateful to have you in my life to share many great memories while traveling together and laughing together.

Thanks to Suzann Ho and her family for taking me in at 15 years old. I am so grateful for your big heart and your caring nature that has always supported and loved me no matter what.

Jenny Chu, you are my ride or die bestie and you have always been a positive light in my life. We've been through so much together and I am so glad we can still support each other through thick or thin.

Jessica Duong, you have always been an amazing friend in my life. You always showed your love and support and was always there for me. Thank you for being an incredible soul.

Thank you Jake Connors and Gia Vuong. You both have taught me a lot about myself and the world. You've pushed my boundaries and helped me grow in so many ways. I appreciate you both.

Jake Connors you always believed in me and pushed me to become a better person. Thanks for loving and supporting me through it all.

Gia Vuong, you've taught me a lot about the universe and I appreciate your gift as a teacher and caring friend.

And thank you to the amazing editors who helped me with my book: Janis Bradfield and Rodney Miles. Janis helped me put the entire book together and I couldn't have done it without her. Rodney Miles helped me finish the last few things before releasing and launching my book. I appreciate both of you so much for turning my dreams of writing a book into reality.

I want to thank *everyone* who has ever said anything positive to me or taught me something about myself and the world. I appreciate and value this gift so much.

Thank you to my amazing clients that allowed me to work with them and shared their stories. You've taught me so much and inspire me greatly with your transformations.

And thank you to the *Universe* for always providing. Thanks for allowing me to have this human experience and all the amazing things that come with it.

APPENDIX:
SELF-HYPNOSIS
RECORDING

"As you are learning new tools to incorporate into your life and to help you facilitate change, I believe that hypnosis can make this change and your efforts easier. I have created a self-guided hypnosis recording so that you can explore self-hypnosis on your own. This will give you the ability to rewire your thoughts and behaviors to adapt to your new way of life."

— Julia

Julia's Self-Hypnosis Recordings

www.thedreamlifefoundation.com/meditations

RECOMMENDED READING

Books That Have Impacted my Life

~

A Guided Tour of the Collected Works of C. G. Jung
by Robert H. Hopcke

Analytical Psychology: Its Theory and Practice the Tavistock Lectures
by Carl Gustav Jung

Boundaries of the Soul: The Practice of Jung's Psychology
by June Singer

Getting Into The Vortex
by Abraham Hicks

Goddesses in Everywoman: A New Psychology of Women
by Jean Shinoda Bolen, M.D.

Gods in Everyman: A New Psychology of Men's Lives and Loves

by Jean Shinoda Bolen, M. D.

Jung to Live By

by Eugene Pascal, Ph.L.

The Hero with a Thousand Faces

by Joseph Campbell

The Power of Now

by Eckhart Tolle

The Success Principles: How to Get from Where You Are to Where You Want to Be

by Jack Canfield and Janet Switzer

The Universe Has Your Back

by Gabby Berstein

NOTES

PREFACE

[1] Llewellyn, Sandra. "7 Phases of Mastery." Pinterest, https://www.pinterest.se/pin/321374123391353252/.

[2] "The Hero's Journey" Image, sourced from: Swapp, Justin. "American Masters – George Lucas and The Hero's Journey." Justin Swapp (Lessons from Myths and Movies), 22 Jun 2013, http://justinswapp.com/american-masters-george-lucas-and-the-heros-journey/.

[3] Boyle, Greg. BrainyQuotes, https://www.brainyquote.com/quotes/greg_boyle_645724.

INTRODUCTION

[1] Campbell, Joseph. The Hero with a Thousand Faces. Pantheon Books, 1949, reprinted 1968, 2008.

[2] Hartman, David, MSW and Diane Zimberoff, M.A. "The Hero's Journey of Self-Transformation: Models of Higher Development from Mythology." Journal of Heart-Centered Therapies, 2009 Vol. 12, No. 2. pp. 3-93, https://www.scribd.com/doc/200471496/The-Hero-s-Journey-of-Self-transformation-Models-of-Higher-Development-from-Mythology.

[3] Schneider, Bruce D. "Uncovering the Life of your Dreams." Bruce D. Schneider, 2018. http://brucedschneider.com/.

[4] McLeod, S. A. "Maslow's Hierarchy of Needs." Simply Psychology, 21 May 2018, https://www.simplypsychology.org/maslow.html.

[5] McLeod, S. A. "Maslow's Hierarchy of Needs." Simply Psychology, 21 May 2018, https://www.simplypsychology.org/maslow.html.

Chapter 1: Self-Discovery

[1] "Self-discovery." Collins English Dictionary, https://www.collinsdictionary.com/us/dictionary/english/self-discovery.

[2] Schimelpfening, N. "The Role of Cortisol in Depression." Very Well Mind, 9 Sept. 2019. https://www.verywellmind.com/cortisol-and-depression-1066764.

[3] Cherry, Kendra. "The Preconscious, Conscious, and Unconscious Minds." VeryWellmind, medically reviewed by Steven Gans, M.D., 28 Sept 2019, https://www.verywellmind.com/the-conscious-and-unconscious-mind-2795946.

[4] "Using the Law of Attraction for Joy, Relationships, Money and Success." Jack Canfield, https://www.jackcanfield.com/blog/using-the-law-of-attraction/.

[5] Tolle, Eckhart. The Power of Now. New World Library, 1st edition, 27 Sept 1999, Navato, CA .

Chapter 2: The Awakening

[1] Campbell, Joseph. The Hero with a Thousand Faces. Pantheon Books, 1949, reprinted 1968, 2008.

[2] Beatles. "Hey Jude." Spin, May 16, 2019. https://www.spin.com/2019/05/beatles-hey-jude-lyrics/.

[3] Levine, Stephen. Turning toward the Mystery: A Seeker's Journey. HarperCollins, 2002, New York, 10-11.

[4] Canfield, Jack. The Success Principles: How to Get from Where You Are to Where You Want to Be. Collins Publishers, 26 Dec 2006.

[5] Rotter, J. "Generalized Expectancies for Internal Versus External Control of Reinforcement." Psychological Monographs, 80 (1), 1966, pp. 1–28.

[6] Peterson, C., Maier, S. F., & Seligman, M. E. Learned Helplessness: A Theory for the Age of Personal Control. Oxford University Press, 1993, New York.

[7] Schultz, D. P., & Schultz, S. E., Martin E. P. Seligman. "Learned Helplessness and the Optimistic/Pessimistic Explanatory Style." Theories of Personality, Tenth Edition, Belmont Wadsworth Cengage Learning, 2009, pp.369-378.

[8] Bandura, Albert. "Self-efficacy: Toward a Unifying Theory of Behavioral Change." Psychological Review, 84, 1977, pp.191-215.

Chapter 3: Refusal of the Call

[1] Mohr, Tara. Playing Big: Practical Wisdom for Women Who Want to Speak Up, Create, and Lead. Penguin Random House, 29 Dec 2015, https://www.penguinrandomhouse.com/books/316209/playing-big-by-tara-mohr/.

Chapter 5: Crossing the First Threshold

[1] Canfield, Jack and Janet Switzer. The Success Principles How to Get from Where You Are to Where You Want to Be. William Morrow, 28 Dec 2004 .

[2] Darwin, Charles. "On the Origin of Species: Chapter III, Struggle for Existence." The Guardian, https://www.theguardian.com/science/2008/feb/09/darwin.struggle, 8 Feb 2008.

[3] "The Key Principles of Cognitive Behavioural Therapy." Sage Pub.com, InnovAiT, 6(9), pp. 79–585, https://journals.sagepub.com/doi/pdf/10.1177/1755738012471029.

[4] Seligman, Martin E.P., Ph.D. Learned Optimism: How to Change Your Mind and Your Life. Knopf Doubleday Publishing Group, 3 Jan 2006.

[5] Littrell, J. "The Mind-Body Connection: Not Just a Theory Anymore," Soc Work Health Care, 2008,46(4):17-37, NBCI National Library of Medicine, National Institutes of Health, https://www.ncbi.nlm.nih.gov/pubmed/18589562#.

[6] Littrell, J. "The mind-Body Connection: Not Just a Theory Anymore." Soc Work Health Care, 2008,46 (4):17-37, NBCI National Library of Medicine, National Institutes of Health, https://www.ncbi.nlm.nih.gov/pubmed/18589562#.

[7] Seligman, Martin E.P., Ph.D. Learned Optimism: How to Change Your Mind and Your Life. Knopf Doubleday Publishing Group, 3 Jan 2006.

[8] "Belief." Lexico, https://www.lexico.com/definition/belief.

[9] Gordon, David and Maribeth Meyers-Anderson. Phoenix: Therapeutic Patterns of Milton H. Erickson. Meta Publications, 1981.

[10] "Pygmalion Leadership: The Power of Positive Expectations." Psychology Today, 18 Apr 2009, https://www.psychologytoday.com/us/blog/cutting-edge-leadership/200904/pygmalion-leadership-the-power-positive-expectations.

[11] Ackerman, Courtney. "Cognitive Distortions: When Your Brain Lies to You." PositivePsychology, 9 Sept 2017 and10 Oct 2019, https://positivepsychology.com/cognitive-distortions/.

[12] Burns, David D. M.D. The Feeling Good Handbook. Plume Book, 1989, New York.

[13] Ackerman, Courtney. "Cognitive Distortions: When Your Brain Lies to You." PositivePsychology, 9 Sept 2017 and10 Oct 2019, https://positivepsychology.com/cognitive-distortions/.

[14] "Top Five Regrets of the Dying." The Guardian, https://www.theguardian.com/lifeandstyle/2012/feb/01/top-five-regrets-of-the-dying.

Chapter 6: Dancing with Fear

[1] Robbins, Tony. Unleash the Power Within. https://www.tonyrobbins.com/events/unleash-the-power-within/losangeles/.

[2] Hill, Napoleon. Brainy Quote, https://www.brainyquote.com/quotes/napoleon_hill_152858.

[3] Williamson, Marianne. A Return to Love: Reflections on the Principles of "A Course in Miracles." Harper One, January 1992, https://www.goodreads.com/quotes/928-our-deepest-fear-is-not-that-we-are-inadequate-our.

Chapter 7: Innermost Cave

[1] Mitchell, David. Cloud Atlas: A Novel. Random House, 17 Aug 2004, p.320.

[2] Quote attributed to John Campbell by Sterns, Maureen. Conscious Courage: Turning Everyday Challenges into Opportunities. Enrichment Books, 2004.

[3] Nguyen, Julia. Thoughts /Beliefs/Actions/Reality model.

[4] Earley, Jay. Self-Therapy. Patterns Systems Books, 2009, Larkspur, CA , p.3.

[5] Johnson, Steven. Mind Wide Open: Your Brain and the Neuroscience of Everyday Life.   Scribner, reprint edition, 27 Feb 2004.

[6] Neill, Conor. "Understanding Personality: The 12 Jungian Archetypes." Conor Neill, 21 Apr 2018, https://conorneill.com/2018/04/21/understanding-personality-the-12-jungian-archetypes/.

[7] Neill, Conor. "Understanding Personality: The 12 Jungian Archetypes." Conor Neill, 21 Apr 2018, https://conorneill.com/2018/04/21/understanding-personality-the-12-jungian-archetypes/.

[8] Neill, Conor. "Understanding Personality: The 12 Jungian Archetypes." Conor Neill, 21 Apr 2018, https://conorneill.com/2018/04/21/understanding-personality-the-12-jungian-archetypes/.

[9] Neill, Conor. "Understanding Personality: The 12 Jungian Archetypes." Conor Neill, 21 Apr 2018, https://conorneill.com/2018/04/21/understanding-personality-the-12-jungian-archetypes/.

[10] Neill, Conor. "Understanding Personality: The 12 Jungian Archetypes." Conor Neill, 21 Apr 2018, https://conorneill.com/2018/04/21/understanding-personality-the-12-jungian-archetypes/.

[11] Schwartz, R.C. Internal Family Systems Therapy. Guilford Press, 1995, New York, NY.

[12] Chart of Dysfunctional Family Roles: https://www.wiseword.org/pg/dysfunctional_family_roles.

[13] Miles, Lisa A. "Early Wounding & Dysfunctional Family Roles." Psycho Central, https://psychcentral.com/blog/early-wounding-dysfunctional-family-roles/.

[14] Miles, Lisa A. "Early Wounding & Dysfunctional Family Roles." Psycho Central, https://psychcentral.com/blog/early-wounding-dysfunctional-family-roles/.

CHAPTER 8: ACTIVATING MY TRUE SELF

[1] "History of Neuroscience Ramon y Cajal." Neuroscientifically Challenged, 30 May 2014, https://www.neuroscientificallychallenged.com/blog/history-of-neuroscience-ramon-y-cajal.

[2] Fuchs, Eberhard and Gabriele Flugge. "Adult Neuroplasticity: More Than 40 Years of Research." Neural Plasticity, 2014(5):541870, May 2014, https://www.researchgate.net/publication/262811332_Adult_Neuroplasticity_More_Than_40_Years_of_Research.

[3] Ackerman, Courtney. "What is Neuroplasticity: A Psychologist Explains." PositivePsychology, 10 Sept 2019, https://positivepsychology.com/neuroplasticity/.

[4] "Hebbian Theory." Wikipedia, https://en.wikipedia.org/wiki/Hebbian_theory.

[5] Lower, S and W Singer. "Selection of Intrinsic Horizontal Connections in the Visual Cortex by Correlated Neuronal Activity." Science, 10 Jan 1992, Vol. 255, Issue 5041, pp. 209-212, https://science.sciencemag.org/content/255/5041/209.

[6] Santos, Edalmarys and Chad A. Noggle. "Synaptic Pruning." Encyclopedia of Child Behavior and Development, https://link.springer.com/referenceworkentry/10.1007%2F978-0-387-79061-9_2856.

[7] Davidson, Richard J., Ph.D. and Sharon Begley. The Emotional Life of The Brain. Penguin Publishing, 2012, https://www.richardjdavidson.com/the-emotional-life-of-your-brain.

[8] Schwartz, Jeffrey M and Sharon Begley. The Mind and the Brain: Neuroplasticity and the Power of Mental Force. Harper Collins Publishers, 14 Oct 2003.

[9] Schwartz, J. M., & Begley, S. The Mind and the Brain: Neuroplasticity and the Power of Mental Force. Regan Books/Harper Collins Publishers, 2002.

[10] Klein, Tim, et al. "Changing Brains, Changing Lives: Researching the Lived Experience of Individuals Practicing Self-Directed Neuroplasticity." Retrieved from Sophia, the St. Catherine University repository website, 2019, https://sophia.stkate.edu/ma_hhs/20.

[11] "The Conscious Competence Ladder." Mind Tools, https://www.mindtools.com/pages/article/newISS_96.htm.

[12] Mosley, Bruce J., M.D., Kimberly O'Malley, Ph.D., Nancy J. Petersen, Ph.D., et al. "A Controlled Trial of Arthroscopic Surgery for Osteoarthritis of the Knee." The New England Journal of Medicine, 11 July 2002, 347, pp.81-88.

[13] Ford, Henry. Goodreads, https://www.goodreads.com/quotes/978-whether-you-think-you-can-or-you-think-you-can-t--you-re.

[14] Pert, Candice B. Molecules of Emotion: The Science Behind Mind-Body Medicine. Simon & Schuster, 17 Feb 1999.

[15] Gordon, David and Maribeth Meyers-Anderson. Phoenix: Therapeutic Patterns of Milton H. Erickson. Meta Publications, 1981.

[16] "Self Hypnosis." Wikihow, https://www.wikihow.com/Perform-Self-Hypnosis.

[17] Sabourin, M. E., Cutcomb, S. D., Crawford, H. J., & Pribram, K. "EEG Correlates of Hypnotic Susceptibility and Hypnotic Trance: Spectral Analysis and Coherence." International Journal of Psychophysiology, 1990, 10(2), 125-142.

[18] Harris, Tom. "How Hypnosis Works." How Stuff Works, https://science.howstuffworks.com/science-vs-myth/extrasensory-perceptions/hypnosis4.htm

[19] Nguyen, Julia. "The Dream Life Foundation Meditations." www.thedreamlifefoundation.com/meditations

[20] Aristotle. Nicomachean Ethics (Book 1). Translated by W.D. Ross, Written 350 B.C.E., http://classics.mit.edu/Aristotle/nicomachaen.1.i.html.

[21] Divola, John et al. "The Pleasure Principle." Pro Artibus, http://sinne.proartibus.fi/en/event/the-pleasure-principle-3/.

[22] Pueblo, Yung. "You are the Answer." Treelove Yoga, http://www.treeloveyoga.com/blog/2019/3/25/5wn93n7etlgyymq5synzgdrdo29ig6.

[23] Rayner, Victoria. "12 Virtues Introduced by Aristotle—The Master of Those Who Know." Aesthetichealingmindset's Blog, 12 Jun 2011, https://aesthetichealingmindset.wordpress.com/2011/06/12/4706/.

[24] McPherson, Miller, Lynn Smith-Lovin, and Matthew E. Brashears. "Social Isolation in America: Changes in Core Discussion Networks over Two Decades." American Sociological Review, 1 Jun 2006, https://journals.sagepub.com/doi/abs/10.1177/000312240607100301.

[25] Winphrey, Oprah. GoodReads, https://www.goodreads.com/quotes/8838701-do-what-you-have-to-do-until-you-can-do.

[26] Wilson, Edward O. Biophilia. Harvard University Press, Jan 1 1984, https://www.amazon.com/dp/B003852K1Q/ref=dp-kindle-redirect?_encoding=UTF8&btkr=1.

[27] Canfield, Jack and Janet Switzer. The Success Principles: How to Get from Where You Are to Where You Want to Be. Collins Publishers, 28 Dec 2004, https://www.goodreads.com/book/show/96593.The_Success_Principl es.

[28] Marie, Carly. "Self-Acceptance." Pinterest, https://www.pinterest.es/pin/AXv0YWTjdhEYv5p1XnkxNqobcxATa6t5 gxqdcYQMvcr_ZN1w3jwiHcl/.

[29] Zweig, Connie Ph.D and Steven Wolf Ph.D. Romancing the Shadow: A Guide to Soul Work for a Vital, Authentic Life. Wellspring/Ballantine, 2 Feb 1999, https://www.penguinrandomhouse.ca/books/196160/romancing-the-shadow-by-steven-wolf-phd-and-connie-zweig-phd/9780345417404

[30] Vitale, Joe. Hypnotic Writing: How to Seduce and Persuade Customers with Only Your Words. John Wiley & Sons, 8 Jun 2010, p.20.

[31] Anderson, Frank, et al. Internal Family Systems Skills Training Manual: Trauma-Informed Treatment for Anxiety, Depression, PTSD & Substance Abuse. PESI HealthCare, 07 Nov 2017.

CHAPTER 9: SHIFT IN PERCEPTION

[1] Sincero, Jen. You Are a Badass: How to Stop Doubting your Greatness and Start Living an Awesome Life. 14 Sept 2018, Running Press, p. 137, http://millerbrian.com/reading-log-2018/you-are-a-badass-by-jen-sincero.

[2] Sincero, Jen. You Are a Badass: How to Stop Doubting your Greatness and Start Living an Awesome Life. 14 Sept 2018, Running Press, p.153, http://millerbrian.com/reading-log-2018/you-are-a-badass-by-jen-sincero.

[3] Robbins, Tony. Unleash the Power Within. https://www.tonyrobbins.com/events/unleash-the-power-within/losangeles/.

[4] Reivich, K. and Shatté, A. The Resilience Factor: 7 Essential Skills for Overcoming Life's Inevitable Obstacles. Broadway Books, 2002.

[5] Davidson, Richard and Sharon Begley. The Emotional Life of Your Brain: How Its Unique Patterns Affect the Way You Think, Feel, and Live— And How You Can Change Them. Hudson Street Press, 2012, https://www.scientificamerican.com/article/mind-reviews-the-emotional-life-of/.

[6] Fehmi, Les and Jim Robbins. The Open-Focus Brain: Harnessing the Power of Attention to Heal Mind and Body. Shambhala Publications, 28 Aug 2007.

[7] https://www.mind-your-reality.com/brain_waves.html.

[8] Tolle, Eckhart. The Power of Now. New World Library, 27 Sept 1999.

[9] Scriven, Amber. "How to Practice Breath of Fire." DoYouYoga, https://www.doyouyoga.com/how-to-practice-breath-of-fire-97945/.

[10] Mitchell, Lisa, "8 Reasons Why We Use Ujjayi Breath in Yoga." MindBodyGreen, https://www.mindbodygreen.com/0-5823/8-Reasons-Why-We-Use-Ujjayi-Breath-in-Yoga.html.

[11] Campbell, Joseph. Pathways to Bliss. Audio, https://billmoyers.com/content/ep-1-joseph-campbell-and-the-power-of-myth-the-hero%E2%80%99s-adventure-audio/.

[12] Robbins, Tony. Unleash the Power Within. https://www.tonyrobbins.com/events/unleash-the-power-within/LosAngeles/.

[13] Value Trap: https://www.effectivealtruism.org/articles/ea-global-2018-intrinsic-values/.

[14] Robbins , Tony. Unleash the Power Within. https://www.tonyrobbins.com/events/unleash-the-power-within/losangeles/.

[15] Clear, James. James Clear, https://jamesclear.com/core-values.

[16] Rath, Tom. Strength Finders 2.0. Gallup Press, 2007, p.144, https://www.amazon.com/StrengthsFinder-2-0-Tom-Rath/dp/159562015X/ref=tmm_hrd_swatch_0?_encoding=UTF8&qid=&sr=.

[17] Garcia, Hector and Francesc Miralles. Ikigai: The Japanese Secret to a Long and Happy Life. Penguin Publishing Group, 29 Aug 2017, https://www.barnesandnoble.com/w/ikigai-hector-garcia/1125366262#/.

[18] Robbins, Tony. Unleash the Power Within. https://www.tonyrobbins.com/events/unleash-the-power-within/losangeles/.

[19] Anthony, Marc. Inspiring Quotes, https://www.inspiringquotes.us/author/1958-marc-anthony.

[20] Steinberg, Amanda. "Personal Mission Statements of 5 Famous CEOs." Proteus Leadership, https://proteusleadership.com/personal-mission-statements-of-5-famous-ceos/.

[21] Hill, Napoleon. The Law of Success: the Master Wealth-Builder's Complete and Original Lesson Plan for Achieving Your Dreams. Penguin Random House, 2020, https://www.penguinrandomhouse.com/books/304333/the-law-of-success-by-napoleon-hill/

[22] Hill, Napoleon. The Law of Success: the Master Wealth-Builder's Complete and Original Lesson Plan for Achieving Your Dreams. Penguin Random House, 2020, https://www.penguinrandomhouse.com/books/304333/the-law-of-success-by-napoleon-hill/

[23] Levitin, Daniel J. The Organized Mind: Thinking Straight in the Age of Information Overload. Dutton, 1 Sep 2015.

[24] Carnegie, Andrew. Brainy Quote, https://www.brainyquote.com/quotes/andrew_carnegie_156212.

[25] S.M.A.R.T.: "Smart Goals: How to Make your Goals Achievable." MindTools, https://www.mindtools.com/pages/article/smart-goals.htm.

CHAPTER 10: FAILING FORWARD

[1] Robbins, Tony. Unleash the Power Within.
https://www.tonyrobbins.com/events/unleash-the-power-within/2019/losangeles.

[2] Camus, Albert. BrainyQuote,
https://www.brainyquote.com/quotes/albert_camus_104177.

[3] Robbins, Tony. Unleash the Power Within.
https://www.tonyrobbins.com/events/unleash-the-power-within/miami/2019/losangeles.

[4] Berstein, Gabrielle. "Manifest & Chill: Advice from Gabby Bernstein."
SobrieTea Party, 15 Jan 2016,
http://www.sobrieteaparty.com/2016/01/15/manifest-chill-advice-from-gabby-bernstein-part-1/.

[5] Singer, Michael. The Surrender Experiment: My Journey into Life's
Perfection. Harmony Books, 2015, New York.

[6] Sanchez, Nouk. "Invoking the Miracle –The Atonement Prayer," Take
Me to Truth, Aug 7, 2013, https://takemetotruth.org/nouks-blog/invoking-the-miracle-the-atonement-prayer/.

[7] Williamson, Jennifer. "Ho'oponopono Prayer for Forgiveness, Healing
and Making Things Right." Healing Brave. 29 Jul 2019,
https://healingbrave.com/blogs/all/hooponopono-prayer-for-forgiveness.

[8] Williamson, Jennifer. "Ho'oponopono Prayer for Forgiveness, Healing
and Making Things Right." Healing Brave, 29 Jul 2019,
https://healingbrave.com/blogs/all/hooponopono-prayer-for-forgiveness.

[9] Hill, Napoleon. "The Twelve Riches of Life." Course Hero: 10560761-Napoleon-Hill-12-Riches-of-Life-and-17-Principles-of-Success.pdf,
https://www.coursehero.com/file/47046546/10560761-Napoleon-Hill-12-Riches-of-Life-and-17-Principles-of-Successpdf/.

CHAPTER 11: RESURRECTION

[1] Markas, Jenny. One Tree Hill: #1 The Beginning. Firefly Bookstore, January 2005, https://www.biblio.com/one-tree-hill-by-markas-jenny/work/1124322.

[2] Hartman, David MSW, Diane Zimberhoff MA. "The Hero's Journey of Self Transformation: Model of Higher Development from Mythology." Journal of Heart-centered Therapies, 2009, Vol 12 No. 2 pp. 3-93,

[3] Hartman, David MSW, Diane Zimberhoff MA. "The Hero's Journey of Self Transformation: Model of Higher Development from Mythology." Journal of Heart-Centered Therapies, 2009, Vol 12 No. 2 pp. 3-93, https://www.scribd.com/doc/200471496/The-Hero-s-Journey-of-Self-transformation-Model of-Higher-Development-from-Mythology.

[4] Campbell, Joseph. Goodreads, https://www.goodreads.com/quotes/83632-we-re-not-on-our-journey-to-save-the-world-but.

[5] Campbell, Joseph with Bill Moyers. The Power of Myth. Doubleday, Jun 1 1991, New York. https://www.biblio.com/the-power-of-myth-by-campbell-joseph/work/33491.

APPENDIX

[1] Rumi. Goodreads, https://www.goodreads.com/quotes/1299504-i-said-what-about-my-eyes-he-said-keep-them.

[2] Nguyen, Julia. Need Title and citation for your Self-Hypnosis Recording